3-9·76

World
Food
Crisis

World Food Crisis

Edited by Lester A. Sobel

Contributing editors: Joseph Fickes, Hal Kosut, Chris Hunt

FACTS ON FILE, INC.   NEW YORK, N.Y.

World
Food
Crisis

Library of Congress Catalog Card No. 75-1
ISBN 0-87196-282-9

9 8 7 6 5 4 3 2 1
PRINTED IN
THE UNITED STATES OF AMERICA

Contents

Dimensions of the Problem

HUNGER IS A FAMILIAR companion to millions of people. United Nations experts estimate that perhaps half a billion of the world's 3.8 billion inhabitants are hungry every day. Up to an additional 1.5 billion are menaced by an ever-present threat of running short of food. Only the developed nations produce enough food—or money for food—to keep the average citizen reasonably well-fed. Malnutrition, at the least, is the fate of most of the 2.5 billion people of the developing countries of Asia, Africa and Latin America. Even when conditions are favorable and crops are good, there often is not enough food to go around in some of these less-favored lands. When the situation deteriorates, the results can be widespread starvation.

A combination of unfavorable food-supply conditions confronted the world in 1972, when world food production dropped for the first time in two decades. Grain reserves in 1961 had been sufficient to feed the world's people for 95 days. By mid-1974, however, there was only a 26-day supply in reserve.

Annual world food output had increased by 26% in the decade prior to 1972, and several of the developing countries had apparently begun to approach self-sufficiency in grain as a result of the Green Revolution. Annual world grain production increased from 833 million tons to 1.264 billion tons between 1961 and 1973, and the developed grain-exporting countries had been restricting production during 1968–71 in an effort to reduce price-depressing surplus stocks. The fertilizer industry had built up to over-capacity, and prices of fertilizer, grain and many other foods had been low.

1

FOOD PRODUCTION & POPULATION, DEVELOPED & DEVELOPING COUNTRIES

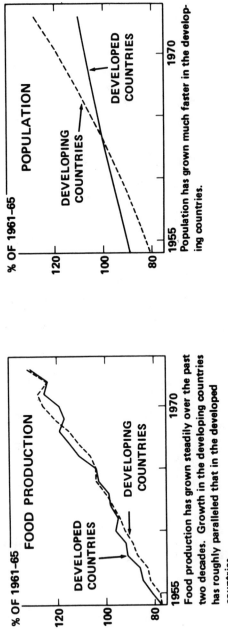

POPULATION

% OF 1961-65

DEVELOPING COUNTRIES

DEVELOPED COUNTRIES

1955   1970

Population has grown much faster in the developing countries.

FOOD PRODUCTION

% OF 1961-65

DEVELOPED COUNTRIES

DEVELOPING COUNTRIES

1955   1970

Food production has grown steadily over the past two decades. Growth in the developing countries has roughly paralleled that in the developed countries.

FOOD PRODUCTION PER CAPITA

DEVELOPING COUNTRIES

% OF 1961-65

1955   1970

DEVELOPED COUNTRIES

% OF 1961-65

1955   1970

Data exclude Communist Asia

From *The World Situation & Prospects to 1985* (Economic Research Service, U.S. Department of Agriculture)

The decline in total food output in 1972 was only 1.6%, but the world's need for food was growing at the same time at a 2% annual rate. Grain production in 1972 was down 4%—rice output off 5% and wheat production off 3%. The 1972 decline in grain output totaled 35 million tons. Although production then increased by 89 million tons in 1973, affected nations once again had to face the possibility that they would run short of food for growing populations.

The world's greatest exporter of grain is the U.S. It currently supplies about 89% of the soybeans, 74% of the corn and 53% of the wheat on the world market. But in 1973 the Soviet Union bought 25% of the U.S. wheat crop. The U.S.S.R., usually a net grain exporter, had suffered so great a crop failure in 1972 that it became the world's largest grain importer in 1972–73, and the 30 million net tons of grain the Soviets bought in this period caused both a drastic reduction in supplies available to food-short developing countries and skyrocketing prices for such grain as was available to them.

The causes of food scarcity are not hard to find. The explosive growth of world population is widely designated as the dominating factor in the problem. In his first *Essay on the Principle of Population*, published in 1798, the English cleric and political economist Thomas Robert Malthus had postulated that since "population, when unchecked, increases in a geometrical ratio" and that "subsistance [food] increases only in an arithmetical ratio," there must be "a strong and constantly operating check on population" or ultimately there would be too many people for the food available. Malthus held that this check was "misery and vice." Malthus' theory has been widely criticized, and he himself revised it in later editions, but the major aspects of his idea have always enjoyed considerable acceptance.

In this context, an excerpt from a World Bank report is quoted frequently: "It took more than 1,800 years for the world population to increase from 10 million to one billion. The second billion required about a century and a quarter, and the third only 30 years. It has now taken only 15 years for the fourth billion people. If the present growth rates are to continue, the current population of more than 3.6 billion would double in 35 years, and by the end of the century it would be increasing at the rate of a half billion every eight years."

Rep. Pierre S. du Pont (R., Del.), in debate in the U.S. House of Representatives March 13, 1975, cited the case of India and its population of 600 million: "In 10 years it [India's population]

INDICES OF WORLD POPULATION & FOOD PRODUCTION

1961-65=100

Calendar year	World			Developed countries			Developing countries		
	Popu-lation	Food production		Popu-lation	Food production		Popu-lation	Food production	
		Total	Per capita		Total	Per capita		Total	Per-capita
1960	94.2	94	100	96.3	96	100	92.8	92	99
1961	96.1	95	99	97.5	95	97	95.1	94	99
1962	98.0	98	100	98.9	98	99	97.5	97	100
1963	100.0	100	100	100.1	99	99	99.9	100	100
1964	101.9	103	101	101.2	103	102	102.4	104	102
1965	103.9	104	100	102.3	104	102	105.0	104	99
1966	105.9	109	103	103.4	111	107	107.7	106	98
1967	107.9	114	106	104.3	115	110	110.4	111	101
1968	109.9	118	107	105.3	119	113	113.2	115	102
1969	112.0	118	105	106.3	117	110	116.1	121	104
1970	114.2	121	106	107.3	119	111	119.0	126	106
1971	116.4	126	108	108.3	125	115	122.1	128	105
1972	118.7	124	104	109.3	124	113	125.3	125	100
1973	120.9	133	110	110.2	133	121	128.5	132	103

Data exclude Communist Asia

From *The World Situation & Prospects to 1985* (Economic Research Service, U.S. Department of Agriculture) is going to be twice as big as that. In the last 20 years, India has doubled its crop yield. They have started double-cropping in terms of getting two yields per year out of their crops. They have almost doubled their land acreage under irrigation; they have almost doubled the land on which they grow crops. And yet they are still falling behind. They are still unable to feed the new mouths that are born into the country of India, even with all this increased technology."

Other factors—long-term or short-term—are also cited as causes of recent food scarcities. These factors, some of them connected, include: (a) Excessive fishing and failure to accept and enforce conservation practices. (b) Long-term changes in climate resulting, among other things, in the southward expansion of the Sahara and famine in the Sahel (the area along the Sahara's southern border). (c) Inadequate conservation of land and water resources. (d) Agricultural disruptions caused by war, recently by the fighting in Indochina and on the Indian subcontinent, where millions of people in India, Pakistan and Bangladesh suffered. (e) The tremendous oil price increases, which in turn caused insupportable increases in the costs of fertilizer and mechanical aids to farming. (f) The large Soviet purchases of grain on world markets after the U.S.S.R.'s 1972 crop failure. (g) The growth of affluence in developed countries and the accompanying increase in the consumption of food, especially animal protein.

It is pointed out that considering income, food is expensive as well as scarce in poor countries (where 70% of the world's population live) but relatively cheap as well as abundant in rich lands. The American consumer spends only about 16% of his disposable income on food. By comparison, the proportion of disposable income spent on food is about 25% in Britain, 35% in Japan, 58% in the Soviet Union, 80% in much of Asia and as high as 90% in many developing countries.

International commerce and politics sometimes acts to shift food from the hungry nations to the well-fed ones in what food scientist Georg Borgstrom has denounced as the "protein swindle." Anne H. and Paul R. Ehrlich asserted in a *Los Angeles Times* article Sept. 8, 1974 that "in the late 1960s, ... fish exported by Peru alone to developed countries would have been enough to make up the protein deficit of all Latin America." They added that "poor nations all too often export food that is needed at home in a world where money, not need, determines international flow of goods. For example, a recent 40% rise in

VALUE OF BILATERAL & MULTILATERAL FOOD AID CONTRIBUTIONS (DISBURSEMENTS) OF DEVELOPED COUNTRIES TO MULTILATERAL AGENCIES

Country	1960	1965	1966	1967	1968	1969	1970	1971	1972	1973	Total 1965-73	Percent of total
						million dollars						
Australia	2.0	10.2	12.6	15.6	8.8	15.1	20.9	12.6	18.5	19.6	133.9	1.22
Austria	—	—	—	—	—	1.0	0.5	0.8	0.8	0.8	3.9	0.04
Belgium	0.1	0.3	0.2	0.2	0.2	2.9	3.3	7.4	11.1	16.0	41.6	0.38
Canada	40.8	57.3	138.3	117.5	63.2	63.3	98.2	88.5	87.8	95.9	810.0	7.37
Denmark	0.1	0.2	0.9	1.6	2.5	8.4	6.7	7.3	8.0	13.9	49.5	0.45
France	0.4	0.7	1.0	1.0	1.0	15.1	14.6	34.8	32.3	66.0	166.5	1.51
Germany	—	2.6	2.6	2.7	2.7	36.6	29.2	46.9	58.4	91.9	273.6	2.49
Italy	—	—	1.5	1.0	0.5	4.5	17.8	24.0	20.0	27.4	96.7	0.88
Japan	0.1	0.4	0.4	0.5	0.5	2.0	23.8	134.5	34.6	105.8	302.5	2.75
Netherlands	—	1.1	0.4	0.9	0.1	13.8	17.1	15.7	20.3	33.0	102.4	0.93
New Zealand	n.a.	n.a.	n.a.	n.a.	n.a.	n.a.	n.a.	n.a.	n.a.	1.2	1.2	0.01
Norway	0.3	0.6	2.0	1.2	8.5	4.5	6.1	4.1	2.5	3.9	33.4	0.30
Portugal	—	—	—	—	—	0.1	—	—	0.1	0.1	0.3	0.00
Sweden	—	—	1.2	2.9	4.2	4.7	9.9	9.4	6.5	11.2	50.0	0.45
Switzerland	0.5	1.1	1.1	3.1	4.1	6.8	6.4	4.1	7.6	8.5	42.8	0.39
U.K.	1.0	1.4	2.3	1.0	1.9	17.4	16.0	17.3	2.7	14.3	74.3	0.68
U.S.	901.0	1,234.4	1,213.0	1,007.0	1,060.0	907.0	860.0	826.0	978.0	730.0	8,815.4	80.15
Total, non-U.S.	45.3	75.9	164.5	149.2	98.2	196.2	270.5	407.4	311.2	509.5	2,182.6	19.85
Total, developed countries	946.3	1,310.3	1,377.5	1,156.2	1,158.2	1,103.2	1,130.5	1,233.4	1,289.2	1,239.5	10,998.0	100.00

Source: OECD, "The Food Situation in the Developing Countries," Feb. 1974, and U.S. Department of Agriculture.

meat production in Guatemala was accompanied by a 6% decline in Guatemalan per capita meat consumption."

James P. Grant, president of the Overseas Development Council, warned in a statement to a Senate Agriculture subcommittee April 4, 1974 that "the international order as we know it cannot long survive if there is a continuation of the 1973 and 1974 trends, whereby the increasingly affluent richest one billion people of the world pre-empt through their purchasing power ever larger shares of the world's grain and fertilizer, leaving less and less for the poorest billion in the world."

"The world produces enough food to feed all its inhabitants," Sen. Mark O. Hatfield (R., Ore.) told the U.S. Senate July 16, 1974. "But when one-third of the world's population—all those who are comparatively the rich—consumes two-thirds of the world's protein sources, then millions of the other two-thirds of the world suffer, starve and die."

Actually, of course, some of the rich nations, led notably by the U.S. had made serious efforts to relieve worldwide hunger. The U.S. was the largest donor of food to the needy that the world had ever seen. Since 1954, the U.S. had provided $25 billion worth of food for hungry citizens of other countries under the Food for Peace (Public Law 480) program. Some critics of the U.S. have pointed out that this aid came almost exclusively from the nation's staggering accumulations of surplus farm products, which, if undisposed of, would continue to depress crop prices and ultimately would spoil. Nevertheless, U.S. food aid in the period 1965–72 amounted to 84% of all food contributions by developed countries and undoubtedly preserved hundreds of thousands of lives.

The overwhelming proportion of the food produced in this world, however, is consumed in the country in which it is grown. There are many practical reasons for this. The most obvious is that the surest way for a country to prevent hunger is for it to grow enough food for its people instead of depending on others to give or sell it this most essential of essentials. Many world leaders involved in the food-supply problem have recently stressed the importance of local production as the solution to food shortage. The most conspicuous international effort in this direction is the often praised (and criticized) Green Revolution.

The Green Revolution was made possible by the development and adoption in underdeveloped countries of a variety of advanced agricultural techniques. The "revolution" was based on the use of new, high-yielding strains of grain—especially wheat and rice. It required heavy inputs of fertilizer, pesticides, irrigation and scientific management to take advantage (or eliminate disadvantages) of climate, soil and other conditions. The first major wheat seed improvements were made at the International Center for Maize & Wheat Improvement in Mexico, founded in 1943, and Dr. Norman E. Borlaug received the 1970 Nobel Peace Prize for directing the center's international wheat research and production program.

The Green Revolution began in Mexico, where the first improved wheat varieties were planted in 1948. By 1960, a succession of improved wheat strains had been planted on 90% of Mexico's wheat land, and yields had doubled. They doubled again in the 1960s after new, semidwarf wheat strains were introduced. Improved wheat and rice varieties were introduced in other underdeveloped countries, largely in Asia and North Africa, in the mid-1960s. The work on rice was started at the International Rice Research Institute, founded at Los Banos, the Philippines in 1960. In Asia, improved strains accounted for about 35% of wheat land and 30% of rice land (Communist countries excluded) by 1972–73. Benefits of the Green Revolution were unevenly distributed, however. About 61% of Asia's improved wheat area and about 55% of the continent's improved rice plantings were in India, where two states accounted for about 48% of the country's improved wheat and another two states accounted for some 40% of the improved rice. Pakistan, with 20% of Asia's improved wheat area, had about 74% of it concentrated in one province and some 77% of its improved rice area in another.

Jon Tinker asserted bluntly in the Nov. 4, 1974 issue of *New Scientist* that "the Green Revolution has failed" as the various long-term and short-term causes of food scarcities converged in 1972. Richard Critchfield, however, rejected any such analysis. "A great many people have misunderstood the nature of the Green Revolution," he declared in a June 15, 1974 *New Republic* article. "... It is no one-shot thing; it is a long-term continuous process of transferring American farm technology, and this requires the continuous presence of American technicians. ... [T]he Green Revolution is not an event but a process that will just go on, transforming for good and bad rural societies all over the earth."

The Green Revolution had already faced other serious criticism for reasons that include the 1972 crop failures. But Robert C. Tetro, senior economist for the Washington Office of the U.N. Food & Agriculture Organization, asserted in a paper on "World

Food Prospects and Problems" that "actually, the Green Revolution probably prevented disasters in 1972 and has been fully as successful as had been anticipated by qualified observers many years ago.... India's increases in wheat production from 1965 to 1972 ... alone added 14 million tons to 1972 availabilities, thus providing the wherewithal for the continued meager existence of the 100 million Indians added to that country's population over the same period of time."

Borlaug himself had tried to explain the limitations of the Green Revolution. He had said in his speech accepting the 1970 Nobel Peace Prize that "the Green Revolution has won a temporary success in man's war against hunger and deprivation; it has given man a breathing space. If fully implemented, the Revolution can provide sufficient food for sustenance during the next three decades. But the frightening power of human reproduction must also be curbed; otherwise the success of the Green Revolution will be ephemeral."

Former U.S. Secretary of Agriculture Orville L. Freeman is among those who express pessimism about the ability of the world to feed its growing population. In a statement presented to a Senate Agriculture subcommittee March 21, 1974, Freeman held that "the recent [food] scarcities reflect important long-term trends in addition to the temporary phenomenon of drought in the Soviet Union and parts of Asia and Africa." According to Freeman:

We are experiencing a fundamental shift from an era of large commercial surpluses to an era of tight supplies of essential food commodities.... [I]t has become clear that, despite the technological breakthroughs that produced the Green Revolution ..., two major growth factors remain in the world demand for food that will result in overall shortages for the foreseeable future. On the global level, population growth is still the dominant source of continuously expanding demand for food. ... In the poor countries, population growth alone accounts for most of the year-to-year increase in the demand for food. In the affluent nations, rising incomes lead to accelerating food consumption. ... All told, the basic agricultural resources—land, water, fertilizer—required to support an average North American are nearly *five times* those of the average Indian, Nigerian or Colombian. ... In 1969, the long period of sustained growth in the world fish catch was interrupted by a sudden decline. ... Many marine biologists now feel that the global catch of table-grade fish is at or near the maximum sustainable level. ... [I]t now turns out that the world was fortunate to have had, in effect, two major food reserves. One was in the form of grain reserves in the principal exporting countries; the other in the form of reserve cropland, virtually all of which was land lying fallow under farm programs in the United States. In recent years, the need to draw down grain reserves and utilize idle cropland had become increasingly apparent. ... The extent of global vulnerability to food supply is underlined by examining the degree of dependence by the rest of the world on North America. . . . [This] ex-treme dependence . . . leaves the world in a very dangerous position in the event of adverse crop years in North America. . . . As matters now stand, a prolonged drought in North America of the kind we have experienced historically about every 20 years, most recently in the early 1950s, would mean widespread famine in many parts of the world.

James P. Grant of the Overseas Development Council warned in a statement to the Senate Foreign Relations Committee July 11, 1974 of the dangers confronting "a new 'Fourth World' . . . made up of some 40 of the poorest and slowest growing countries with a total population of nearly one billion people." Grant said that "these countries are so seriously threatened by the combination of soaring food and fertilizer prices on the one hand, and of skyrocketing oil prices on the other, that they face the prospect of disaster during the next several years unless there is a major, stepped-up international effort to assist them. . . ." "It has been apparent for approximately a year now," Grant asserted, "that the current international scarcity of major agricultural commodities . . . reflects important long-term trends as well as the more temporary factor of lack of rainfall in the Soviet Union and large areas of Asia." Echoing Freeman's pessimism, Grant suggested that "we probably are witnessing in the world food economy a fundamental change from two decades of relative global abundance to an era of more or less chronically tight supplies of essential foodstuffs."

A mixture of pessimism and optimism colors Robert C. Tetro's forecasts in his paper "World Food Prospects and Problems":

In the longer run, the food prospects for the world continue to be of growing concern, with cautious optimism on the adequacy of global food resources. All statistical projections point to larger supplies of grain and oilseeds and to probably modest increases in food availability. However, I would prefer to state a corollary that the serious food shortages on a global scale are likely to be more frequent. The caution arises from a number of questions and responses, such as:

1. Is there a reasonable prospect that population can soon be controlled? Probably not.

2. Can increased food from developed countries and developing countries be distributed to meet all foreseeable needs? Only with great difficulty and substantial improvement in developing countries' technology.

3. What are the more serious immediate problems for world food technology?

a. Water conservation.

b. Improved fisheries culture—sea and fresh water.

c. Increased fertilizer production *and* improved use.

d. New impetus to the Green Revolution.

e. A food security system that includes provision for disaster relief.

f. Global adjustment of production and trade to achieve the most efficient use of food resources.

A summary of present thinking on the supply of and demand for food points to a concern relative to availability and cost which seems to grow in direct proportion to population increases. It is fortunate that agriculture deals with renewable resources that are responsive to intelligent handling; however, present famine threats and unusual price changes suggest the need for the closest cooperation among governments.

This book is a record of the food-supply problems that reached world proportions during 1970–75. It demonstrates the worldwide effect of international trade and diplomatic links in the matter of hunger and world food supply. The material that follows consists largely of the record compiled by FACTS ON FILE in its weekly coverage of world events. As in all FACTS ON FILE works, a conscientious effort was made to keep this volume free of bias and to make it a balanced and accurate reference tool.

LESTER A. SOBEL

New York, N.Y.
July, 1975

Problems & Progress (1970-72)

World Leaders Attack Problems

Although major achievements were reported in the international struggle against hunger during the years 1970–71 and early 1972, some world leaders warned that the worst was yet to come. They asserted that the problems of explosive population growth, environmental pollution and climatic change as well as shorter term difficulties might threaten hundreds of millions of people with famine in the years ahead.

World Food Congress. The second World Food Congress, sponsored by the United Nations Food and Agriculture Organization (FAO), met in The Hague June 16–30, 1970. In a declaration approved June 29, the 1,500 delegates, including 300 youth delegates, stressed that food was a "fundamental human right," the denial of which was "intolerable."

The declaration asserted that "the battle against hunger and underdevelopment can be won," but it added that "victory depends on a massive effort by the entire world community." "It is not enough to think only of food," the delegates said. "The total development of every man, woman and child is at stake."

Among the recommendations of the congress:

"All governments must drastically increase the supply of resources for development and channel an increasing proportion through an improved system of international cooperation. Is it not insane to spend such vast sums on armaments when resources for development are so desperately needed?"

"Governments must ensure that knowledge of different population policies is available to all, and that people are free to follow the mandates of their own conscience in the matter of family size."

"We urge governments to transform inequitable trade arrangements which are a barrier to development. Increased export opportunities must be provided for the developing countries."

"We urge governments to provide farmers and fishermen with the means, services and incentives required to meet growing food needs."

"We urge FAO and other international agencies to marshal their resources to alleviate the growing threat of contamination and destruction of the environment."

In conclusion, the declaration said: "The dialogue initiated at this congress must continue. Food and development are too important to be left only to the experts."

In an opening address June 16, U.N. Secretary General U Thant had urged a meeting of the leaders of the great powers, including Communist China, to discuss world problems. Thant, emphasizing the problems of developing countries, particularly acute shortages of food, said the big five must "have the vision, the wisdom and the human elevation to set aside their fractricidal course."

Sicco L. Mansholt, a vice president of the Common Market's Executive Commission, June 17 recommended the establishment of a world-wide agency with powers to deal with employment and population. Mansholt asserted that the FAO had not achieved its goals because it could not compel governments to carry out its decisions.

Dr. Addeke H. Boerma, director general of the FAO, predicted the same day that unemployment in developing countries would grow as their economies expanded.

(Boerma June 8 had proposed an international dairy development plan to fight malnutrition among the world's children. Boerma told an FAO meeting in Rome that two-thirds of the world's pre-school children suffered enough malnutrition to retard their physical growth and permanently damage their health.)

WFP pledges. Forty-nine countries pledged a total of $215,423,580 at the fourth World Food Program (WFP) pledging conference, which ended Jan. 23, 1970. The donations would go to the WFP and FAO for the two-year period 1971–72. The pledges assured that the goal of $300 million would be reached, WFP officials said.

In a related development, the FAO indicated that fears of a world famine had been rendered groundless by new developments in agricultural technology, according to a Jan. 6 report. The report cited new strains of crops, fertilizers, irrigation and pesticides as among the new developments, and said food production had increased faster than the population. But Secretary General U Thant, in a report to the U.N. Economic & Social Council, gave warning that the "Green Revolution" could prove to be "a Pandora's box rather than a cornucopia" unless it were accompanied by land reform in developing countries. According to a

Jan. 11 report, Thant said that while the threat of famine had been dispelled by the new technology, its likely long-range effect could be a displacement that would prove advantageous only to large-scale commercial farmers.

The WFP's Intergovernmental Committee April 15 announced food-aid projects totaling $126.6 million in 22 countries. Recommendations on channeling more food aid through multilateral channels were also discussed during the committee's 10-day meeting.

Europe food aid ends. An American aid program that in 24 years provided $2.3 billion in food assistance to Europeans ended June 30, 1970 when new shipments to Poland ceased.

The program, called "PL-480" after U.S. Government Public Law 480 for the distribution of surplus food, had helped feed up to three million Poles each day with such basic commodities as wheat flour, dried milk and butter.

(U.S. Controller General Elmer B. Staats told the U.S. Joint Congressional Subcommittee on Economy in Government Jan. 4, 1971 that foreign countries had used PL-480—the Food for Peace program—to finance $693 million worth of military equipment in the past five years.)

Nobel Prize to Borlaug. Dr. Norman E. Borlaug, Iowa-born crop expert and a founder of the Green Revolution, was awarded the 1970 Nobel Peace Prize Oct. 21. Borlaug, who headed a team of scientists from 17 countries experimenting in Mexico with high-yield grains, was given the $78,000 prize for his "great contribution" in spurring food production, especially in Mexico, India and Pakistan. He developed a dwarf strain of wheat that increased Indian and Pakistani harvests by more than 60% in five years. Mexican wheat production was increased by six times in 20 years.

(Borlaug said in Mexico Oct. 21 that his research in developing new foods "is not the solution" and warned, "We have only delayed the world food crisis for another 30 years. If the world population continues to increase at the same rate we will destroy the species.")

MIT study asks end to growth. "The Limits of Growth," a study of current world production and population trends financed by the Club of Rome, predicted a catastrophic world economic and population decline in the next century, unless production and consumption habits were put under deliberate international control. The study was made public in early 1972.

The study, conducted at the Massachusetts Institute of Technology (MIT), centered on a computer model of the interrelations between such economic factors as population, natural resources, industrial and food production, and pollution.

If current trends continued, the report said, growing population and rising demand for production would deplete the dwindling supply of natural resources, including arable land. Recovery of resources would become far more expensive, leaving less capital to replace aging productive capacity, eventually causing a decline in production. This would in turn devastate the population through lack of food and adequate medical services, both of which require heavy investment of capital goods.

Various alternative sets of trends were fed into the computer, but zero population growth alone, even combined with new resource discovery, would only postpone the day of reckoning. A stable world economy with minimally adequate living standards would require "a Copernican revolution of the mind" away from growth and wastefulness.

Specifically, the report called for a halt to population and industrial growth, a reduction in pollution, an increased use of recycling, the production of lasting, repairable goods, and an emphasis on services such as recreation and education rather than consumer goods.

The study was directed by MIT professor Dennis L. Meadows, at the request of the Club of Rome, an international group of business and economic leaders.

Criticism of the study, reported Feb. 26, included charges by economists that the computer model bore little resemblance to complex reality, and that the study ignored possible new technological breakthroughs in energy and food production and in pollution control. Critics also feared that a halt to production would freeze current income distribution patterns, to the detriment of poorer nations and less affluent classes everywhere, or require a substantial drop in American living standards.

Population slowdown urged. The Commission on Population Growth and the American Future issued three reports March 11–25, 1972 urging a U.S. population policy limiting growth and guiding the distribution of the population between urban, suburban and rural areas.

The commission, established by Congress at the request of President Richard M. Nixon, had undertaken a two-year investigation of the effects of continued growth on the economy, the environment, natural resources, living standards and the relations between government and the individual. The March 11 report concluded that "the pluses seem to be on the side of slowing growth and eventually stopping it altogether."

This goal could be largely achieved if unwanted births were prevented, the commission found, by making "freedom of choice and equality of access to the means of fertility control" a matter of government policy.

The commission projected that by the year 2000, U.S. population could reach 322 million if American families averaged three children, but would rise from the current 209 million to only 271 million if the two-child family were the norm.

Ever greater population levels would tend to cause increased bureaucratic controls and regulation of scarce resources and space, so that "the population of 2020 may look back with envy on what, from their vantage point, appears to be our relatively unfettered way of life."

However slowly the population might grow, the commission predicted that "sooner or later we will have to deal with water as a scarce resource," although technological progress would probably assure an adequate supply of energy and clean air. Farm production could handle the lower population growth estimate, but a three-child family norm would cause food prices to rise by as much as 50% in 50 years.

Replying to fears that a population slowdown would hamper economic growth, the commission said that slower growth in the next 10–15 years would result in higher levels of per capita and national income. In addition, slower growth would "buy time for the development of sensible solutions" to environmental problems that might otherwise provoke more drastic and damaging measures. In any case, "changes in consumer tastes and technological development" would affect business and employment far more than population rates.

The commission predicted that average U.S. family income would rise from the current $12,000 a year to over $21,-000 by the year 2000, even with a 30-hour work week and a three-child family. Poverty would be reduced, but some groups would still be excluded from the prevailing prosperity.

In its March 25 report, the commission asked for creation of a federal office to develop population growth and distribution guidelines for regional, state and local governments, and to oversee all government actions affecting population policy.

Although nearly all population growth was expected to take place in the metropolitan areas, the commission recommended that further migration from rural areas be channeled into small cities, whose economic development would be encouraged.

Within metropolitan areas, government planning would aim at controlled, balanced development, without which the growing outer cities would face the same problems of pollution and decay as the inner cities.

The commission also recommended a complete national census every five years, instead of the current 10.

The commission was headed by John D. Rockefeller 3rd and included congressmen, business, labor and educa-tional executives, and representatives of youth, women and minority groups.

Disaster relief program. The U.N. General Assembly Dec. 14, 1971 approved a program for relief to countries stricken by disaster and for assistance in disaster planning. The vote was 86–0 with nine abstentions, among them the Soviet Union. Secretary General U Thant had proposed such a program in July.

The relief program, to be headquartered in Geneva, would also concern man-made disaster situation. It provided for a disaster relief center that would act as the central clearing house for information on plans formulated by U.N. members to assist the victims, and on location, availability and nature of emergency food, clothing, medical and other relief supplies.

Youths hike to combat hunger. Hundreds of thousands of young people hiked up to 30 miles in 285 U.S. communities May 8–9, 1971 to draw attention to world hunger and to raise funds for anti-poverty projects in the U.S. and abroad. The walks were part of a weekend effort sponsored by the U.N. Food and Agriculture Organization. "International Walk for Development" hikes were organized in more than 50 countries around the world.

The American Freedom From Hunger Foundation, a Washington-based organization that coordinated the walks in the U.S., had sponsored such anti-hunger hikes each year since 1968. Private individuals and organizations supported the hikes by pledging sums ranging from a penny to $10 per mile hiked. The money, an estimated $5.1 million in pledges over the two days, was raised for domestic and international programs.

The coordinators said the largest group May 8, 14,000 young people, hiked in Denver. In Reno, Nev., Gov. Mike O'Callaghan joined 1,000 youths for a 27-mile walk. New York City's 1,000 marchers walked 16 miles in a heavy rain. In Washington, 4,000 hikers were joined by the ambassadors of a number of foreign nations.

Biafra & Bangla Desh

Much of the misery and death that accompanies war is often caused by starvation as fighting interrupts agriculture and commerce and requires shifts of populations. Such was the case in the unsuccessful Biafran secession from Nigeria and in the strife that resulted in the creation of the independent state of Bangla Desh from what had formerly been East Pakistan.

Starvation in Biafra. International relief sources estimated that between July 1967 (two months after Biafra seceded from Nigeria) and January 1970 (when the Biafran army was defeated and the Republic of Biafra extinguished), some two to three million people in the stricken area died of the effects of war and starvation. Starvation deaths were said to total sometimes as many as 10,000 a day. As in almost all situations of this kind, however, the reports were often contradictory and never fully reconciled.

During the period of the fighting, ad hoc pro-Biafran groups sprang up in many countries because of the starvation issue. Citizens of the U.S., Great Britain, France and West Germany were extremely influential in pressuring their governments to send food and supplies to the Biafrans. World efforts to aid the starving in Nigeria were stepped up as the fighting ended in January 1970.

Reports from the scene estimated that nearly a million refugees were clogging the roads in search for food. Some relief officials predicted that a million persons would die of famine within a few days, according to Jan. 11 reports, and aid workers described scenes of horror and mass starvation along the refugee routes. The New York Times reported Jan. 13 that 1.5 million persons "at the very least" needed quick relief assistance.

British Prime Minister Harold Wilson Jan. 13 convened a meeting of the heads of all British aid organizations and ordered Lord Hunt, a member of the British relief advisory mission to Nigeria in 1968, to fly to that country to assess the situation.

President Richard M. Nixon Jan. 11 ordered eight U.S. Air Force C 130 cargo aircraft and four helicopters on ready alert to help distribute food and supplies "as soon as the military situation permits." The President authorized an additional $10 million in food and medicine for Biafran relief. Other aid offers poured in from Canada, France, and smaller nations around the globe.

The U.N. Children's Fund (UNICEF) announced Jan. 12 that adequate relief supplies were on hand if clearance to move them to the hunger areas could be obtained from the Nigerian government. An estimated 10,000 to 12,000 tons of foodstocks were said to be warehoused on the Portuguese island of Sao Tome, off the African mainland, while relief personnel awaited Lagos' approval to move the supplies into Biafra.

But Maj. Gen. Yakubu Gowon, the Nigerian leader, denounced the numerous foreign relief agencies that had aided Biafra during the civil war and insisted that Nigeria would handle the job itself. Gowon announced Jan. 14 that his government would accept no assistance from France, Portugal, South Africa, Rhodesia or any other country or agency that had been "studiously hostile" toward Nigeria during the civil war. Joint Church Aid, Caritas, Canairelief and the Nordic Red Cross were listed as unwelcome agencies, and the announcement also declared that relief personnel who had participated in relief flight operations would not be permitted to assist in relief efforts.

Nigerian officials insisted later that the problem was not as serious as had been reported by many foreign observers.

Federal Information Commissioner Anthony Enahoro said at a Lagos news conference Jan. 16 that "the relief situation is well under control" and that there was no need for immediate foreign airlifting of food. Enahoro predicted that the urgent relief problem would be "overcome this month."

An international team of observers reported in Lagos Jan. 16 they had found neither widespread starvation nor mistreatment of inhabitants in the area of Biafra which they visited between Port Harcourt and Owerri. The observers, who began their inspection tour Jan. 10, said they had not gone north of Owerri, where conditions were said to be the worst, because they wanted to return to Lagos to issue their report. The military officers who made up the team reported seeing children suffering from malnutrition, "but they were walking, so they could not have been so badly off," according to Brig. Gen. Yngve Berglund of Sweden. Canadian Brig. Gen. John Drewry reported enough food "in the ground and on the trees."

U.N. Secretary General U Thant arrived in Lagos Jan. 18 and was met by Gowon and other federal leaders. Thant was feted at a state banquet that night. He canceled a scheduled trip to Port Harcourt for a first-hand inspection of relief needs Jan. 19. Thant said in Lagos Jan. 19 before flying to Paris that he had seen "no hint, nor even the slightest, remotest evidence of any violence or mistreatment of the civilian population" in his one-day stay in Nigeria.

Henrik Beer, secretary general of the League of Red Cross Societies, returning Jan. 18 from an inspection tour of former Biafran areas, supported Thant's views. The threat of mass starvation might be "less serious than we thought," Beer said.

The first international group of newsmen authorized to visit former Biafran territory left for Port Harcourt Jan. 18. A report Jan. 20 said some newsmen reported the situation in the conquered areas was "more serious" than had been supposed, citing examples of mass starvation.

The White House announced Jan. 22 that President Nixon had received an urgent request from the Nigerian government for refugee aid. Nixon ordered an immediate renewal of aid efforts. A State Department spokesman said Jan. 22 that reports showed a "problem of greater magnitude than earlier . . . indicated."

A United Nations observer reported Jan. 26 that the relief program was inadequate. Prince Sadruddin Aga Khan said "the question of malnutrition, poverty and death will remain a cause of alarm for many months, and will need a major effort by all the voluntary and governmental agencies." Khan's report,

based on a five-day tour in the area ending Jan. 20, emphasized the need for transport and said Nigerian Red Cross action was "not enough to meet the situation."

By March 11, reports indicated that while an estimated 750,000 people were suffering from malnutrition in the former Biafran territory, few were actually starving.

The federal government continued to ban foreign newsmen from the area, but relief workers and others returning from the eastern region reported that nearly everyone in the former war zone was receiving some food regularly. The Red Cross distribution of 3,000 tons of food a week to three million people was considered to be only subsistence rations, but there were indications that many people were obtaining food on their own and that commerce and small farming had been reactivated.

In an April 11 dispatch, the New York Times reported that 50,000 persons had died of starvation since the end of the civil war, a figure far below the earlier estimates.

The Red Cross announced May 2 that it would end its relief operation and turn responsibility over to the government by June 30. Red Cross President Sir Adetokunbo Ademola explained that "we feel that the emergency is over."

Starvation accompanies emergence of Bangla Desh. The uneasy union of East and West Pakistan broke under the strain during 1971. Nine months of fighting, which began in March as civil war but escalated into conflict between India and West Pakistan in early December, ended in mid-December with victory for the Indian forces and the emergence of a new nation, Bangla Desh, in the area that had been East Pakistan. During the fighting, nearly 10 million Bengalis ultimately fled from East Pakistan to India. These refugees posed an international hunger and health problem in a country chronically short of food but over-endowed with disease. It took more than a year before all the refugees were repatriated to Bangla Desh.

India had called on the U.N. April 22 and May 6, 1971 to provide food and other aid for the Bengali refugees in India.

Pakistan called on the U.N. May 17 to provide food and other relief for suffering people still in East Pakistan.

A Chinese Communist plane carrying two tons of powdered milk arrived in Dacca, East Pakistan May 16 to ease the food shortage in the province.

The Indian Foreign Ministry reported May 22 that Prime Minister Indira Gandhi had written to all heads of state informing them of the problem created by the huge influx of refugees into India.

Mrs. Gandhi said May 24 that the refugees were moving into her country at a rate "unprecedented in recorded history." She said the number totaled 3.5 million and that 60,000 a day continued to cross the frontier. The refugee problem threatened to disrupt India's economy and drain the government's resources, Mrs. Gandhi said.

Pakistani President Agha Mohammad Yahya Khan had charged May 21 that the number of refugees estimated by India were "highly exaggerated and distorted." He claimed that India had added to the total of East Pakistanis on its territory the unemployed and homeless of India's West Bengal State.

Indian Health Minister Uma Shankar Dixit reported to parliament June 7 that as of June 4 the East Pakistani influx totaled 4,738,054 and was growing.

Dixit said 2,722,561 refugees were inhabiting camps in the Indian states of West Bengal, Assam, Bihar and the territories of Meghalaya and Tripura. In addition, 2,015,493 were living outside camps, largely sleeping in the open, he said. Parliament had convened in special session to consider the cholera outbreak.

India had appealed May 31 for international assistance to help it combat a cholera outbreak and to cope with the refugee problem in general. Various governments and private charitable organizations were reported June 8 to have responded by providing or pledging to donate food, medicine, clothing and funds.

U.S. officials in Washington July 31 disclosed agreement by the U.N. and Pakistan on an American plan for establishment of a 153-member U.N. relief and rehabilitation unit in strife-torn East Pakistan. The relief effort was to be financed by non-U.N. funds. An initial U.S. contribution of $1 million for the program was granted by Secretary of State William P. Rogers to U.N. Secretary General U Thant Aug. 9. The U.S. pledged another $1 million.

According to a U.N. informant, the principal purpose of the U.N. force was to deal primarily with helping Pakistani authorities prevent starvation and disease and with rehabilitating homes and shelters.

The U.N. was also extending its relief efforts to eastern India, which contained nearly seven million East Pakistani refugees, it was announced July 31. UNICEF was to establish 1,000 centers in the border region Aug. 15 to distribute high-protein foods to prevent deaths from malnutrition among refugee children.

New Delhi July 30 had ordered foreign relief workers among East Pakistani refugees in India to cease their operations within 48 hours. An Indian official explained "the least possible number of foreign volunteers should be permitted for a variety of reasons. If none at all are there, that would be the best possible alternative."

Meeting with representatives of 28 countries, the U.N.'s U Thant Aug. 18 renewed his appeal for more funds to assist the victims of the fighting in East Pakistan and of the cyclone there in 1970.

Thant said $51 million in cash had been received and another $54.5 million had been pledged through U.N. channels for the relief program. Canada earlier Aug. 18 had donated $7 million in supplies and France gave about $200,000.

The plight of East Pakistanis deteriorated further as flood waters from rivers swollen by monsoon rains since Aug. 22 claimed the lives of more than 70 persons and ruined an estimated three million acres of crops, the government reported Aug. 25.

The U.S. agreed Sept. 17 to provide the U.N. with two helicopters, 200 trucks and 210,000 more tons of grain and food blend for relief in East Pakistan.

The increased assistance brought total American aid to East Pakistan to $137 million compared with $82 million provided for East Pakistani refugees in India.

A 13-nation consortium agreed at an emergency meeting in Paris Oct. 26 to give India a "substantial part" of the $700 million that, it was estimated, was needed for the relief of the nearly 10 million East Pakistani refugees in India until March 1972. The meeting was held under World Bank auspices.

A communique issued by the conferees "noted that worldwide contributions pledged to date came to over $200 million." The statement said "the assistance [to New Delhi] should preferably be in the form of grants to prevent drastic cutbacks of development expenditures in India."

The consortium consisted of the U.S., Britain, France, West Germany, Canada, the Netherlands, Belgium, Norway, Sweden, Denmark, Italy, Japan and Austria.

New, major fighting in East Pakistan brought a virtual halt to U.N. relief operations in East Pakistan, a U.N. spokesman reported Nov. 23. The spokesman said the distribution of food supplies had been stopped outside Dacca and Chittagong after mines had damaged two food-storage containers and after the Pakistani army had confiscated six trucks.

The U.S. State Department disclosed Jan. 8, 1972 that the U.S. was continuing to provide India with a $90 million relief program for the nine million Bengali refugees still there despite reluctance by many Nixon Administration officials to discuss it.

India had appealed to the U.N. High Commissioner for Refugees for an additional $50–$60 million to care for Bengali refugees still in India, it was reported Jan. 21. Three–five million of the 10 million Bengalis who had fled to India in 1971 had returned to their homes in Bangla Desh. The additional funds would bring total refugee assistance to India to $250 million.

Kurt Waldheim, who had succeeded U Thant as U.N. Secretary General, Feb. 16 proposed a massive relief program for Bangla Desh and issued an international appeal for $565 million in contributions before the end of 1972. These funds, he said in a report, would just meet "the most immediate needs of the area so as to avert large-scale misery and hunger."

Waldheim's report in effect gave the U.N. sole responsibility for the task of food distribution and refugee resettlement in Bangla Desh.

Waldheim met Feb. 18 with representatives of 30 prospective contributing countries. Among those attending were diplomats from the U.S., Britain, France and the Soviet Union.

The U.N. was reported Feb. 22 to have urged the U.S. to provide more funds for Bangla Desh relief. Maurice J. Williams, deputy administrator of the U.S. Agency for International Development, replied that the U.S. would give the request sympathetic consideration. But he said Washington would insist on two provisions: the U.N. must seek greater contributions from other countries and the U.N. must coordinate relief shipments.

Appropriations including $200 million for Bangla Desh refugees won U.S. Congressional approval Feb. 24 and March 2.

The Indian government announced March 16 that 9,777,000 Bengali refugees had returned to Bangla Desh from India, with 122,451 awaiting repatriation. New Delhi had spent $367 million on the refugees as of Feb. 29 and foreign assistance for them had totaled $170 million, Deputy Minister P. B. Mehta told parliament.

The U.S. March 23 contributed $35.3 million to be spent for Bangla Desh relief. The money was to be funneled through the U.N. Relief Operation Dacca (UNROD).

George Bush, chief U.S. delegate to the U.N., said the latest American contribution would be used to help ease transportation bottlenecks that had impeded food and other supplies from reaching their destination. In addition, the U.S. was providing $36.5 million worth of grain, $20 million worth of vegetable oils and $3.7 million worth of shelter supplies, Bush said.

The U.S. had given Bangla Desh $267.5 million to help prevent starvation and suffering, the Agency for International Development announced Aug. 12 in Washington.

Indian Labor Minister R. K. Khadilkar reported Dec. 20 that virtually all Bengalis who had taken refuge in India during the 1971 Indian-Pakistani war had been repatriated to Bangla Desh.

Struggle Over Fishing Rights

Many national and scientific leaders had regarded the oceans as a virtually inexhaustible reservoir of protein in the form of fish. The world's annual catch zoomed from 21 million tons in 1950 to 63 million in 1968, with each year setting a record. This average annual growth in fish catch of nearly 5% far exceeded the 2% world population growth rate. But a sudden decline in the world catch took place in 1969, and although 1970 was another record year, the fishing industry is in trouble. Individual fishing areas had been showing signs of depletion long before 1969, and several nations have tried to protect their protein resources from foreign fishermen by unilaterally announcing extensions of their sovereignty to up to 200 miles from their coasts. Foreign fishermen, however, generally resisted efforts to bar them from their traditional fishing areas.

(Eight nations were reported to claim territorial waters or fishing limits of 200 miles, according to a 106-nation survey released during February 1970 by the U.N. Food and Agriculture Organization. The eight countries were Argentina, Chile, Ecuador, El Salvador, Nicaragua, Panama, Peru and Uruguay.)

World fishing catch up 10% in 1970. The U.N. Food and Agriculture Organization reported Jan. 6, 1972 that the world fish catch during 1970 rose more than 10%, reaching a new record of 69.3 million metric tons.

Peru remained the leading fishing nation in 1970 with a total of 12.6 million tons of fish caught. Japan was second with 9.3 million tons, followed by the Soviet Union with 7.3 million tons.

China, Norway and the U.S. followed, with 5.8, 3, and 2.7 million tons respectively.

Peru's catch, up 25% from 1969, consisted almost entirely of anchoveta, which was processed into fish meal for export.

Latin nations seize U.S. boats. Peru and Ecuador each seized and fined U.S. tuna boats in early 1970 for fishing within their declared 200-mile "territorial waters." The first incident took place Jan. 21 when a Peruvian gunboat intercepted the U.S. tuna boat Hornet about 25 miles off the coast; this was the first seizure of a U.S. fishing boat since June 1969.

The second seizure of 1970 was that of the U.S. tuna clipper City of Panama by Ecuador Feb. 14. A Peruvian gunboat then seized the U.S. tuna boat Western King about 75 miles out to sea Feb. 23. Ecuador seized two tuna boats—the Japanese schooner Seiyo Maru (reported Feb. 26) and the U.S. tuna boat Day Island Feb. 26. Another U.S. tuna schooner was seized by Peru April 17. In each case, the boats were released on the payment of fines.

Mexico June 26 released 24 U.S. tuna fishermen held for three weeks in a dispute over territorial waters.

The 24 men and their two tuna clippers had been seized June 5 off the islands of Las Tres Marias and taken to the western port of Mazatlan. Following negotiations between the U.S. embassy and the Mexican government and the subsequent payment of $41,000 in fines, the crew was released. A spokesman for the American Tunaboat Association said the two boats had "accidentally" drifted into the 12-mile limit surrounding the Mexican-owned islands when a skiff overturned. (Mexico claimed a 12-mile territorial water limit.)

Brazil said June 1, 1971 that warships and planes would begin immediate patrol of a 200-mile territorial water limit. In a communique, the government declared that the new limits would be "rigorously observed beginning July 30." President Emilio Garrastazu Medici March 25, 1970 had ordered extension of Brazil's territorial waters from 12 miles to 200 miles along the country's 4,600-mile coastline.

France and Trinidad & Tobago, according to press reports June 1, had begun negotiations with Brazil on the application for fishing licenses within the new limits. The U.S. had insisted that such unilateral claims were not bound by international law and thus it would not recognize them. It accordingly advised U.S. shrimpers to ignore the 200-mile limit. Brazil was the ninth Latin American country to claim the extended limit on its coastal waters. In a related development, Brazil charged the U.S. June 9 with "intolerable economic pressure" after the Ways and Means Committee of the U.S. House of Representatives was reported to have indefinitely postponed a vote on continued U.S. participation in the International Coffee Agreement in apparent retaliation for the new Brazilian territorial claim. Coffee accounted for one-third of Brazil's exports in 1970.

The Brazilian Foreign Ministry expressed the "shock" of the government over the House move, stating that the coffee agreement should not be bound to the issue of the extension of territorial waters, a subject "touching the sovereignty of Brazil."

Brazilian Foreign Minister Mario Gibson Barbosa and U.S. Ambassador William M. Rountree May 9, 1972 signed an agreement allowing Brazil to regulate the operations of U.S. shrimp boats within 200 miles of Brazil's coasts. The accord was effective through 1973.

The agreement was the first signed by the U.S. with a nation claiming 200-mile offshore sovereignty. However, it did not recognize the 200-mile claim as legal.

The treaty limited the number of U.S. boats permitted to operate within the area and allowed Brazilian authorities to tax, license, board and search the boats. Shrimp boats found to have violated catch and seasonal restrictions would be subject to seizure, but would be released after payment of fines.

U.S. Assistant State Secretary Charles A. Meyer had conferred with officials in Peru and Ecuador in December 1971 over the fishing-rights dispute.

On his departure from Peru Dec. 17 Meyer announced that in talks Dec. 16 with Peruvian Foreign Minister Edgardo Mercado Jarrin, agreement was reached on a conference early in 1972 between the U.S., Peru, Ecuador and Chile on the territorial waters issue.

(The Miami Herald reported Dec. 22 that the U.S. had eased its position during the talks by suggesting that the U.S. would buy licenses for its fishing boats in Latin waters, but under protest to preserve legally the U.S. 12-mile position.)

Meyer had begun his trip Dec. 10 in Ecuador. He met with Ecuadorian Foreign Minister Rafael Garcia Velasco Dec. 10 and Dec. 12 and with Ecuadorian President Jose Maria Velasco Ibarra Dec. 13.

Velasco Ibarra said Dec. 12 that Ecuador could not reach any agreement with the U.S. while economic sanctions were in effect against Ecuador. (On Dec. 8 the U.S. House of Representatives had voted to cut off all aid to Ecuador because of its seizure of American tuna boats.)

Fifteen California tuna boats had spurned U.S. State Department requests and purchased licenses to fish within Ecuador's disputed 200-mile offshore territorial limits, the Miami Herald reported Feb. 7, 1972.

According to August Felando, general manager of the American Tuna Boat Association, the boat operators bought permits because they could no longer afford to pay the stiff fines levied when their ships were captured in the disputed waters.

The U.S. government reimbursed the operators for the fines, but only after delays of as long as a year.

Three U.S. tuna boats were seized by Ecuador Nov. 21, 1972 and six were taken Nov. 22 for fishing within Ecuador's declared 200-mile offshore territorial limits. Their capture brought to 19 the number of U.S.-owned boats seized by Ecuador since Nov. 12. The boats seized Nov. 22 reportedly returned to the U.S. after paying $444,562 in fines and taxes.

Soviet aid for Latin fishing industry. Peru and the U.S.S.R. Sept. 6, 1971 signed an accord for the construction of a fishing port at Paita with Soviet technical and financial assistance. The cost was estimated at $54 million.

The agreement, signed by Soviet Minister of Fisheries Alexander Iskhov and Peruvian Foreign Minister Edgardo Mercado Jarrin, also called for Soviet training of Peruvian personnel to operate the port and in manning Soviet fishing vessels that would sail from it.

The news agency Tass reported Dec. 9 that Russia and Chile had signed a "program of cooperation for 1972" which would provide Russian aid for Chile's fishing industry. It would include the use of Soviet fishing boats and construction of new fishing harbors in Chile with Soviet technical aid.

Canada charges raids. Canadian Fisheries Minister Jack Davis accused Russia, Poland and East Germany of "callous actions" in overfishing waters along Canada's continental shelf, according to a Feb. 7, 1970 report.

Davis said the overfishing was "being practiced today on an awesome scale by the Russians and the Poles. The East Germans are also moving in on our continental shelf," Davis charged, and he added that "these massive raids are leaving gaping holes in our fish stocks." The fisheries minister said the intrusions were also threatening to "upset the balance of nature" in the North Atlantic.

Davis urged an agreement on an overall quota on all fish stocks in the North Atlantic, with quotas to be set by an international panel.

(Canadian sources reported that the Russian boats carry on 24-hour operations and process their catch on board, and that Canadian fishermen are not allowed to use lights at night because they attract fish, but the Russian boats are well lit. Canadians were forbidden to catch herring in 1968 due to serious depletion of the species, but the Russians continued to catch them.)

A Soviet trawler rammed a Canadian fishing boat in international waters off the coast of Vancouver Island early July 26. The incident, the fourth in less than a year and the second in July, caused Canada to deliver a strong protest to the Soviet government.

Canada and the U.S.S.R. signed their first fishing agreement, Reuters reported Jan. 24, 1971. The Soviet Union agreed to discontinue fishing off Vancouver Island in return for fishing rights in Canadian territorial waters off Queen Charlotte Islands. Soviet ships were also authorized to take on supplies at the ports of Vancouver and Prince Rupert. (The Canadian parliament had banned

the port facilities to Soviet trawlers in 1969 to obstruct large-scale Soviet fishing operations in the area.)

Norway and Canada July 15, 1971 exchanged notes authorizing up to 20 Norwegian boats to fish for cod in the Gulf of St. Lawrence,—at least 12 miles from shore—from mid-August to mid-December, until Jan. 1, 1975. No other Norwegian fishing vessels would be permitted in Canada's fisheries zone.

U.S.-Soviet fishing pact. An agreement limiting fishing rights off the New England and Middle Atlantic coast was signed in Washington Dec. 11, 1970 by Soviet and U.S. representatives.

The pact increased by 15 days the length of time certain species of fish could not be caught, enlarged the restricted area by 75 miles and added protection for menhaden and black sea bass.

Sen. William B. Spong Jr. (D, Va.) and Sen. B. Everett Jordan (D, N.C.) criticized the accord Dec. 11 on the grounds that it did not sufficiently restrict catches of sea and river herring. The two-year agreement, to take effect Jan. 1, 1971 and to extend until April 15 of each year of its duration, was signed by V. M. Kamentsev, Soviet first deputy minister of fisheries, and by Donald L. McKernan, special assistant for fisheries and wildlife to the U.S. secretary of state. McKernan said additional discussions would be held to renegotiate northern Pacific fisheries agreements and that the question of herring could then be raised as well as a Soviet request to use U.S. ports for repairs on its fishing vessels.

(President Nixon Oct. 30 had signed legislation increasing from $10,000 to $100,000 the maximum penalty for illegal operation of foreign fishing vessels in U.S. waters.)

The U.S. lodged a protest with the Soviet embassy May 14, 1971 over the seventh case in 10 days of Soviet herring trawlers running through the fishing gear of U.S. lobster boats in international waters off Nantucket Island, Mass. Talks aboard a Soviet vessel appeared to end the trouble May 19 but harassment occurred again May 20.

Donald L. McKernan, a U.S. State Department special assistant for fisheries, met May 19 near Nantucket Lightship aboard the S. S. Robert Eikhe with Yuri I. Radtsev, commander of the 120-boat Soviet fleet.

McKernan said later that Radtsev had "recognized our position that their boats were violating international law of the seas and would work to rectify the situation. . . . The Soviets acknowledge, generally, that it was their job to look out for our gear . . . they indicated that their government did not want any difficulty over this." Radtsev was said to have agreed "that U.S. fishermen could contact a Soviet inspection vessel in the area which would react immediately if there were trouble, or potential trouble."

Only hours after the agreement, two U.S. lobster boats were reported May 20 to be suffering new harassment by Soviet trawlers "zigzagging . . . at various speeds, deliberately destroying our gear." Charles W. Bray 3rd, a State Department press officer, said the U.S. believed "the [Soviet] commander did not have time to contact all of his ship captains."

Four days of talks ending Nov. 12 produced an offer by the Soviet fishing fleet to compensate a U.S. lobster company for damage caused by Soviet trawlers. Armenak S. Babaev, president of the Soviet fleet, known as SovRyb-Flot, offered the Prelude Lobster Company $89,000 after flying from Moscow to Westport Point, Mass. Babaev recommended that a bilateral U.S.-Soviet commission be set up to handle future disputes. The U.S. company's president, Joseph S. Gaziano, said that although Prelude had originally asked for more he was accepting the Soviet offer in the interest of "good will among fishermen."

U.S.-Soviet ship incident. A U.S. Coast Guard icebreaker which had sent men aboard a Soviet vessel accused of breaking fishing laws in the Bering Sea Jan. 17, 1972 got permission to fire across the bow of the Soviet ship Jan. 18 when it "appeared to flee."

The incident, related Jan. 18 by Lt. Cmdr. Gilbert Shaw, a Coast Guard spokesman, involved the U.S. icebreaker Storis and two Soviet ships, the factory vessel Lamut and the trawler Kolyvan.

The Storis had come upon the Kolyvan Jan. 17 transferring fish to the Lamut nine and a half miles from Saint Matthew Island in the Bering Sea, about 200 miles west of the Alaskan coast. Coast Guard personnel from the Storis sent men aboard the two vessels, determined they were violating a U.S. regulation against transfer of fish within a 12-mile zone contiguous to land and ordered them to follow the Storis to Adak Island for a court hearing.

Some time after beginning the journey to Adak, the two Soviet ships refused to go on. The Lamut then attempted to escape the Storis, which caught up with it and took the Soviet fishing fleet's commander into custody. It was during the chase of approximately one hour that the Storis' commander, William P. Allen, obtained but was not required to act on permission from Coast Guard headquarters in Washington to fire warning shots in the direction of the Lamut.

Salmon ban. At a meeting of Scandinavian fisheries ministers in Copenhagen March 19, Sweden and Denmark decided to join West Germany in rejecting British proposals for a total ban on salmon fishing for the North Atlantic. Norway refused to join in the rejection of the proposal made in February by then British Prime Minister Harold Wilson.

A year later an unofficial U.S. delegation of the Committee on the Atlantic Salmon Emergency disclosed April 23, 1971 that it had failed to persuade Danish government leaders to ban salmon fishing in the Atlantic Ocean.

The committee contended, during a visit to Denmark, that Danish fishing in the Davis Strait, off Greenland, deprived North American rivers of salmon. The Danes had already limited the catch for 1971.

Canada and the U.S. Dec. 24, 1971 called jointly for immediately halting salmon fishing in international waters. The statement was said to be aimed at Danish vessels which had been taking salmon on high seas west of Greenland despite an international conservation agreement to ban salmon fishing beyond 12 miles offshore.

In a related move, President Nixon signed a bill Dec. 24 authorizing him to prohibit fish imports from nations whose fishing operations diminish the effectiveness of international fishery conservation programs.

Canada and the U.S., which had spent millions of dollars to promote salmon runs from their rivers, contended the fishing should be restricted mainly to domestic waters.

Canada May 29, 1972 banned commercial salmon fishing off the tip of the Gaspe peninsula in a further effort to protect the species. Gaspe fishermen would be compensated for their losses, as would salmon fishermen in New Brunswick and Newfoundland, who had been ordered to put away their nets May 1.

Fisheries Minister Jack Davis charged that unless Denmark imposed similar curbs on Atlantic salmon fishing, the species would wither away and the annual spawning runs up Canadian rivers would end, the Miami Herald reported May 10. However, Danish officials insisted Danish fishermen were adhering to international conservation agreements, and that their small fleet could not possibly endanger the species, the Herald said.

The Danish parliament Dec. 15, 1972 narrowly approved an international agreement banning high-seas salmon fishing off the west coast of Greenland by 1976. Critics charged the government had bowed to U.S. pressures.

Iceland sets 50-mile limit. Iceland July 14, 1972 published regulations extending its fishing limits from 12 to 50 nautical miles effective Sept. 1.

Talks between Icelandic and British officials, held in Reykjavik July 10-13, had broken down after the two sides failed to reach an interim accord on British fishing off the Icelandic coast.

The Icelandic government added three helicopters and a reconnaissance plane to its fleet, indicating preparations for a possible showdown, the New York Times reported July 15.

In an interim decision Aug. 17, the International Court of Justice (World Court) in The Hague ruled that the new limit was invalid. But Iceland held that the court lacked jurisdiction.

The World Court ruled 14-1 that the trawlers of Britain and West Germany, which had filed the suit, must not be interfered with outside the 12-mile limit pending a final decision by the tribunal. The court also ordered Britain to restrict its annual catch in Icelandic waters to 170,000 tons and West Germany to 119,000 tons.

The Icelandic Cabinet formally rejected the World Court decision Aug. 18. Fisheries Minister Ludvik Josefsson said after the meeting that if British ships "come within the 50-mile limit we shall warn them that they are breaking the rules." If the ships failed to comply with the new restrictions, they would be towed into port and their captains would be subject to fines, Josefsson said.

The Norwegian, Swedish, Danish and Finnish foreign ministers assured their Icelandic counterpart Sept. 2 that they supported Iceland's extension of its fishing limits to 50 miles.

About 100 British, West German and Belgian trawlers Sept. 1 defied the new limit and continued to fish within 50 miles of Iceland's coasts.

For several days after the new limit went into effect, Icelandic aircraft and gunboats patrolling the coast restricted themselves to merely photographing the unmarked vessels. The coast guard took its first direct action Sept. 5 when the gunboat Aegir cut the trawling wires of an unmarked British trawler, which had refused to identify itself or comply with an order to quit the 50-mile zone. A second gunboat tried to cut the wires of another British trawler Sept. 5, but the trawling crew outmaneuvered it.

The British government protested the cutting of the wires as a dangerous practice Sept. 5, but Icelandic Foreign Minister Einar Agustsson rejected the protest the following day.

Fisheries Minister Josefsson warned Sept. 6 that Iceland would not resume negotiations with Britain if warships were dispatched to protect the fishing vessels. The warning came amid reports that the warship Aurora was headed for the Icelandic coast, recalling the 1958–61 so-called "cod war" in which British men-of-war ships escorted trawlers fishing off the Icelandic coast in defiance of the then new 12-mile fishing limit.

U.S.-Japanese pact. The U.S. and Japan reached agreement Nov. 27, 1972 on fishing rights in the North Pacific.

Under one accord, Japan was to restrict crab fishing for two years in the Bering Sea by 70%, but would continue these operations north and west of the Pribilof Islands. A second agreement gave Japan continued rights to fish in selected areas off Alaska's Aleutian Islands within the nine-mile fishing zone contiguous to the three-mile territorial limit. Japan in turn would refrain from fishing in "certain areas of the high seas" off Alaska during certain times of the year to avoid conflict with American fishermen.

EEC accord. Britain, Ireland and Denmark, then applicants for EEC (European Economic Community) membership, reached agreement with the EEC in Brussels Dec. 12, 1971 on fishing rights in the applicants' inshore waters.

The agreement would bar access by member nations to coastal waters of the applicant countries for the first 10 years after their entry into the EEC. At the end of 10 years, the EEC Council of Ministers would decide on future arrangements.

The special regulations meant that about 95% of the fish then caught inside the 12-mile limit would be protected from foreign fishermen during the 10-year period, according to the London Times Dec. 13. The 12-mile limit would operate around approximately 30% of Britain's coasts, 70% of the Irish coast, and a stretch of Denmark's western Jutland, as well as its Faroe Islands and Greenland. France was also granted a 12-mile limit for the coasts of five departments in Brittany and Normandy. The six-mile limit would apply in other areas off the applicant nations' coasts. The agreement constituted a major retreat by Britain's chief negotiator, Geoffrey Rippon, who had previously insisted on exclusive national fishing rights after the 10-year period. British fishing industry leaders and parliamentary opponents of EEC membership immediately denounced the accord.

Norway, the fourth applicant for EEC membership, rejected the agreement on the ground it did not provide a "reasonable assurance" for Norwegian fishermen.

Peru's anchovy catch fails. Peru's Fisheries Ministry announced Aug. 1,

1972 the indefinite suspension of fishmeal sales abroad due to a large drop in the anchovy catch during several previous months. Anchovy fishing would be permitted near three ports on the extreme southern Pacific coast, but a ban on activities in all other coastal areas, decreed June 30, would remain in effect indefinitely.

According to the New York Times Aug. 11, ecological changes not fully understood by oceanographers had caused anchovies and related species to all but vanish from Peruvian coastal waters. Fishmeal exports were down by 500,000 tons thus far in 1972, leaving Peru with far less than the volume already contracted for by foreign buyers.

The drop in fish production, which accounted for more than one-third of Peru's export earnings, was accompanied by a sharp decrease in food production and in exports of cotton, sugar and wool, the Times reported.

Peru announced Sept. 26 that exports of fish oil and fishmeal would be stopped indefinitely Oct. 1, confirming that the fishing industry was experiencing the worst crisis in its history.

With the decree, the government reportedly sought to avoid penalty clauses in contracts to deliver 400,000 metric tons of fishmeal to buyers throughout the world by the end of 1972.

(The crisis was aggravated by a sharp drop in domestic food production by the agricultural sector, reported Sept. 20. Due to poor harvests, the Agriculture Ministry would enforce a law requiring owners of agricultural land in Lima, Ancash and Ica to use not less than 40% of their acreage to grow vegetables, potatoes, sorghum, maize or wheat.)

In an attempt to alleviate the fishing crisis, Gen. Javier Tantalean Vianini, fisheries minister, had recently traveled to the U.S. to ask for assistance in determining the factors affecting the behavior of the ocean currents off the Peruvian coast. However, the U.S. had refused such assistance until Peru signed a bilateral agreement allowing California fishing boats unlimited access to its waters, the newsletter Latin America reported Sept. 22.

Tantalean also visited Cuba, which agreed Sept. 13 to accept a postponement on deliveries of Peruvian fishmeal in 1972.

The resumption of limited anchovy fishing off the southern coast was permitted Dec. 4 after a ban of several months.

U.S. proposes policy. An ocean policy statement released by the White House May 23, 1970 proposed reservation of the ocean floors beyond the continental shelf "as the common heritage of mankind." It called for a treaty to "establish an international regime for the exploitation of seabed resources" beyond the depth of 660 feet (200 meter).

President Nixon suggested that coastal nations waive claims to the ocean bed beyond the continental shelf and "act as trustees for the international community" in return for "a share of the international revenues" from the zone.

In a separate statement, the State Department reiterated U.S. policy that "it is not obliged to recognize territorial seas which exceed three miles" but supported the 12-mile limit if a treaty could be negotiated with widespread international acceptance and providing for freedom of navigation in international straits. It said the U.S. also would seek "to accommodate the interests of coastal states in the fishery resources off their coasts."

The U.S. Aug. 3 offered a modified draft of its proposal. The offer was made in Geneva at the opening session of a four-week meeting of the U.N. Seabed Committee.

According to an Aug. 1 report, the Nixon Administration had hoped to present a draft treaty that would preserve the common use of the ocean floor beyond the continental shelf by creating an organization to regulate its exploitation and funnel royalties to emerging nations for economic development. This draft was opposed by four members of the Senate Interior and Insular Affairs Committee in a letter dated July 21. The four—Henry M. Jackson (D, Wash.), Gordon Allott (R, Colo.), Lee Metcalf (D, Mont.) and Henry L. Bellmon (R, Okla.)—claimed that the proposed treaty was "inconsistent with the national interest." Three committee members met July 27 with officials of the State, Defense and Interior Departments and succeeded in modifying some points of the draft.

The resulting proposal was labeled only a "working paper for discussion purposes" that "did not necessarily represent the definitive views of the U.S. government." The proposals called for a limit of the international seabed at a depth of 200 meters. Future exploitation or exploration beyond that would be under licenses granted by an International Seabed Resource Authority whose income would be channeled through development organizations to underdeveloped nations. Under an International Trusteeship Area, coastal nations would administer licensing and share in fees beyond the 200-meter depth.

The U.S. proposed Aug. 3, 1971 that all nations have the right to set their territorial sea limits at 12 miles from shore. The proposal was made by U.S. delegate John R. Stevenson in Geneva at a new series of meetings of the U.N. Seabed Committee.

Stevenson said that while the U.S. continued to favor the three-mile limit, it recognized that a 12-mile zone represented "probably the only possibility for reaching agreement" between the widely differing positions. He said it was "apparent that the overwhelming majority of states are prepared to accept the 12-mile limit." (In a related development, Iceland announced Aug. 6 that its fishing limit would be extended to a 50–70 mile limit from its present 12-mile limit, effective Sept. 1, 1972).

The U.S. also called for international bodies for regulating fisheries and for measures to insure conservation of the "living resources of the sea."

Soviet & Far East Food Output

Food output up in 1970. Food production in the Far East was increasing ahead of the population growth, the U.N. Food and Agriculture Organization reported Aug. 22, 1971.

The survey said Communist China's 1970 grain harvest totaled 230 million tons, compared with about 220 million tons reported for the previous year. Cambodia showed a 25% increase in agricultural production in 1970, according to the report. The rise was attributed largely to a recovery of rice output following a sharp drop in 1969 because of drought. Farm production in South Vietnam increased in 1970 by 8%, which the report said "reflects more settled conditions in the rice-producing areas which are being rapidly planted to high-yielding varieties."

According to the U.N. survey, farm production in Eastern Europe in 1970 was down 1% compared with 1969. The exception was the Soviet Union which showed a 9% gain following a loss of almost 4% in 1969.

U.S.S.R. seeks greater output. A plenary session of the Soviet Communist Party Central Committee July 3, 1970 approved a Politburo agriculture report submitted July 2 by party General Secretary Leonid I. Brezhnev. The report condemned agricultural mismanagement during the previous five-year period and called for increased production of meat and grains.

Brezhnev complained that in the past "some agricultural, government and party bodies slackened guidance and control over the financial and economic activities of the collective and state farms." This had resulted in a grain output which "still does not satisfy us" and insufficient livestock produce, "especially meat," to satisfy demand.

In order to remedy this, the 1971-75 economic development plan would provide for an increase in agricultural investments of 70% (about $85 billion) for "the intensification of production and its technical reequipment." Average annual production of grain and meat would rise to 195 million tons by 1975 (as against 162 million tons during 1965-70) and 15.6 million (as against 11.4 million for 1965-70), under the plan.

In a related development, all major Soviet newspapers carried July 18 a notice of government plans to increase the price paid producers of meat and dairy products. The directive said that, retroactive to May, the government would pay 20% more for milk and cream and 35-50% more for beef. The newspapers published July 19 a directive saying that 50% more would be paid for cattle, poultry, wool and dairy products supplied in excess of planned quotas. Both decisions were considered to be aimed at stimulating efforts by private producers, estimated to provide as much as 40% of the Soviet Union's meat supply.

These farm incentives were reported July 21 to have been extended to other types of garden produce.

An announcement in the CP newspaper Pravda said collective farms would be guaranteed "not less than an average 15%" profit for fruit and vegetables and "not less than 25% for onions and garlic." In addition, central and republic ministries were told July 21 to increase efficiency in insuring supplies to the consumers of fruit, vegetables and potatoes.

Announcing the results of the 1970 plan, the Central Statistical Board reported Feb. 3, 1971 that agricultural productivity had increased by 8.7%. (The board listed Soviet population as 243,900,000 as of Jan. 1.)

A draft version of the 1971-75 five-year plan was approved by the Central Committee Feb. 13 and published Feb. 14. An estimated $90 million was to be invested in agriculture in order to "meet more fully the population's growing demand for foodstuffs and industry's for raw materials."

Brezhnev reported at the 24th Soviet Communist Party Congress March 30 that 1970's grain harvest had totaled 186 million metric tons. Indications that this was insufficient were reinforced by a U.S. disclosure Nov. 5 that the U.S. had agreed to sell $136 million worth of grain to the U.S.S.R. for livestock feed.

A further indication of unsatisfactory Soviet grain output was the report by Brezhnev at the opening of the Supreme Soviet's winter session Nov. 26, 1971 that 1971 Soviet grain production was expected to total only 180 million metric tons. But he predicted that by 1975 the "total industrial and agricultural output of the U.S.S.R. would exceed the present production level of the U.S."

In a related development, Soviet Minister of Agriculture Vladimir V. Matskevich said Dec. 9 in Washington that his country wanted to buy agricultural machinery and licenses from the U.S. for production in the U.S.S.R. of tractors, combines and other equipment "by the millions."

The Central Statistical Board, reporting Jan. 23, 1972 on 1971 production, said that agricultural output was stationary at approximately $105 billion.

Soviet newspapers revealed Feb. 18 that Brezhnev had called party and government leaders of the union republics to Moscow Feb. 17 to discuss "problems of preparing and carrying out spring field work, as well as the further development of animal husbandry." Western agricultural specialists believed that as much as one-third of the 1972 crop of winter wheat, barley and rye had been lost because of unusually cold weather.

Chinese output up. The U.S. Agriculture Department reported April 28, 1971 that China had achieved a record grain output in 1970 and that its soybean production was the highest in three years. The increased food yield was assisted by record large use of fertilizers, more irrigation, mechanization and newer seeds, the report said.

According to statistical estimates released by the Japanese Foreign Office March 4, Chinese agricultural production in 1970 had exceeded 1969's output by 5% to 10%.

Chinese Premier Chou En-lai had said in an interview with U.S. writer Edgar Snow (published in the Italian magazine Epoca) that China's grain production in 1970 totaled 240 million metric tons (well below the 1959 output of 270 million tons), with state grain reserves currently at 40 million tons.

Chou added that chemical fertilizer output had increased from 1.3 million metric tons in 1959 to 14 million in 1970.

(Communist China had reported Dec. 30, 1970 that its food harvest that year was the largest in its history, but it did not provide statistical details.)

Although China's increase in food output did not yet make the country independent of foreign supplies, apparently it did give Peking more leverage in deciding where to buy grain. This was bad news for Australia, a major grain exporter, which did not recognize Peking.

According to an April 13, 1971 report in the weekly publication Australian Comment, Prime Minister William McMahon had confirmed that he had received information through British diplomatic channels that China had canceled its annual wheat order. News reports cited "political reasons" for the cancellation. China, which had bought about 32% of the wheat exported by Australia since 1960, wanted to buy wheat in the future from Canada, which recognized the Peking government.

In a communique July 3, Peking promised Canada priority treatment as a supplier of wheat to China.

It was announced Sept. 14 that Canada had contracted to sell about 500,000 tons of wheat with a market value of $34 million to China. The total was 18.7 million bushels, compared with a 98 millionbushel, $160 million sale (the largest one-year sale ever made by the Canadian Wheat Board) in October 1970.

The Nixon Administration's policy of detente made the U.S. another potential supplier of grain to China. President Richard M. Nixon June 10, 1971 authorized the export of farm products and a list of other nonstrategic goods to China.

In a related development, Nixon also lifted a requirement by which 50% of grain shipments to China, the Soviet Union and other Eastern European countries were to be carried in U.S. ships.

According to a report made public by the Chinese press agency Hsinhua Jan. 1, 1972, China's industrial and agricultural output had increased by "about 10%" in 1971 and grain output had gone up to 246 million tons.

A U.S. Congressional report released May 20, 1972, however, suggested that population pressure was adding to China's food problems. According to the report, China faced a population explosion in the next two decades that would put a tremendous strain on its limited economic resources and diminish any "serious military danger" to the U.S.

The report, released by the Joint Economic Committee, had been prepared by the Central Intelligence Agency, the Library of Congress and the State and Commerce Departments. One Commerce Department official, John S. Aird, forecast in the report that China's population would increase to no less than 1,301,260,000 by 1990 and might go as high as 1,333,128,000. Peking's efforts to reduce population growth through various planning measures would have little effect because the program to curb births also tended to reduce deaths, Aird said.

Another contributor to the report, Arthur G. Ashbrook Jr., said the Chinese themselves had no exact population figures. He noted that Vice Premier

GROWTH RATES (PER CENT) IN FACTORS

AFFECTING GRAIN PRODUCTION & CONSUMPTION

Country	Area	Yield	Pro-duction	Con-sumption	Popu-lation	Income
	Compound rate of growth, 1960-62 to 1969-71					
Developed countries	-0.1	2.8	2.7	2.5	1.1	4.4
United States	-1.0	3.4	2.4	2.1	1.3	3.9
Canada	0.0	3.3	3.3	2.9	1.8	4.0
EC	0.7	2.5	3.2	2.2	0.7	3.7
EC 6	-0.2	3.3	3.2	2.2	0.8	4.2
EC 3	2.1	1.3	3.4	2.1	0.5	2.6
Other West Europe	0.2	3.5	3.8	3.5	0.9	5.1
South Africa	3.2	1.1	4.2	4.5	3.0	5.7
Japan	3.5	1.3	-2.2	3.3	1.1	9.8
Australia & New Zealand	3.6	0.2	3.7	3.9	2.0	4.2
Centrally planned countries	0.0	3.0	3.0	3.4	1.4	5.2
East Europe	-0.6	3.7	3.0	2.9	0.6	4.5
USSR	-0.1	3.4	3.3	4.3	1.3	6.5
China (PRC)	0.5	2.2	2.7	2.6	1.8	2.7
Developing countries	1.4	1.9	3.5	3.7	2.6	4.6
East Asia	1.6	3.1	4.8	5.6	2.4	4.3
Indonesia	1.3	2.0	3.6	3.7	2.5	2.0
Southeast Asia	1.3	2.2	3.6	5.0	2.6	3.9
South Asia	1.3	2.2	3.2	3.1	2.6	3.4
India	1.0	2.0	3.0	3.4	2.6	3.3
No. Africa/Middle East	0.6	2.4	3.1	3.9	2.7	6.2
Central Africa	3.5	-0.5	3.0	4.4	2.4	2.9
East Africa	5.0	+.5	5.6	5.7	2.5	4.1
Mexico/Central America	2.7	3.0	5.7	5.6	3.3	6.5
Venezuela	4.9	0.6	5.5	7.8	3.0	5.4
Brazil	5.0	0.0	5.0	4.3	2.9	7.0
Argentina	2.6	1.7	4.4	3.2	1.5	4.1
Other South America	0.2	1.8	2.1	3.2	2.8	3.8
World	0.4	2.6	3.1	3.3	2.0	4.6

Source: U.S. Agriculture Department's Foreign Agricultural Service and Economic Research Service for area, yield, production and consumption data; U.N. for population and income data

Li Hsien-nien had said in November 1971 that the current population varied from 750 million to 830 million, depending on requirements of different government departments. Ashbrook quoted Li as having said: "The Ministry of Commerce insists on the bigger number in order to be able to provide goods in larger quantities. The planning men reduce the figure in order to strike a balance in the plans of the various state departments."

China's population in 1970 was 697,260,000, according to figures published Aug. 5, 1972 by the China Cartographic Institute in Peking. It was the first time since the mid-1960s that an official document containing census information had been published in Peking.

China was reported Jan. 27, 1973 to have begun a new birth control campaign to reduce a population growth of more than 15 million annually.

At a conference in Hupeh Province, Tseng Ssy-yu, first secretary of the provincial Communist party committee, declared in a work report that "We must pay attention to and carry out propaganda for later marriage and family planning." A broadcast said the conference had called on CP officials to "take the lead in practicing birth control."

Keeping Grain Prices Up

A major concern of the U.S. and other grain producers during this period was to prevent what they considered potentially diastrous declines in the prices of grain and other farm products.

U.S.-British corn pact. The U.S. Agriculture Department announced March 17, 1971 a new grain agreement between the U.S. and Britain. The pact would set a higher minimum British import price for U.S. corn, below which a levy would be imposed.

Under the accord, the minimum import price for corn would be increased in stages from $54.21 a metric ton to $63.19 a ton in the August-September 1972 period. No levy would be placed on corn imported for industrial uses—generally a

third of all foreign corn consumption in Britain.

U.S. corn was sold in Britain at prices well above the new minimum prices. The pact was seen as an attempt, in the light of Britain's application for membership in the European Economic Community (EEC), to establish minimum corn prices below those used in the EEC.

The pact would be in effect from July 1 through 1972.

EEC-U.S. trade pact. The U.S. and the EEC Feb. 11, 1972 made public the terms of their Feb. 4 trade agreement, following formal approval of the accord in Brussels by the EEC Council of Ministers.

The pact gave the U.S. short-term trade concessions on its agricultural exports. The Common Market agreed (1) to add 1.5 million tons of surplus wheat during the 1972–1973 crop year to its wheat stockpile, rather than sell it in competition against the U.S., (2) to lower tariffs on certain citrus fruit imports in 1972 and 1973, (3) to apply export subsidies to grains to prevent "trade diversions" favoring the EEC, (4) to make proposed taxes on tobacco "neutral" as between domestic tobacco and imports and consult with the U.S. before putting the taxes into effect.

In return for the concessions won from the EEC, the U.S. agreed not to plant 26 million acres of wheat and feed grains during the 1972–1973 crop year.

EEC price agreement. The EEC ministers of agriculture agreed March 24, 1972 on a program of farm price increases.

Under the accord, the guaranteed prices for the 1972–73 crop year would rise 4%–5% for grain and 8% for dairy products. Beef prices would rise 4% immediately, with additional increases to be worked out later. The increases largely followed a compromise recommended by the EEC Commission, but were lower than the average 8% rise in cereal prices and 12% rise in milk product prices demanded by farmers' organizations.

WHEAT AREA & PRODUCTION
IN THE U.S., CANADA, AUSTRALIA & ARGENTINA

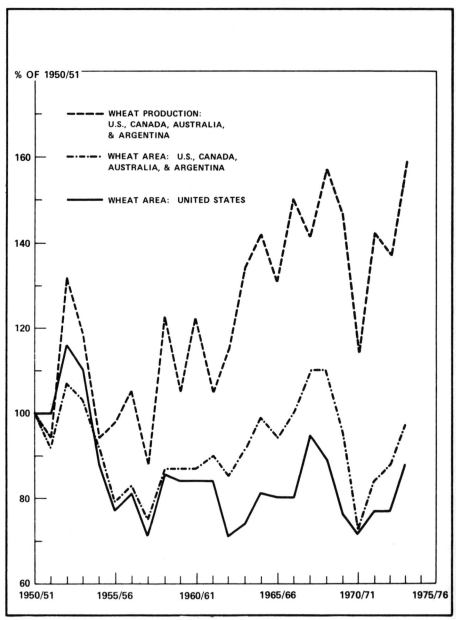

U.S. Department of Agriculture: Economic Research Service

The major price dispute was between France and West Germany, with France urging higher prices for beef than for crops to encourage animal production and West Germany seeking to protect its grain farmers with higher grain prices.

U.S. subsidies up. U.S. Agriculture Secretary Clifford M. Hardin Oct. 18, 1971 announced a program to increase farm subsidies in 1972 to reduce surplus production of corn and other livestock feed grains. The program called for more acreage to be taken out of production and higher subsidies to farmers idling the acreage. The new program was designed as a result of a record 1971 corn crop of 5.4 million bushels, almost one-third more than in 1970, when the corn blight cut output. The blight was not a factor in 1971.

The new program was expected to cost $1.5 billion–$1.75 billion compared with costs of $1.2 billion in 1971. The goal was to reduce acreage by 38 million acres for feed grains, including corn, grain sorghums and barley. This would compare with an idling of 18.2 million acres in 1971 for farmers to qualify for federal price support loans.

Hunger in the U.S.

Even in the U.S., a country whose agricultural bounty made it the envied benefactor of starvation-threatened multitudes throughout the Third World, there were widespread instances of hunger and malnutrition due to poverty. The major means of attacking hunger in the U.S. were direct payments of welfare money and the food stamp plan; the latter enabled the poor to buy coupons that were redeemable in food worth much more than the coupons had cost.

Budget for poor raised. In his budget for fiscal 1971, submitted to Congress Feb. 2, 1970, President Richard Nixon proposed a 10% increase in programs to aid the poor.

Outlays for food programs were hiked $623 million to a total of $1.6 billion, of which $1.2 billion was for the food stamp program (a $674 million increase), which was expected to reach about 7.5 million persons by the end of the budget year. Child nutrition programs also were funded higher—by $12 million to a $314 million level accommodating 6.6 million children.

The Administration planned to reduce spending for the special milk program by $64 million.

In a related development, Dr. Arnold Shaefer, director of the National Nutrition Survey, told the Senate Committee on Nutrition and Human Needs April 27 that the government survey conducted in Texas and Louisiana had found "widespread malnutrition." In testimony updating preliminary findings reported to the committee in January 1969, Shaefer said: "There is no longer any doubt that the incidence of malnutrition is related to poverty income levels."

Shaefer said data on 13,373 persons examined in the two states confirmed preliminary findings of serious malnutrition and also showed evidence of widespread growth retardation, anemia and dental decay. He reported finding two or more nutritional deficiencies in 48.5% of children aged one to nine; 39.5% aged 10 to 12; and 54.5% aged 13 to 16.

Food stamp program. Secretary of Agriculture Clifford M. Hardin said Jan. 7, 1970 that 31 communities across the nation had been authorized to begin food stamp programs for the first time and that 180 other areas would be allowed to switch from food distribution programs to food stamps.

Hardin said the food stamp extension had been possible because funding had been increased from $340 million to $610 million.

A department spokesman said the new food stamp programs, expected to reach as many as 900,000 persons, would begin "as soon as state and local welfare officials get their operations moving" by making arrangements to train personnel, certify eligibility and determine distribution procedures.

The action reduced the number of counties in the U.S. without plans for food programs to 279. After the new plans went into operation, food programs would be established in 1,865 communities in 46 states and the District of Columbia. One state, Delaware, joined the stamp program for the first time.

The Senate Dec. 31 passed and sent to the President compromise legislation continuing the food stamp program for three years but barring such assistance to any family in which an able-bodied adult refused to work.

A $1.75 billion expenditure for fiscal 1971 was authorized. The bill with its work requirement was approved by the House Dec. 16 by a 290–68 vote in contrast to a more liberal version approved in 1969 by the Senate. A deadlock developed in the Senate-House conference, but a compromise was worked out to retain the "must work" provision but free the states from sharing the cost of the program.

Pres. Nixon said Jan. 21, 1971 that the number of participants in the food stamp program had tripled in 1970, but he added "this is no time to sit back or ease off in our efforts." The President's comments were released with a White House report on accomplishments in the year following the White House Conference on Food, Nutrition and Health.

The report said those participating in the food stamp program rose from 3.6 million to 9.3 million between December 1969 (when the conference was held) and November 1970. It said nearly 300 cities and counties had joined the program during the year and that all but 10 of the nation's cities and counties had established some kind of food program. Federal expenditures for the program were $248 million in 1969, $576 million in 1970.

New food stamp rules issued. The Agriculture Department July 22, 1971 issued new food stamp regulations that would make 1.7 million persons eligible for the first time but would eliminate or decrease benefits for more than 2 million other persons currently participating in the program. The rules, which implemented the 1970 Food Stamp Reform Act, also included a new "work requirement" that would make registration for and acceptance of jobs by able-bodied adults a prerequisite for food aid.

The regulations set a uniform national eligibility standard, which would allow a family of four with a monthly income of $360 or less to receive some aid. Of the 45 states participating in the program, only New York, New Jersey and Alaska had eligibility levels at or above the new standard. Other states had ceilings ranging down to $180 per month for a South Carolina family of four.

The Administration changed the final rules from a version proposed April 15 so that a family on welfare could get food stamp aid even if its household income exceeded the national eligibility level. In announcing the regulations, Assistant Agriculture Secretary Richard E. Lyng said the revised rules would particularly benefit "the poorest of the poor"—the, estimated 900,000 persons who would receive free food stamps for the first time. For example, a family of four with less than $30 monthly income could now receive free stamps where formerly the stamps cost $2 a month.

However, the new rules cut off aid altogether for some 600,000 current participants with incomes above the new national standard.

The new rules raised the monthly food stamp allocation for a family of four by $2 to $108. However, families with incomes near the maximum eligibility level would have to pay more for their stamps. For example, a family of four earning $360 a month formerly paid $82 for stamps valued at $106. Under the new rules, this family would have to pay $99 for $108 in stamps.

School lunch bill enacted. Congress completed action May 4, 1970 on a bill to provide free or reduced-price school lunches to an estimated eight million needy school children. President Nixon May 14 signed the bill, which had been approved by a Senate-House conference committee April 27.

The legislation made it mandatory for schools to provide free or reduced-rate lunches for all children whose families fell under the poverty level, currently $3,600 a year for a family of four. Although a school lunch program operated under previous legislation, no more than four million children received subsidized lunches. The conference report, passed by the Senate April 30 and by the House May 4, adopted the House provision of subsidized lunches for children whose families fell under the poverty level rather than the Senate version, which set the standard at $4,000 or less a year.

The report accepted the Senate provision for $25 million to be spent on a pilot school breakfast program in fiscal 1971 but eliminated authorizations for the program in fiscal '72 and '73.

A bill to make the milk program for children permanent and to authorize appropriations of up to $120 million annually for the program was passed by the Senate May 11 and House June 16. The Administration had opposed the legislation on the ground that the milk could be provided under child nutrition programs. President Nixon announced June 30 he had allowed the bill to become law automatically (that day) without his signature on expiration of the 10-day period permitted for Presidential action.

Inaction on hunger charged. Leaders of a national hunger conference said Feb. 5, 1971 that despite "real progress" in the fight against hunger in the U.S., the Nixon Administration's response to the conference's recommendations had been inadequate. The critique of the nation's actions to eliminate hunger came during a one-day followup meeting in Williamsburg, Va. of 79 panel chairmen and vice chairmen at the 1969 White House Conference on Food, Nutrition and Health.

Mrs. Patricia Young, who had chaired the Women's Task Force at the conference, said: "I assumed this job with the understanding that our real work would begin after the first conference ended—to press for public, private and governmental action against hunger. But we've had almost no support at all for this from the Administration." She said the delegates had "to put pressure on the White House even to have the followup meeting."

Dr. Jean Mayer, general chairman of the 1969 conference, lauded the "gigantic progress" toward eliminating hunger, but he spoke of groups of people "who somehow fall between the cracks of existing progress." He described migrant workers as "men who are killing their wives and their children trying to get work—and subsidizing both the food in-

dustry and the consumers out of their misery." He said their "wives and children could receive better care, better housing and better education if they moved north and went on welfare."

Among related developments:

■ South Carolina Gov. John C. West (D), who had pledged in his inaugural address to end hunger and malnutrition in the state, toured poverty communities on John's Island and in Charleston Feb. 3. West was accompanied by Sen. Ernest F. Hollings (D, S.C.), who said 15 million people in the U.S. suffered from malnutrition. He said the purpose of the tour was to "bring the problem to the public's attention." Hollings said conditions had improved since his last tour two years before. He said: "Now they at least know about the food stamp program."

■ An Agriculture Department spokesman said Feb. 3 that federal school lunch aid had been cut off from 92 school districts in January because of failure to provide "policy statements" of terms under which needy children would be eligible for free or token-priced lunches.

■ Assistant Secretary of Agriculture Richard E. Lyng said Feb. 19 that the federal government would not undertake food distribution centers in 10 "holdout" counties that had refused to establish federally aided food programs. Lyng said efforts to induce voluntary cooperation in the 10 counties would continue and "I think we'll get most of them." When the Nixon Administration took office, 480 counties and cities had not established locally administered food programs. By Aug. 31, 1970, all but 10 had established programs.

Hunger session held. Witnesses from 12 states testified at a public meeting in Washington Feb. 16, 1971 to call attention to hunger in the U.S. The session was held by the Citizens Board of Inquiry Into Hunger & Malnutrition.

Leslie W. Dunbar, executive director of the Field Foundation and chairman of the meeting, said testimony from the 100 participants demonstrated "a pattern of official lawlessness, at that point where government comes most into contact with poor people."

Many of the witnesses recounted incidents of official callousness and bureaucratic bottlenecks confronting persons seeking relief. Dunbar said, "I have a feeling, and I think it's widely shared, of despair. . . . A feeling that we—our institutions—don't know where we're going. We make the poor fight, clutch and claw for everything they can get."

Senators hear plight of migrants. In testimony before the Senate Select Committee on Nutrition Feb. 23, 1971, a pediatrician said malnutrition among the children of migrant workers was 10 times greater than among the nation's children generally. The hearing was the first of a series called to review the results of the 1969 White House Conference on Food, Nutrition and Health.

Sen. George S. McGovern (D, S.D.), chairman of the committee, said the testimony of Dr. H. Peter Chase of the University of Colorado medical center was "among the most dramatic and disturbing evidence" heard by the committee since its inception in December 1968. Chase, 34, was conducting his third study of Mexican-American migrant children in Texas and Colorado.

Chase reported instances of severe cases of malnutrition and disease among the children he examined. He said that while extreme cases were rare, malnutrition serious enough to stunt growth and endanger mental development "definitely exists in this [migrant] population and must be corrected."

In a letter to the committee, Dr. Jean Mayer, chairman of the 1969 conference, said "the biggest deficiencies at the federal level" of the fight against hunger "are the underfunding of practically every program, and the lack of clearcut, unambiguous federal directives to local authorities."

McGovern, in a hearing March 2, criticized a Nixon Administration proposal that would eliminate the food stamp program by incorporating part of the benefits into the President's welfare reform proposal. In the original Family Assistance Plan, a family of four would receive $1,600 annually plus food stamp benefits, currently worth $800 a year. Health, Education and Welfare Undersecretary John Veneman said Feb. 24 that the Administration "would be receptive" to a plan which would give a family of four $2,200 a year and no food stamps.

The plan would eliminate food aid for low-income families not on welfare.

In the McGovern committee hearing March 2, Assistant Secretary of Agriculture Richard Lyng agreed with the chairman that a family with about $2,000 in annual income would have a hard time meeting food needs without food stamp aid. Lyng said 10 million persons currently participated in the food stamp program and that the figure was expected to reach 12.5 million to 13 million in the next fiscal year. He said a family of four earning $200 per month typically spent $60 monthly for stamps worth $108 in groceries.

Food stamp cutback restored. The Nixon Administration Jan. 16, 1972 reversed its planned cutback in the food stamp program after the change had drawn protest from senators and governors.

The Agriculture Department had set $360 as the top monthly income limit for participants in the food stamp program. The change would allow an additional 1.7 million persons, mostly in Southern and Western states, into the program while eliminating from it, or reducing benefits to, some 2.1 million persons, mostly in Northeastern states where the cost of living was higher.

The change had been protested Dec. 19, 1971 by 28 senators in a letter to the Agriculture Department.

Sens. George McGovern (D, S.D.) and Clifford P. Case (R, N.J.), in separate statements Jan. 3, warned that they would take legislative action, if necessary, to counter the change.

The protest gained momentum when it was joined by the governors of 15 states and New York Mayor John V. Lindsay, whose representatives met in Hartford, Conn. Jan. 7 to mount an effort to preserve current benefits. They demanded that no family be dropped from the program and that benefits be increased to reflect the cost of an adequate diet.

The New York Times reported from confidential budgetary documents Jan. 12 that the Nixon Administration had impounded $202 million of funds allocated for food assistance, almost 10% of the $2.2 billion appropriated by Congress for the food stamp program. The Administration's budget request for food stamps was $2 billion for fiscal 1972, and Congress had added $200 million to the program.

Sen. Hubert H. Humphrey (D, Minn.) and McGovern protested the impounding Jan. 12. Assistant Agriculture Secretary Frank B. Elliott said that day the $202 million had not been impounded, except in a technical sense, and the money, while not requested by the department for its budget, was "available from the Office of Management and Budget any time we need it."

The policy reversal was announced Jan. 16 by Agriculture Secretary Earl L. Butz, who said he had issued new regulations to insure that "the benefits available to each household are as high or higher than they were under the old regulations." He made clear that the "impounded" funds would be used.

A department report Jan. 1 put enrollment in the food stamp program at 10.9 million persons in November 1971. The combined enrollment in the food stamp program and the program of distributing surplus commodities to needy families was estimated at 14.4 million in November. This compared with a 13.1 million combined enrollment a year earlier and 7.1 million two years previously.

Cash food aid urged. A public interest organization urged that federal food programs to aid the poor be replaced by direct cash payments, it was reported Oct. 26, 1972.

The Citizens' Board of Inquiry into Hunger and Malnutrition, whose reports in 1967 and 1968 had been largely responsible for Congress' increasing food aid, said that while vastly increased federal food stamp and school lunch programs now reached 57% of the nation's poor, bureaucratic waste, private profit and budget-cutting by the Department of Agriculture had kept individual payments to a minimum.

The report said the programs had spawned a "vast bureaucratic mechanism" with a large payroll and high profits to companies providing supplies and help, following a pattern set in antipoverty and defense programs. Nevertheless, the report charged, the Department of Agriculture had returned $418 million in 1972 food aid money to the Treasury, and would have curtailed several programs if Congressional and public pressure had not materialized.

Total federal food aid had risen to $4.3 billion a year, to provide food stamps for 11.8 million recipients and school lunches to 8.4 million poor children. But 43% of the nation's 27 million poor people received no food assistance, and an additional 12% "receive less than three-fourths of the recommended dietary allowances."

1972's Crop Failures, Competition for Food

Food Output Decline in 1972

"During the two decades between 1954 and 1973, food production declined on a global basis only once—in 1972," the U.S. Agriculture Department's Economic Research Service (ERS) noted in its 1974 publication "The World Food Situation and Prospects to 1985." This decline was disastrous for some developing countries despite the fact that, as the ERS publication further noted, the two-decade increase in world food output, which exceeded the period's population growth (by an annual rate of 2.8% to 2%), meant that "on the average, the 3.8 billion people in the world in 1973 had about one-fifth more food to eat per person than did the 2.7 billion people in 1954." The problem for the developing countries was that the per capita increase in food output (and consumption) in the developed countries far exceeded the increase in the developing ones. And after the 1972 shortfall, poor countries had to compete with the rich for the available food.

In a 1974 report entitled "U.S. and World Food Security," a U.S. Senate Agriculture subcommittee listed "leading factors" in the 18 million-ton shortfall in world grain production in the 1972–73 crop year: "Soviet grain production dropped sharply due to winter kill and a dry summer; Australia's grain production was crippled by drought; India had a below-normal monsoon, which cut grain crop expectations;

the Philippine rice and corn crops were reduced by drought and typhoons; West African nations suffered their fifth consecutive year of drought; production in Canada was below trend because of the cumulative effect of government policies that reduced grain acreage considerably . . . ; the United States, while maintaining production above trend, had reduced its grain acreage from 1971 levels because of stock buildup resulting from the bumper crop in 1971."

The Senate report emphasized the impact of two factors on the 1972 world grain situation: "First, the major exporters . . . were following a policy of shrinking their production to reduce their stocks. Second, U.S.S.R. made a major shift in its import policy. . . .[I]n 1972–73, while the shortfall was 15 million tons below trend in production, net imports of grain amounted to 25 million tons above trend. . . . " In the past, the U.S.S.R. had slaughtered livestock to make up for shortfalls in grain output, but in 1972 the Soviets continued a two- or-three-year policy of increasing their herds.

Food output in developing world lags. The world's developing nations were not producing enough food to keep pace with their expanding populations, according to the U.N. Food and Agriculture Organization (FAO) Nov. 20, 1972.

The FAO annual report said food production in developing countries had

FOOD PRODUCTION PER CAPITA

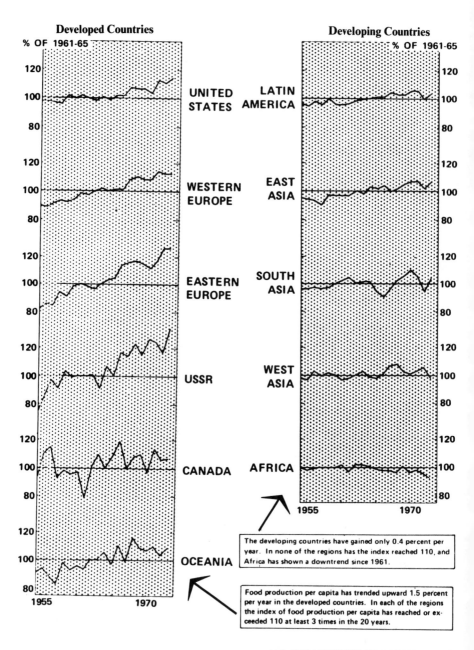

The developing countries have gained only 0.4 percent per year. In none of the regions has the index reached 110, and Africa has shown a downtrend since 1961.

Food production per capita has trended upward 1.5 percent per year in the developed countries. In each of the regions the index of food production per capita has reached or exceeded 110 at least 3 times in the 20 years.

U.S. DEPARTMENT OF AGRICULTURE
ECONOMIC RESEARCH SERVICE

increased by only 1%-2% in 1971-72, far below the 4% annual increase needed to feed their growing populations.

According to the report, conditions had improved somewhat in Latin America and food production was up substantially in the Middle East. However, there was no improvement in Africa, and production was down in the Far East, where 1973 harvests would determine whether a regional food crisis could be avoided. Food production in developed nations was expected to remain stable after a 9% increase in North America and a 5% rise in Western Europe in 1971.

U.S. wheat record. The U.S. Agriculture Department reported Dec. 12 that the U.S.' 1972 wheat crop exceeded a 25-year record in reaching sales of $3.4 billion. Total production was 1.54 billion bushels worth an average of $2.23 a bushel, up from $1.89 a bushel in 1971.

The U.S.S.R.'s Grain Purchases

The Soviet Union bought more than 700 million bushels of grain from the U.S. in the summer of 1972 after the U.S.S.R.'s own crops failed. The biggest grain sale in U.S. history, the deal included nearly 440 million bushels of wheat, 25% of the U.S.' total crop.

Nixon Administration officials hailed the sale as providing markets for U.S. farmers, reducing U.S.-Soviet tensions and improving the U.S.' balance of international payments. Critics charged that the sale depleted U.S. grain reserves, caused higher prices for food in the U.S. and abroad, cheated U.S. farmers of the higher prices they would have charged had they been informed of the U.S.S.R.'s situation, cost the U.S. heavily in subsidy payments and unduly enriched international grain traders.

The U.S. sale of 18 million tons of grain to the U.S.S.R. in 1972 was preceded and accompanied by Soviet purchases of 10 million tons of grain from other producers the same year.

Canadian-Soviet deal. The signing of a contract obligating the Soviet Union to purchase 130 million bushels of Canadian wheat, with an option to buy 55 million bushels more, was reported Feb.

29, 1972. The price: about $330 million. To complete the deal, the Soviet Union agreed July 18 to take an option in its last wheat sale agreement with Canada and buy 55 million bushels of Canadian wheat for about $100 million.

(Statistics Canada estimated Canada's 1972 wheat crop at 526.2 million bushels, the Wall Street Journal reported Oct. 5.)

Butz visits Soviet Union. U.S. Secretary of Agriculture Earl L. Butz ended a five-day visit to the Soviet Union April 12, 1972 with the prediction of a big U.S. sale of grain to the U.S.S.R.

(The agriculture attache at the U.S. embassy in Moscow had informed the U.S. State Department in reports filed Feb. 9 and 18 that the Soviet winter grain crop had been heavily damaged and that the U.S.S.R. would probably try to buy large quantities of feed grain later in 1972. The U.S. embassy reported to Washington March 31 that the Soviet Union's winter wheat loss totaled 25 million acres and that low soil moisture made conditions unfavorable for the spring planting.)

Butz, who began talks during his stay on a proposed $200 million grain transaction, was returning the visit of his Soviet counterpart Vladimir V. Matskevich, who traveled to the U.S. in 1971.

Soviets to buy U.S. grain. President Nixon announced July 8 that the U.S. had concluded a three-year agreement for the sale of at least $750 million of American wheat, corn and other grains to the Soviet Union.

Some Administration officials said they expected actual Soviet purchases of American grain to be considerably higher than $750 million.

Under the agreement, the Soviet Union would purchase grain on the commercial market from private grain dealers in the U.S.

Also included in the agreement was a U.S. pledge that it would provide long-term credits to the Soviet Union from the Agriculture Department's Commodity Credit Corporation.

In cash terms, the Soviet Union would purchase $200 million worth of

American wheat for delivery during
the first year of the agreement—Aug. 1
through July 31, 1973. Loans from the
Commodity Credit Corp., which the
Soviet Union would use to finance the
purchases, had to be repaid within three
years of delivery.

In a related development, U.S. Agriculture Department officials said Aug. 9
that Cook Grains had formalized the
sale of $100 million worth of soybeans to
the Soviet Union for use as cattle feed.

Grain harvest poor. According to the
Journal of Commerce Aug. 17, the Soviet Central Statistical Office was estimating that the country's grain yield was
15% behind the figure for 1971, itself
below the 1970 total.

With most winter wheat harvested, the
average yield for the Ukraine, where
much of the crop was grown, was 31.4
bushels per acre.

The Washington Post Aug. 22 cited
Minsk newspaper reports revealing that
grain harvests in the Byelorussian Republic were running 20% below the 1971
figure and that the republic's minister of
agriculture, Stephen G. Skoropanov, had
been dismissed.

In a related development, the Communist party newspaper Pravda said
Aug. 29 that large quantities of potatoes
were being brought into the Moscow region from Byelorussia, Latvia, Lithuania
and Estonia to make up for a fall in
local production because of "complicated weather conditions."

Soviet Agriculture Minister Vladimir
V. Matskevich declared Oct. 4 that
although the recent drought was the
worst "in 100 years of recorded meteorological history" there would be "no
question of starvation." Much of the
summer crop had been lost in the south-
eastern Ukraine, the middle and lower
Volga and some areas of the northern
Caucasus and central Russia, Matskevich said. Good crops had been achieved
in the virgin lands of Kazakhstan and
Siberia. (The journal Economicheskaya
Gazeta reported Oct. 11, however, that
rain and frost had "seriously impeded"
the harvest in eastern regions of the
country. The paper said some of the "wet
and green grain is sent to central parts
of the country" for drying but that "there

are still cases when the transport is being
delayed—and with wet material this is
wasteful.")

Matskevich said Nov. 4 that the poor
1972 harvest would cause a redirection
of funds to agriculture from other areas
but he denied that such allocations would
reach the $24 billion reported by West-
ern news sources.

Matskevich noted that the Soviet
Union was having "certain difficulties"
in providing forage for livestock and
that hay for this purpose was being
shipped from Byelorussia to the Volga
valley and to regions south of Moscow,
a distance of about 1,000 miles.

Matskevich was "relieved" of his post
Feb. 3, 1973, and Dimitri S. Polyansky,
a first deputy premier and member of the
Politburo in charge of farm policy, was
demoted to agriculture minister.

More Soviet grain purchases expected.
An Agriculture Department analysis
released Oct. 2 predicted that the Soviet
Union would continue to be "a major
importer of grain" for the next three to
five years.

The forecast came in an appraisal of
current Soviet crop conditions. The
report said poor harvests had jeopar-
dized plans to increase meat and dairy
stocks by 1975.

Crop difficulties had also depleted
grain stores for the population, and
rather than divert that grain to livestock feeding requirements, the report
said the Soviet Union would be forced
to import.

"With Soviet living standards at a new
high, people have been led to expect a
more dependable supply of better foods,
and it also appears that the Soviet government is determined that the Russian
people aren't to be disappointed," the
study said.

USDA ends wheat subsidy. The Agriculture Department (USDA) announced Sept. 22 that it was eliminating
the export subsidy by setting the payment rate at zero because of the "strong
demand for wheat and supplies."

The subsidy had been used to pay the
difference between the relatively high
domestic price of wheat and a lower

world price to keep U.S. grain competitive on the world market.

The USDA had been criticized for using the subsidy to permit sales to the Soviet Union at prices of $1.63–$1.65 a bushel (while the U.S. price was climbing to $2.10 a bushel) when the U.S. was the Soviet's only supplier of grain and could have demanded a higher price.

Dropping the subsidy had the effect of raising the export price of wheat 14¢, the difference between the world price and the domestic price. The domestic price al o rose 4¢, bringing the export price to $2.44 a bushel, up 18¢ from the world price of $2.26 on Sept. 22.

U.S.-Soviet maritime accord. The U.S. and the Soviet Union signed a three-year maritime agreement in Washington Oct. 14 establishing premium rates for U.S. vessels carrying Soviet grain purchases and substantially increasing the number of ports in each country open to ships of the other nation.

The Soviet Union was to pay U.S. shippers either $8.05 a ton from Gulf Coast to Black Sea ports or 110% of the prevailing world rate, whichever was higher. American shipowners were to receive from the Maritime Administration a subsidy covering the difference between the Soviet rate and the cost of shipping.

The first U.S. ship carrying wheat to the U.S.S.R. docked in Odessa Dec. 20 after negotiations deadlocked over shipping rates were settled Nov. 22 in Washington.

A complex agreement covering only the period until Jan. 25, 1973 was arranged by Assistant Secretary of Commerce Robert J. Blackwell on the basis of a sliding scale of $10.34–$9.90 per ton of grain.

Another pact was signed Dec. 20 setting the carrier rate at $10.34 per ton until July 1, 1973.

Renewed shipping talks had become necessary after world charter rates climbed.

Third nation carriers had already shipped 3 million of the 17 million tons of grain bought by the Soviet Union, according to the Commerce Department Nov. 22.

Total grain sale loss estimated. The Washington Star News Nov. 1 estimated

the net loss to U.S. taxpayers as a result of the Soviet purchase of grain at $27 million.

Taxpayer Gains (In Millions)
Rise in value of surplus wheat	$183.5
Cut in 1972 farm subsidy	$120.
Cut in 1973 farm subsidy	$189.
Storage and interest savings	$ 73.
Total Gains	$565.5

Taxpayer Costs
Rise in bread price	$178.5
Rise in flour price	$ 20.
Wheat export subsidy	$300.
Shipping subsidy	$ 40.
Subsidy cost to farmers who sold early	$ 54.
Total Costs	$592.5

Fertilizer financing set. The U.S. Export-Import Bank approved a preliminary commitment to lend the Soviet Union $180 million at 6% to help finance purchase of $400 million–500 million worth of equipment and engineering services for the huge fertilizer manufacturing and pipeline complex to be built with the aid of Occidental Petroleum Corp., it was reported May 31, 1973.

Ten major U.S. banks announced Sept. 12 an agreement to provide a $180 million loan to build the project.

Controversy Over Grain Deal

Conflict of interests? Charges made Aug. 30, 1972 by Consumers Union that two Agriculture Department officials violated federal conflict of interest laws in connection with the recent sale of wheat to the Soviet Union escalated Sept. 8 when Democratic Presidential nominee George McGovern charged that the Nixon Administration and large grain exporters and speculators engaged in a "conspiracy of silence" to exploit U.S. grain farmers.

Consumers Union asked the Justice and Agriculture Departments to investigate the role in the grain deal of Clarence D. Palmby, formerly assistant agriculture secretary for international affairs and chief negotiator with the Soviets, and Clifford G. Pulvermacher, a former general manager of the Export Marketing Service in the Agriculture Department (USDA).

Both had resigned their federal posts

in June after taking part in April credit negotiations with the Soviet Union related to the forthcoming wheat sale, according to the Washington Post Aug. 31.

Their present employers, Continental Grain Co. and Bunge Corp., participated as grain exporters in the U.S.-Soviet wheat deal.

The General Accounting Office (GAO) announced Sept. 6 it would investigate related charges brought by Rep. Pierre S. du Pont 4th (R, Del.) that exporters benefitted from the wheat sale by acquiring inside information of the transaction, thereby purchasing grains at low cost and defrauding farmers of a rightful share in profits from the Soviet transaction, and by obtaining heavy subsidies for their subsequent sales.

A Senate Agriculture Committee staff memorandum, reported Aug. 27 in the Post, noted that its investigations uncovered a "coziness between the Department of Agriculture and private grain exporters" which "is clearly working out as both a windfall for the Russians and exporters at the direct expense of the U.S. taxpayer."

Rep. Graham Purcell (D, Tex.), chairman of the House Agriculture Subcommittee on Livestock and Grain, announced Sept. 1 his group would examine the allegations.

Purcell also claimed that most producers of hard red winter wheat would show fewer overall 1972 profits than in 1971 and fewer profits from the Soviet trade than if the deal had not been made.

Farmers sold grain to the exporters at lower prices before the Soviet wheat purchases were known and the subsequent rise in price then reduced wheat subsidies by $100 million, Purcell said.

In his speech at Superior, Wis., McGovern contended that "there is now evidence that these big grain companies had quietly gone into the open market during July to buy up as much wheat as possible at the lowest domestic prices before the farmers could get wind of the magnitude of the Russian deal."

McGovern claimed that when terms of the U.S.-Soviet transaction were announced July 8, farmers thought the purchases would be spread evenly over

three years and that grains other than wheat would comprise the bulk of the transaction.

"Many unsuspecting farmers from early harvest states sold their wheat at July prices, about $1.32 per bushel, unaware that if they held their production, prices would rise to current levels of around $1.65."

The National Farmers Union Sept. 10 corroborated McGovern's charges of heavy losses taken by farmers who had no prior knowledge of the impending Soviet purchases.

McGovern also charged that under a special one-week grace period between Aug. 25 and Sept. 1, exporters were able to get certification of grain subsidies on proposed sales to the Russians at the 47¢ a bushel rate, which was being discontinued.

"That one deal cost the American taxpayers more than $128 million alone," McGovern declared.

(The 47¢ level was based on the difference between the domestic wheat price of $2.10 a bushel Aug. 24 and the $1.63 basic export price. Exporters registered 280 million bushels for the subsidy during that week, according to the Times Sept. 10.)

Assistant Agriculture Secretary Carroll Brunthaver told reporters Aug. 26 that the department had assured grain exporters that the U.S. would raise the export subsidy if necessary so that they could sell at the then price of $1.63 per bushel for wheat, even if the sale to the Soviets pushed up the domestic purchase price of wheat and increased the exporters' costs.

Agriculture Secretary Earl L. Butz acknowledged before Purcell's subcommittee Sept. 14 that a report by the Agriculture Department's Economic Research Service (ERS), which could have driven up domestic wheat prices, had been withheld from the public as "too controversial."

The mid-August ERS report analyzed Soviet crop conditions and concluded that the department had overestimated Soviet wheat production.

The study, which was classified confidential, would have provided farmers with some evidence of the magnitude of the Soviet purchases through U.S. exporters. Instead of the 7 million tons of wheat originally thought to be needed by the Soviet Union, the report predicted 11 million tons would be bought. In making the July 8 credit announcement, the Administration had said U.S. farmers could expect initial wheat sales of 1.3 million tons. The USDA Aug. 26 had estimated total Soviet wheat purchases to date at 10.4 million tons.

The Wall Street Journal reported Sept. 14 that a McGovern supporter, John Schnittker, a former Johnson Administration official in the USDA, charged that the U.S. agriculture attache in Moscow had filed reports in June and August which had also indicated the worsening prospects for Soviet grain harvests.

The reports were suppressed, Schnittker said. USDA officials confirmed that the studies were labeled confidential and were not available to the public.

Butz said Sept. 15: "The facts are that this is the greatest transaction of its kind in world history—that wheat has gone up 50¢ a bushel—that nobody, including the Russians themselves, realized how great their need for wheat would be until their crop reports started coming in during July, after the government negotiations had been completed and announced."

Clarence Palmby, the former Agriculture Department official who became a vice president of Continental Grain Co., Sept. 19 denied "categorically" that he had taken part in his company's negotiation with the Soviet Union after he left the government in June.

In testimony before the House subcommittee, Palmby denied that he had discussed the grain transaction with company officials because of possible conflict of interest violations.

Palmby said it was an "outright lie" that he had carried inside information on the transaction to his new employer. But he also disclosed that Continental contracted to sell 4 million tons of wheat and 4½ million tons of feed grains to the Russians July 5, three days before the Administration announced the credit arrangements permitting further grain purchases.

Another contract for a million tons of wheat was let on July 11. The Continental transactions comprised nearly half the total Soviet purchases of wheat.

Palmby said the export company knew nothing of the pending credit agreement

with the Soviets, and that Continental kept its own transaction of July 5 secret from the Agriculture Department.

President Nixon called a news conference Oct. 5 to deny McGovern's charges of corruption in his administration.

Nixon added he had been "rather amused" by some comments that the wheat agreement was "a bad one" for the U.S., that "we got schnookered by the Russians." The farmers "got $1 billion in more farm income" from the wheat deal, he said, the taxpayers "were saved $200 million" that it would have cost to keep the wheat in storage and "thousands of jobs were created on the farm, in the merchant marine and in processing areas."

Cargill, Inc., which was the third largest exporter of wheat to the Soviet Union, reported Nov. 2 that the firm had lost $661,386 or .9¢ a bushel on its sale of nearly 74 million bushels of wheat to the Russians.

In making its first financial disclosure in company history to counteract charges of windfall profits, Cargill attributed the loss to "the need to purchase the wheat at rapidly rising prices and, at the same time, failure of the government's export differential [subsidy] to keep pace with those rising prices."

Cargill denied that it had received inside information regarding Soviet intentions to purchase huge supplies of grain and said it had not begun to make large purchases of grain until after its second deal with the Russian negotiators Aug. 1, when the price of wheat had started its rise.

According to Cargill, the firm was committed to supplying 30 million bushels of wheat more than it held in storage after the first contract was signed with the Russians July 10. After the second deal Aug. 1, spokesmen claimed, the company was short more than 60 million bushels.

The company claimed that its purchase price of wheat averaged $2.009 per bushel, while its sale price was an estimated $1.621 per bushel. Cargill said it received an average subsidy payment from the USDA of 33.4¢ per bushel and denied that it had waited until the end of August to apply for most of its federal subsidy when the support price had reached a record high of 47¢.

USDA corn subsidy attacked. The Agribusiness Accountability Project released a report Oct. 7 which was critical of the USDA subsidies given to Continental Grain Co. and Cargill Corp. for the 1971 sale of corn to the Soviet Union.

The nonprofit research group, which was funded by the Field Foundation Inc., entitled the report, 'The Great Grain Robbery and Other Stories.'

The study contended that the controversial government subsidy to U.S. wheat exporters during 1972 was part of standard USDA policy. That policy of favoring exporters began with the Nixon Administration "gutting the International Grains Agreement," the study stated.

In late 1971, according to the report, the USDA bought barley "at inflated prices" of $1.18 or more per bushel, and sold it to Cargil and Continental for 83¢ to 91¢ per bushel. The export companies then sold the barley to the Soviet Union.

The USDA defended the barley sale, the report said, as a necessary inducement to encourage Soviet purchases of corn (also surplus). The report, however, noted that another grain exporter, Louis Dreyfus Co., subsequently sold corn to the Soviet Union without special conditions and that the USDA permitted exporters to fulfill contracts with corn, half of which was taken from U.S. stocks.

GAO criticizes deal. In 1973 a Government Accounting Office (GAO) report held that the Agriculture Department had subsidized the 1972 U.S. grain sale to the U.S.S.R. "much beyond what appeared necessary or desirable" and had provided the Soviets with wheat at "bargain prices."

Comptroller General Elmer B. Staats presented the GAO report to the House Agriculture Committee March 8. Although there was "no indication of law violations," Staats noted that "farmers were not generally provided timely information with appropriate interpretive comments. Agriculture reports presented a distorted picture of market conditions."

Senate inquiry. The Senate Permanent Investigations Subcommittee held open hearings on the issue July 20–24, 1973.

Congressional attention was focused on charges of mismanagement against the Agriculture Department (USDA) and allegations that the nation's grain exporters had reaped huge profits, at the expense of U.S. farmers and consumers, through secret negotiations and by manipulation of government export subsidy levels.

Sen. Henry M. Jackson (D, Wash.), chairman of the investigations subcommittee, had charged July 19 that preliminary evidence indicated that the USDA had received advance notice of the planned grain sale.

Jackson said, "If the USDA in fact was aware of the negotiations, it is guilty of a deliberate attempt to conceal them from the public, particularly American farmers" who sold crops to the export companies at bargain prices before the export sales were concluded.

Jackson's charges against the USDA were corroborated July 20 by the testimony of Bernard Steinweg, senior vice president of Continental Grain Co., the largest U.S. grain exporter.

Steinweg claimed he had informed Assistant Agriculture Secretary Carroll G. Brunthaver "both before and after" negotiating his firm's massive wheat and corn deal. Steinweg said he met with Brunthaver July 3, 1972 to seek assurances that the USDA export subsidies would be maintained at then-current levels. According to Steinweg, he also telephoned Brunthaver July 6, 1972 one day after reaching an agreement with Soviet representatives.

The grain sale was announced publicly July 8, 1972.

Steinweg added that he had not asked USDA officials to keep secret the information about the pending purchases.

Affidavits supporting Steinweg's testimony were also filed with the subcommittee by two Continental officials who accompanied Steinweg to the Washington meeting July 3, 1972. Officials of other participants in the grain sale—Cargill, Inc., Louis Dreyfus Corp. and Bunge Corp.—also claimed to have notified the USDA of their intentions to sign large export contracts.

Agriculture Secretary Earl L. Butz and Brunthaver appeared before the subcommittee July 23 to refute charges of prior knowledge.

Butz reacted angrily to Jackson's questioning, claiming that the chairman's earlier statements "certainly prejudge the case." Butz also denied that the large grain sale had contributed to the current grain shortage and soaring food prices. He repeated his previous assertions that "a broad growth in world demand" for grain, coupled with adverse weather conditions, had been responsible for increased wheat prices.

Shultz: U.S. 'burned' on grain deal. Treasury Secretary George P. Shultz conceded at a White House press conference Sept. 7, 1973 that the U.S. had been "burned" in the Soviet grain deal.

"I think it is a fair statement that they [Soviet traders] were very skillful in their buying practices, and I think that we should follow the adage [that] if we are burned the first time, why, maybe they did it, but if we get burned twice, that is our fault and we shouldn't have that happen," Shultz said.

Sen. Walter D. Huddleston (D, Ky.) had charged earlier Sept. 7 that the Soviet Union had profited doubly from the U.S. grain deal. In addition to obtaining U.S. supplies at very low prices, Huddleston said, the Soviet Union had resold some of its U.S. wheat to Italian dealers at inflated prices.

Assistant Agriculture Secretary Carroll G. Brunthaver, a defender of the U.S.-Soviet grain deal, told the New York Times Sept. 7 that the disputed purchases had been made by Swiss exporters and that the Soviet Union had not been involved. Italian officials also denied the charges Sept. 8.

China Also Buys Grain

China has been suffering drought since 1963. After a series of optimistic reports and predictions, the Chinese government conceded that the 1972 grain crop was about 10 million metric tons below the 1971 crop. Although good yields in other crops were reported, China had to go back to the world market to buy enough grain

in 1972, and it made similarly large purchases in 1973.

China, however, remains a large producer and exporter of food. K. H. J. Clarke noted in a report presented at the National Industrial Conference in San Francisco Sept. 20, 1973, that "China competes with the Soviet Union for second place behind the United States in the value of agricultural commodities produced. It produces more rice, millet, sweet potatoes, sesame and rapeseed than any other nation and ranks second or third in soy beans ... [and] wheat...." During the 1960s, Clarke reported, "foodstuffs accounted for 20–30% of [China's] total exports. Major items were pork, beef, poultry, canned meat and mushrooms, rice, corn, fruit, vegetables, fish, dairy products, sugar, tea and feed." But he described the wheat situation as "complicated": "China has imported 4–7 million tons of wheat each year since 1962 except for 1971, when 3.2 million tons were purchased." Clarke reported that "China has become the world's largest importer of nitrogenous and other fertilizers and, as a consumer, is exceeded only by the Soviet Union and the United States."

Grain output down in 1972. China's grain production in 1972 was 240 million metric tons compared with 250 million in 1971, it was reported Jan. 1, 1973. The figures were made public by the official Hsinhua press agency. The decline was attributed to drought in the north and to floods and windstorms in the south.

However, Hsinhua reported good yields of cotton, sesame and peanuts and an increase in such industrial crops as hemp, silk cocoons, tea, tobacco, fruit and sugar-bearing plants.

Premier Chou En-lai had told Warren H. Phillips of the Wall Street Journal Oct. 9, 1972 that China expected its 1972 grain output to exceed 250 million metric tons.

In an earlier report, China had said June 9 that the three northern provinces of Hopei, Shantung and Honan "have become basically self-sufficient in grain since 1970." The press agency Hsinhua said the production increase, achieved despite "serious natural disasters," permitted a reduction in the amount of rice and other crops normally shipped from the south to the north.

The Chinese army newspaper Hung Chi called on the Chinese people to save grain following predictions of a 4% drop in the country's grain output in 1972, it was reported Dec. 7. A New York Times report from Hong Kong Dec. 4 confirmed that widespread and prolonged drought in the west and north of China would seriously affect the country's 1972 grain production.

China buys Canadian wheat. Canadian Justice Minister Otto Lang, who also had responsibility for the Canadian Wheat Board, announced June 2, 1972 the sale of 58.8 million bushels of wheat to China for $100 million.

Lang said nearly half the amount would be shipped in 1972, raising to 117.6 million bushels the total volume of wheat shipped to China by the end of the year, with the rest being sent between January and March 1973.

(Argentina and China had signed an agreement under which China would buy 100,000 tons of Argentine corn, according to the Argentine Foreign Ministry June 16.)

Canadian External Affairs Minister Mitchell W. Sharp visited China in August. At a meeting with Premier Chou En-lai Aug. 19, Sharp was given a pledge that Canada could "count on China as a continuing market for Canadian wheat."

China buys U.S. wheat. U.S. Agriculture Secretary Early L. Butz said Sept. 14 that China had placed an order for wheat with the U.S. subsidiary of a French-based company.

Later Sept. 14, an official of the Louis Dreyfus Corp., the New York branch of the French firm Societe Anonyme Louis-Dreyfus et Cie., said the Chinese had agreed to purchase 18 million bushels of soft red wheat. The U.S. firm would "de-Americanize" the grain by selling it first to the parent firm in France for "business reasons."

During a political radio broadcast Oct. 27, President Nixon announced that China had purchased on the U.S. market in the past few days some 12 million bushels of corn at a cost of $18 million.

Nixon said the sale, reportedly made through the Louis Dreyfus Corp., pointed to an "immense trade potential between our two countries."

The Department of Agriculture announced Nov. 1 that China had purchased 970,000 bushels of U.S. wheat valued at about $2.5 million. The department said the sale had been made through the Louis Dreyfus Corp.

Australian sale. John Cass, chairman of the Australian Wheat Board, announced Sept. 27, 1972 the sale by Australia of one million tons of wheat, worth about $A60 million ($US72 million), to China. The sale—reportedly Australia's first to Peking since 1969—was negotiated in China by a four-man Wheat Board delegation. Cass said Oct. 2 that Australian resources would have to be stretched to meet the order.

(Cass reported Jan. 8, 1973 that severe drought had cut the wheat harvest to 192 million bushels, less than half the 470 million-bushel quota. Exports were to be cut from 1971's 337 million bushels to about 120 million bushels.)

India's 1972 Crop Failure

Insufficient rain during the 1972 monsoon season resulted in serious crop failures in India. Grain production declined from the record 93 million metric tons of 1970 to 91.2 million in 1971 and 83.8 million in 1972. Coupled with runaway population growth, the food scarcity resulted in widespread hunger, malnutrition, starvation and death. Indian officials, however, at first refused to admit that there was a disaster in the making and said that record food production could be expected. Foreign observers indicated that if relief were to be supplied from abroad, it would have to be sent without Indian government request.

Grain surplus claimed. Indian officials asserted April 29, 1972 that India's grain output was expected to increase to the point where New Delhi would export about eight million tons by the end of 1972.

According to preliminary figures, grain production since Jan. 1 was exceeding by five million tons 1971's record level of 108 million tons. The principal gain was in wheat, with the output expected to reach a total of 26 million tons. State Minister for Food Annasaheb Shinde said that at this rate India would "outstrip the United States in seven to eight years."

Iqbal Singh, chairman of the government-owned Food Corp. of India, said India would be exporting wheat to west Asia in six months. India already had launched its own Food-for-Peace drive by providing Bangla Desh with 700,000 tons of grain to help it overcome a severe food shortage.

Poor crops as 1972 advanced disproved the claims of a potential surplus, but Food Minister Shinde said Dec. 16 that late rains in September and government warnings about food shortages had prevented a possible famine in the country.

Although several large areas of severe drought conditions existed in four states along the western coast, Shinde said "The situation today is vastly better than it was six years ago" when India had to import 10 million tons of grain to make up for a shortage. Negotiations were currently under way with wheat-surplus countries for purchase of at least two million tons of grain. Rains that were due in July arrived two months late, saving most of the grain crops in northern and central India.

India buys U.S. grain. Food Minister Fakhruddin Ali Ahmed announced Jan. 17, 1973 that the country was in the grip of its worst drought in a decade and was purchasing at least two million tons of food grains, mostly from the U.S., to ease the shortage affecting 200 million people, about a third of the population.

Ahmed estimated that food grain production during the agricultural year ending June 30 would total about 100 million tons, compared with 104 million the previous year.

A Food Ministry official said the new grain imports would include 400,000 tons from Canada, 200,000–300,000 tons from Argentina and the remainder from the U.S.

(The Food Ministry March 13 halted the further import of U.S. sorghum following discovery of a poisonous weed in a recent shipment of 150,000 tons of the grain. A ministry official said such adulteration had been detected before, but never in "such magnitude.")

The government's alleged inability to cope with the drought had been protested as a new parliament opened Feb. 15. Five major opposition parties boycotted the session to also show their displeasure with the government's handling of other matters, including food shortages, price rises and unemployment. The only major opposition party that did not stay away was the pro-Moscow Communist party of India.

An Agriculture Ministry statement said "The drought now is serious, it is here." The ministry, however, expressed hope that the monsoon season, which was to start in June, "will be good."

Prime Minister Indira Gandhi Feb. 27 announced relief measures to combat the threat of famine in six drought-ridden states.

Describing the drought as of "unusual magnitude," Gandhi told parliament that starting March 15 the government would assume control of the wholesale trade in food grains. The prime minister said this action was necessary because "vested interests" had resorted to hoarding to create a "psychology of scarcity" in order to force price increases in grain. The government had allocated $600 million for direct relief work in the drought areas, she said.

Food riots in Nagpur. Riots over shortages of food and yarn erupted April 18–20 in the city of Nagpur in northeastern Maharashtra State. Shops selling grain, clothing, wine and groceries were looted by stone-throwing demonstrators. Nearly 300 persons were arrested for possessing looted property. Businesses and transport in Nagpur were shut down.

Maharashtra had been more severely affected than any other Indian state by the failure of monsoon rains in 1972 and loss of crops. The shortage of yarn caused widespread unemployment among weavers.

CALORIES PER PERSON PER DAY FROM 11 FOOD GROUPS
(1964–66 average)

Country	Region	Cereals	Starchy crops	Sugar	Pulses, nuts & cocoa	Vegetables	Fruit	Meat	Eggs	Fish	Milk	Fats & oils
Developed												
United States	3,156	649	95	513	103	73	101	598	71	26	397	530
Canada	3,142	670	155	520	73	62	101	622	57	23	378	481
Australia & N. Zealand	3,192	821	101	550	61	47	102	655	52	23	403	377
USSR	3,182	1,544	265	412	60	41	27	240	27	21	252	293
EC-9	3,111	878	179	391	68	59	109	474	50	30	305	568
Eastern Europe	3,080	1,498	183	307	59	49	58	314	31	13	189	379
Japan	2,416	1,397	134	197	146	90	53	53	38	85	62	174
South Africa	2,734	1,583	33	403	55	14	37	254	11	28	147	167
Other Western Europe	2,897	978	191	304	103	69	126	288	38	50	267	483
Average	3,043	1,127	175	388	82	59	76	371	44	32	270	419
Less Developed												
Argentina	2,885	999	180	378	28	30	88	614	24	12	206	326
Mexico & Cent. America	2,425	1,197	107	388	188	14	82	131	16	11	104	187
Other South America	2,276	898	291	363	80	23	62	203	13	21	142	180
West Asia	2,316	1,480	41	187	91	39	113	78	7	4	91	185
China (PRC)	2,045	1,383	224	35	134	33	6	134	12	14	5	65
Brazil	2,541	861	410	401	312	11	48	203	18	13	135	129
East Asia & Pacific	1,969	1,271	245	99	107	27	31	58	7	31	8	85
North Africa	2,290	1,461	104	198	72	43	67	69	5	6	78	187
South Asia	1,975	1,300	29	192	176	35	26	8	1	5	89	114
Southeast Asia	2,121	1,589	70	84	78	29	58	77	8	39	18	71
Africa South of Sahara	2,154	1,109	568	53	180	13	18	61	3	13	32	104
Average	2,097	1,300	191	135	146	30	30	89	8	13	50	105
World	2,386	1,247	186	212	127	39	44	175	19	19	117	201

The Indian government informed the U.N. Disaster Relief office in Geneva April 17 that there was no food crisis in India and that it did not need outside help.

Meat Shortages

Shortages in Latin America. Argentina, Uruguay, Colombia, Chile, Bolivia, Peru and Venezuela faced bans, limitations or restrictions on meat consumption, and most other Latin American nations were making serious efforts to increase domestic production, according to El Nacional of Caracas Oct. 5, 1972. But the meat shortage was a worldwide problem, the newspaper noted.

In Argentina, where a partial ban on domestic consumption was in effect, meat exports had fallen from 668,000 tons in 1970 to 494,000 in 1971, due in part to a reduction in livestock. The ban and rising prices had cut domestic beef consumption from a record 220 pounds per person in 1956 to about 140 pounds in 1971.

Uruguay was in the midst of a full four-month ban on beef consumption, with the government agency Coprin in control of prices. The National Meats Institute said August exports were 6,109 tons, a considerable rise from 2,392 tons in August 1971 but below the 8,000 tons of August 1970. The ban ended Nov. 15, but prices for various cuts rose by an estimated 83%. The National Meats Institute said 92,400 tons of beef had been exported during the first 10 months of 1972, compared with more than 126,000 tons for the same period in 1970, but 1972 revenue had been $10 million higher than the 1970 sum. Extensive smuggling of cattle into Brazil was reported. Illegal trade in cattle and sheep on the hoof was put at 600,000 head annually.

(A new three-month ban on domestic beef sales went into effect in Uruguay Aug. 19, 1973 to stimulate beef exports. It ended Nov. 15.)

The Colombian government had imposed partial bans on domestic meat sales to stimulate exports, and was working with the Venezuelan government to cut contraband in livestock across the Colombian border. Smugglers reportedly took 300,000 head of cattle into Venezuela annually, valued at $40 million.

In Peru, the government had imposed stringent measures to increase domestic production to more than 418,000 tons and reduce meat imports to 8,000 tons by 1975. The country would import 39,300 tons of meat, mostly beef, in 1972, principally from Colombia, Bolivia, Argentina and New Zealand.

Cuba Feb. 1, 1973 further reduced meat quotas in view of a shortage attributed to higher prices of imported feed grass, a shortage of fishmeal, droughts during the past three years and the 1971 epidemic of African porcine fever, which necessitated the killing of 600,000 pigs and hogs.

The Brazilian government was reported Nov. 4, 1973 to have decided to cut meat exports to 80,000 tons in 1974–75 to avert a domestic shortage. Meat exports in 1972 had totaled 110,000 tons. The government had decreed measures Oct. 21 to facilitate meat imports, and the Agriculture Ministry, according to a report Aug. 3, had announced $338 million would be invested in the cattle industry in 1974–75.

U.S. situation. U.S. beef production reached 22.3 billion pounds in 1972, an increase of 430 million pounds over 1971; during 1973, 8% more cattle were being fattened for market compared with the previous year, the Agriculture Department reported April 12.

Increased livestock production was attributed to population growth, calculated for food consumption purposes at 1.2 million persons a year, and to rising per capita consumption of beef—from 88.9 pounds a year in 1962 to 115.9 pounds in 1972.

Per capita consumption of veal declined from 5.5 pounds a year in 1962 to 2.6 pounds in 1972. There was a corresponding drop in the number of calves slaughtered for veal—down from 1 billion pounds a year in 1962 to 544 million pounds in 1971.

New York City wholesalers' supplies of beef were down by 67%, the city reported. Supermarkets reportedly showed a 33% drop in beef supplies.

Following the imposition of a freeze on beef, lamb and pork prices in March 1973, a nationwide consumer boycott of meat took place April 1–7, but meat prices continued at their previous high levels despite an estimated 50%–80% drop in retail meat sales during the week beginning April 1.

(The beef price freeze was ended Sept. 9.)

Supplies of beef had been sharply reduced during the boycott period as farmers withheld livestock from market, causing wholesale prices to remain at high levels.

Herrell Degraff, American Meat Institute president, reported Aug. 1 that across the nation, 46 beef packing houses had closed, 37 were cutting back operations and 6,000 packers had been laid off because cattle men were refusing to sell livestock while prices were frozen.

As fears of shortages mounted and consumers began to hoard meat supplies, large beef retailers were buying cattle directly, contracting to have it slaughtered and absorbing the price increases.

The Agriculture Department reported Aug. 1 that cattle slaughter was 80% lower than during the previous week, and was at its lowest level since the consumer boycott of April.

Institutional buyers were among the first to notice diminishing meat supplies. Pentagon spokesmen reported purchasing problems July 28 and New York City was unable to obtain a two-week supply of meat for the Aug. 6–17 period, spokesmen said.

A special federal grand jury was impaneled Aug. 1 in Brooklyn, N.Y. to investigate charges that "artificially created" meat shortage had resulted in a "wholesale holdup of consumers."

A suit brought by New York City Aug. 21 asked a federal district court to order Agriculture Secretary Earl L. Butz to declare a national beef shortage. The move would require President Nixon to utilize the recently-passed farm bill and take "appropriate action" to relieve the shortage.

Fears of shortages were causing some consumers to buy meat in Canada and Mexico where supplies were both cheaper and plentiful. U.S. customs officials at the California-Mexico border termed he shopping trips "nothing less than a s‹ m-pede" and refused to allow travelers to import more than $100 worth of meat (at Mexican retail prices), the New York Times reported Aug. 13.

U.S. shoppers in Canada were purchasing poultry and grocery products in addition to meat, according to the Times. Canadian merchants claimed that U.S. demand for their meat had not been equaled since World War II.

Canada curbs exports. Canadian Prime Minister Pierre Trudeau announced Aug. 13, 1973 that controls would be placed on the export of beef and pork because of market distortions caused by the U.S. beef price freeze.

Trudeau said there was "no shortage of food in Canada and none will be allowed to develop."

Industry, Trade and Commerce Minister Alastair Gillespie said controls would not affect "traditional" customers, who could continue purchases "provided they don't exceed last year's level." He said export licenses would be denied in cases of "raids" by U.S. buyers, and licenses would be revoked on profiteering companies.

The U.S. price freeze did not apply to imported beef, and increased exports to the U.S. had helped drive up prices for steer in Toronto to over $60 a hundredweight by Aug. 8.

Beryl Plumptre, head of the federal Food Prices Review Board, charged Aug. 10 that the news media were creating a panic in Canada over an artificial shortage of meat.

Australia heads world meat exporters. Roy Durand, a member of the Australian Meat Board, said Sept. 11, 1972 that the latest statistics showed Australia was the world's largest meat exporter. Durand cited an 11%–15% annual rise in shipping costs as the only serious problem confronting beef exporters.

Australian exports of beef and mutton to the U.S. had risen to 290,000 tons so far in 1972 following a U.S. suspension of meat import quotas in June, it was reported Oct. 10. This figure was 20,000 tons above the original quota for 1972. An Australian Meat Board spokesman said the increased exports to the U.S. had not affected Australia's exports to other nations.

Australian meat exports increased by 57% to $A841.5 million in fiscal 1972-73, a $A299 million rise over the previous record set in 1971-72, according to the annual report of the Australian Meat Board.

Australia remained the world's largest beef exporter; exports comprised 61% of national production, a 6% increase over 1971-72, the report stated. Beef and sheep meat prices had risen an average 30% since 1970.

The U.S. remained the major importer of Australian meat during the year, obtaining 317,600 tons worth more than $A366 million, an $A87 million rise. Japan remained the next highest importer of Australian meat, with a 157% jump in one year to $A188 million.

N.Z. halts curb on export to U.K. The New Zealand Meat Producers Board announced March 9, 1973 that it would suspend its restrictions on meat exports to Great Britain for the rest of the current season. The move was made in response to Britain's concern over diminishing meat supplies, a condition that had contributed to soaring prices. For the past seven years New Zealand had progressively increased the proportion of its exports to countries other than Britain.

Food Shortages Grow

Grain Stocks Low, Famines Foreseen

Declines in food stocks, fertilizer shortages and unfavorable climate changes threatened millions of people with possible famine in the years ahead, food, agriculture and science experts warned during 1973-74. World population, meanwhile, continued to grow.

Grain warning issued. World grain reserves had dropped to the point where rich and poor countries alike would depend on "the vagaries of a single year's weather" for adequate supplies, a Food and Agriculture Organization official said May 11, 1973.

Remaining stocks no longer provided an adequate buffer against crop failure, and consequently food supplies for millions in the coming year would depend almost entirely on 1973 harvests, the official reported to the U.N. Economic and Social Council.

The International Wheat Council said July 3 that world wheat demand in 1973–74 could exceed supplies, which might decrease to its lowest level in 20 years. Despite the abundance of the current wheat harvest, the council estimated that import demand could reach 64 million tons and the supply only 56 million tons.

The projected shortage was blamed on the high import demands of the Soviet Union, India, Bangla Desh and Pakistan.

According to the Food & Agriculture Organization Sept. 1, world wheat stocks were at a 20-year low.

Despite predictions of an easing of the shortage by 1974, officials anticipated no reduction in the price of grains and grain-fed livestock because there was "strong unabated world demand" for the crops. World wheat production dropped 3% in 1972 to 342.4 million tons.

Massive famines predicted. Dr. Norman E. Borlaug, Nobel Peace Prize-winning developer of high-yield grains, warned that 20 million people in developing countries might die in the next year as a result of fertilizer shortages and climate shifts, it was reported Jan. 26, 1974.

Borlaug said Arab oil cutbacks had drastically curtailed fertilizer production, which required heavy energy use and which used petroleum by-products as a base. Japan had cut nitrate fertilizer output by half since the oil crisis began in October 1973. Most of the deficit was expected to hit India, Indonesia and Southeast Asia.

A worldwide southward migration of monsoon rains was reported to be a major factor in droughts in West Africa, India and Latin America, according to participants at a New York meeting of cli-

WORLD GRAIN SUPPLY & DISTRIBUTION[1]

Marketing year	Area harvested (million hectares)	Yield (quintals/hectare)	Beginning stocks[2]	Production	Total exports	Consumption total[3]
			million metric tons			
1960/61	473.5	13.9	169.8	657.0	69.9	640.6
1961/62	466.9	13.4	182.7	624.2	80.8	648.1
1962/63	468.0	14.3	156.0	671.3	78.0	664.8
1963/64	475.1	13.9	159.6	661.7	94.1	664.5
1964/65	480.0	14.5	154.8	696.3	92.4	686.0
1965/66	476.3	14.7	157.7	701.9	108.1	734.7
1966/67	475.6	16.2	122.2	771.1	100.0	744.1
1967/68	485.7	16.2	151.1	785.6	97.4	767.4
1968/69	491.1	16.7	163.1	822.4	89.7	794.4
1969/70	487.4	16.9	191.3	825.7	102.1	839.3
1970/71	476.1	17.3	168.6	823.7	109.2	855.5
1971/72	484.4	18.8	131.5	911.4	111.2	892.8
1972/73	479.4	18.5	149.3	888.1	141.8	925.4
1973/74	499.6	19.4	108.1	970.4	151.0	959.5

NOTE: Includes wheat, rye, barley, oats, corn and sorghum.

[1]Data are based on an aggregate of differing local marketing years. [2]Stocks data are for selected countries and exclude such important countries as the U.S.S.R., China and part of Eastern Europe, for which stocks data are not available; the aggregate stock levels, however, have been adjusted for estimated year-to-year changes in Soviet grain stocks. [3]For countries in which stock data are not available or for which no adjustments have been made for year-to-year changes, consumption estimates assume a constant stock level.

Source: Foreign Agricultural Service and Economic Research Service, *Grain Data Base*, Nov. 1974.

mate and food experts at the Rockefeller Foundation in New York Jan. 24–25.

Northwest India had reported steadily declining monsoon rains in the past decade. The drought in India was not yet as severe as in the early twentieth century, but the region's population and food needs were far greater. The southward drift of the monsoon in Africa was pushing the Sahara desert southward by as much as 30 miles a year in some regions.

All these conditions had reduced grain reserves in exporting countries to a level adequate to feed the world for 29 days, compared with 95-day reserves in 1961.

World population up. The United Nations Demographic Yearbook (Feb. 14, 1973) reported that world population had reached 3.706 billion in mid-1970, and was increasing at about 2% a year, a rate that would double the total by 2006.

The Yearbook said Shanghai had become the world's most populous city, with 10,820,000 people, followed by Tokyo, with 8,841,000, New York, with 7,895,-000, Peking, with 7,570,000 and London, with 7,379,000. The figures did not include suburbs.

Food output & population increase. Despite annual fluctuations, world food production had grown at a faster rate than population during 1954–73:

	Total increase 1954-1973	Annual rate of increase
	percent	
Food production		
World _____ 69		2.8
Developed countries _ 65		2.7
Developing countries _ 75		3.0
Population		
World _____ 44		2.0
Developed countries _ 22		1.0
Developing countries 61		2.5
Per capita food production		
World _____ 17		0.8
Developed countries __ 33		1.5
Developing countries 8		0.4

Based on linear trends

Drought & Famine in Sahel & Other African Areas

A tragic example of famine-causing climate change is that of the Sahel (from the Arabic word for "coast"), the strip of non-desert land on the southern border of the Sahara. Six Sahelian countries of West Africa have been suffering drought that since 1969 has pushed the desert south by up to 30 miles a year in some areas. The Sahelian land, never well-watered, has been further depleted since at least World War II by large increases in population and livestock and by overcultivation, overgrazing and deforestation. Cattle have died by the hundreds of thousand, and starving people have left their homes to migrate with their livestock, as their ancestors had done, in search of food and water.

Famine threatens West Africa. The United Nations Food & Agriculture Organization reported May 12, 1973 that six million people in six Sahelian nations of West Africa faced famine as a result of the five-year drought.

Relief efforts in the countries—Senegal, Mauritania, Mali, Upper Volta, Niger and Chad—were hampered by inadequate transport to isolated areas. Nomads were reported moving toward settled regions, threatening fights for dwinding food stocks.

The U.S. and the European Economic Community had sent about 600,000 metric tons of food to the area, as well as vaccines for cattle and seed for new planting. West German, French, U.S. and Soviet aircraft were being used in an airlift program designed to distribute food before the rainy season made transport impossible.

FAO officials said long-term planning aid would be needed by the Sahara nations, whose economies were almost entirely agricultural and dependent on weather conditions.

Leaders of the six sub-Sahara nations presented a $1.5 billion plan for immediate and long-term aid projects to representatives of over 20 countries and international organizations Sept. 12, at the end of a 14-day conference in Ouagadougou, Upper Volta.

The plans included emergency food aid, construction of dams, wells and irrigation projects, and road, rail and river transport systems. About 625,000 tons of food had been delivered by Aug. 21, when the U.S. Agency for International Development reported that food supplies were adequate to prevent mass famine. (Niger President Hamani Diori had said July 23 it was "probable that many young Niger children had died of malnutrition" during the drought.) The U.S. had provided more than half the 470,000 tons of grain that was the mainstay of the relief effort.

U.N. Secretary General Kurt Waldheim and FAO Director General Addeke Boerma appealed Nov. 26 for $30 million and 500,000 tons of food to help the Sahel's drought sufferers.

The two leaders said that despite "some improvement in the rains and harvest this year in some areas, local production will not cover the food needs of the zone."

Drought spreads. By mid-1973 it had become obvious that the sub-Saharan drought had spread across the entire width of Africa—from Senegal to Ethiopia. Parts of Ethiopia and Kenya on Africa's east coast were reported to be especially hard hit.

According to a survey in Ethiopia by the U.N. Children's Fund, at least 50,000 people had died of famine caused by drought in Wollo Province (Ethiopia), it was reported Sept. 16. Ethiopian authorities said 670,000 persons were in need of assistance. The drought had caused clashes over grazing rights among tribesmen near the border of the French territory of Afars and Issas, it was reported July 29.

As 1973 advanced, the death toll mounted. The United Kingdom Disasters Emergency Fund reported by Oct. 29 that 100,000 to 150,000 people had died in the famine and drought in central and northern Ethiopia.

About two million others suffered from malnutrition and faced death. About 1,-000 were dying each week, according to Agence France-Presse Nov. 8. About 88% of Ethiopia's cattle had died in the drought.

The United Nations Food and Agriculture Organization (FAO) had arranged a shipment of 5,000 tons of grains, in addition to 10,000 tons already supplied, it was reported Oct. 28. Most of the grain had been supplied by Kenya at prices below world levels.

Diplomatic sources in Ethiopia charged that the government had delayed seeking international assistance in the early months of 1973, according to press reports. It was reported in February 1974 that government mismanagement had actually exacerbated the effects of the drought. Formerly confined to Wallo and Tigre Provinces, famine had spread to southern and eastern regions.

Although export of cereals had been banned as of April 13, 1973, hundreds of tons of grain and beans were being exported to Western Europe and Arab nations in October and November of that year, according to a Jan. 2 Washington Post report. The New York Times noted Feb. 6 that while grain exports had halted, bean exports continued. A 10,000-ton stock of privately-owned grain in Addis Ababa which the government could have purchased for immediate distribution to the most seriously affected regions was also cited in the Washington Post report.

It was reported Jan. 11, 1974 that more than 60,000 people were suffering from the effects of prolonged drought in northern Kenya and south of Nairobi.

According to the Kenya News Agency, an unknown number of people had starved to death, and some children were suffering from diseases of malnutrition. About 50% of the cattle in the northern regions had died, as well as a significant number of animals in Nairobi National Park.

The government said the situation had been brought under control by food shipments, it was reported Jan. 18.

The central highlands, which produced most of Kenya's food grains, had not been affected, and record crops were reported.

Sahel drought worse in 1974. Addeke H. Boerma, director general of the FAO, said Jan. 23 that the Sahelian drought had become worse that at the same time in 1973. He warned that pledges of aid received so far would not be enough to prevent widespread starvation and malnutrition.

Boerma said some crops had come up during the rainy season, but had died when the rains stopped prematurely. Unknown thousands had already died, many from normally nonfatal diseases complicated by malnutrition. Thousands more were continuing to move south from the region. Only 300,000 tons of grain had been committed by donor nations, out of 500,-000 needed. About $15 million needed for transporting the food was as yet uncommitted.

FAO reported Jan. 23 that more than 3.5 million head of cattle—about 25% of the region's cattle—worth $400 million may have died in 1973 because of the drought.

The drought had begun to affect Nigeria and Cameroon to a substantial degree, it was reported Feb. 11.

Argument over relief. Criticism of international relief efforts was voiced by U.N. Secretary General Waldheim March 7, 1974 after he had returned from an inspection of African drought areas. While hundreds of thousands were dying of disease and starvation throughout the sub-Sahara, international organizations, national governments and private foundations expended their energies in acrimonious denials of guilt and accusations of blame for the slowness with which assistance programs were undertaken.

In a study released March 3, the Carnegie Endowment for International Peace charged that, through "a pattern of neglect and inertia," relief organizations throughout the world had responded belatedly and inadequately to the drought.

In his March 7 comments, Waldheim, apparently in response to such accusations, stressed that the six affected countries had themselves long refused to acknowledge the gravity of the situation and had deferred appeals for assistance. "I should not criticize too much the international organizations," he said.

Addeke H. Boerma, director general of the U.N. Food and Agricultural Organization (FAO), March 7 rejected the Carnegie report charges as "grossly unfair" and declared that its estimate of 100,000 resulting deaths was "not supported by authoritative evidence."

The League of Red Cross Societies issued an appeal March 8 for renewed efforts to help save the two million people, mostly of the cattle-breeding Tuareg tribe, starving in Niger alone. A Red Cross spokesman remarked March 4 that in 1973 the cattle had died because of the drought; in 1974, the people were dying. Untold numbers were already eating boiled tree bark, a March 10 report said.

Drought & famine intensify. Famine conditions intensified across sub-Saharan Africa throughout the first half of 1974 as drought persisted in the west African Sahel region and torrential rains destroyed food crops in the east. According to an April 7 report, the drought had reached proportions of a national disaster in Mali, Niger, Chad, Mauritania and Ethiopia; famine had also spread to countries previously unaffected.

Despite numerous bilateral and multilateral assistance programs, a food deficit of 700,000 tons was anticipated for the six countries of the Sahel (Mauritania, Senegal, Upper Volta, Mali, Niger and Chad) in 1974, it was reported May 9, notwithstanding a United Nations Food and Agricultural Organization (FAO) announcement April 9 that the Sahel countries would receive about 700,000 tons of food for the year.

Throughout the Sahel and eastern Africa, a number of problems, chiefly the embryonic state of transportation and communications infrastructures, were thwarting attempts to provide relief. Typical was a March 22 report that 26,-000 tons of food for Ethiopian drought victims were waiting in Djibouti, capital of the French Territory of the Afars and Issas, for want of transport. The remoteness of villages and lack of reliable population records also impeded the development of adequate assistance programs.

The U.S. Agency for International Development pointed out that the U.S. had contributed $129 million, or 35% of the total from all nations, to the relief funds, but admitted that its effort was not "a model operation." U.S. officials also complained, according to a March 8 New York Times report, that the development of a U.S. assistance program had been hindered by French authorities who feared that political leverage in the former French territories which comprised the Sahel might be affected. The French Ministry of Foreign Affairs published a booklet, the French newspaper Le Monde reported March 7, describing its own aid program,which totaled 124 million francs ($24.8 million) in 1973.

Among reports of the situation:

Ethiopia—More people had died in one year of the Ethiopian famine than in the several years of the sub-Saharan famine in the six west African countries, according to figures released March 16 by Ethiopian Relief Coordinator Kassa Kebede. Official statistics showed that more than 700,000 persons were suffering from famine as a result of the drought in four southern provinces (Harar, Gemu Goffa, Balle and Sidamo), while another 1.3 million– 1.7 million were starving in the northern provinces of Wollo and Tigre and the central province of Shoa, in which the nation's capital, Addis Ababa, was located.

Statistics for deaths in the south were not available, Kebede said, but he reported that some 100,000 had died of starvation in Wollo in 1973.

In the midst of Ethiopia's six-year drought, torrential rains had fallen in Wollo and Danakyls Provinces, leaving several thousand people without shelter and decimating cotton and other crops, it was reported March 23. Relief efforts were paralyzed by floods which washed away several vital bridges along the route from the Red Sea port of Assab to Dessie, Wollo's chief town.

The Red Cross announced April 18 that it had mobilized 700 camels to transport grain to famine victims in the north. The British Royal Air Force June 20 flew trucks to the northern regions in an attempt to distribute food in the famine area before rains began again.

A Harrar official said Oct. 18 that one million people faced starvation in 12 of the eastern province's 13 districts. A grave water shortage also threatened, particularly in the Dagabur district, where more than one-third of the estimated 300,-000 inhabitants lacked adequate water supplies. As much as $2.50 was being charged for a barrel of water in that district, he said, and more than 80% of the cattle and camels had succumbed, depriving the nomadic population of its livelihood.

According to a Washington Post report Oct. 23, almost total crop failure was observed in parts of northern Eritrea, Ethiopia's northernmost province. The report noted that Eritrea had its own private relief and rehabilitation association, which said that 700,000 persons were seriously affected by the prolonged drought, complicated by the state of war existing for more than a decade because of the province's secessionist movements.

There also was an emerging dispute between Ethiopian and international relief agencies over the nature and extent of the crisis. Most international relief groups were closing down their emergency feeding stations in Ethiopia, according to an Oct. 23 Washington Post report, in the wake of the dispute and other pressing international demands for assistance.

A serious factor was Addis Ababa's reported reluctance to tap its available resources—including over $300 million in gold and foreign exchange holdings—to purchase grain for relief. The Oct. 23 report cited sources in Washington which said that Ethiopia was planning instead to spend more than $100 million to buy military equipment.

Donors also noted that Ethiopia's grain exports for the first six months of 1974 totaled 11,000 tons, twice the figure for the first six months of 1973, the report said. The government Relief and Rehabilitation Commission had issued an appeal for 278,-000 tons of grain, a figure challenged by foreign relief sources since the results of the November harvest were not yet known. The relief commissioner, however, cited caterpillar and locust attacks on crops which foreshadowed a poor harvest and added that "donors have a tendency to wait until a catastrophe has hit."

Mali—Minister of Production Sidi Coulibaly defended Mali's assistance program March 18, denying allegations published by the French newspaper Le Monde Feb. 18 that the government had not responded adequately to the drought. He acknowledged that it had affected 1,-835,000 of the country's 5 million people. Le Monde reiterated its charges March 21 and accused Mali of prohibiting distribution of food and other assistance to the Tuareg population by a Belgian relief unit approaching Mali from Algeria. Le Monde also suggested that the Tuaregs were fleeing northward and eastward to escape government repression. It was reported March 24–25 that 37,000 nomads were living in refugee camps near Gao and Tombouctou.

According to a June 10 report, cereal production had fallen in 1972–73 by at least 37% against a normal year; cotton production had failed by one-third to reach the expected level; and cattle losses were estimated at 40%, with as many as 90%–100% dead in the northeast.

The U.S. announced June 13 that the Air Force would begin a 90-day relief operation to Mali June 15, to provide the famine-stricken nation with 5,000 tons of grain.

Mauritania—Authorities in Nouakchott had adopted a program in 1972 to counter the effects of the drought, allocating about 20% of the nation's 1973 budget for the plan. To mobilize the funds, the government collected one day's earnings per month from every wage or salary earner and 1% of business earnings.

Relief assistance was impeded by the FAO which reduced Mauritania's original request for 100,000 tons of food to 60,000 tons, it was reported April 13, 1974. The FAO attributed the cut to "either a misinterpretation . . . or a misunderstanding." Further FAO aid reductions lowered daily rations in the country to below 300 grams of food per person, the report said.

It was reported March 20 that nearly 80% of Mauritania's livestock had been lost.

Chad—David Smithers, deputy director of Christian Aid, a relief organization, said April 9 that villages in droughtstricken Chad were reminiscent of concentration camps, so desperate was the situation. There were, he said, virtually no drugs or medicines and only 44 doctors to serve a population of nearly 4 million.

The French government April 11 donated 5,000 tons of grain to Chad.

President Ngarta Tombalbaye said Oct. 25 that Chad would accept no relief assistance from the U.S. and ordered returned to Washington thousands of tons of grain intended to aid the more than two million Chadians believed to be suffering from famine.

Tombalbaye said the decision was reached because U.S. officials had refused to allow Chadian authorities "the right to discuss and plan the distribution of the aid." He also criticized the Americans for expecting his government to assume responsibility for the payment of their hotel bills.

The brunt of his attack, however, was leveled against "an American journalist" who had written articles discrediting him and his government. (New York Times correspondent Henry Kamm had reported Oct. 6 and 10 on the state of affairs in drought-ravaged Chad, alleging that the relief program was being grossly mismanaged due to "incompetence, apathy and participation in or toleration of profiteering on the part of persons close to the national leadership.")

Niger—The Red Cross announced that 15,000 starving nomads were being settled in a refugee camp near Niamey, the capital, it was reported March 23–24. In the face of charges that the government of deposed President Hamani Diori had not responded to the ravages of the drought and had engaged in studied neglect in order to exterminate the Tuareg tribesmen, the new military regime had undertaken a program to mobilize action against the drought.

Upper Volta—Tuareg refugees had alleged that Upper Volta, like Niger and Mali, was using the drought to exterminate the tribe, according to an April 2 report. The charges were denied, but a local official said "we do not pity the Tuaregs because they are being fed while we must work for everything we get."

Senegal—Hundreds of thousands of cattle had died in Senegal and the peanut crop had been seriously affected, it was reported May 28. Peanuts represented 33%–50% of Senegal's total export earnings.

Algeria—The Algiers newspaper El Moudjahid reported Nov. 24, 1973 that about 2 million peasants in the south were affected by the drought.

Guinea—Drought conditions had appeared in Guinea, it was reported April 7, but government authorities said they would not permit U.S. officials to visit stricken regions.

Liberia—The minister of foreign affairs announced March 25 that drought condi-

BILATERAL & MULTILATERAL FOOD AID CONTRIBUTIONS OF DEVELOPED COUNTRIES (estimated disbursements 1973)

Countries	Bilateral			Multilateral grants				Total
	Grants	Loans	Total bilateral	EC	WFP	Other	Total multilateral	
	million dollars							
Australia	18.7	–	18.7		0.9	–	0.9	19.6
Austria	–	–	–		0.8	–	0.8	0.8
Belgium	5.0	–	5.0	10.7	0.3	–	11.0	16.0
Canada	65.3	9.8	75.1		19.9	(0.9)	20.8	95.9
Denmark	2.6	–	2.6	1.7	9.6	–	11.3	13.9
France	30.3	–	30.3	35.6	0.1	–	35.7	66.0
Germany	37.5	–	37.5	41.8	12.6	–	54.4	91.9
Italy	–	–	–	27.4	–	–	27.4	27.4
Japan	7.5	97.0	104.5		1.3	–	1.3	105.8
Netherlands	6.1	–	6.1	16.0	10.9	–	26.9	33.0
New Zealand	(0.8)	–	(0.8)		0.4	–	0.4	1.2
Norway	0.2	–	0.2		3.7	–	3.7	3.9
Portugal	(0.1)	–	(0.1)		–	–	–	0.1
Sweden	–	–	–		6.6	4.6	11.2	11.2
Switzerland	5.5	–	5.5		2.6	0.4	3.0	8.5
United Kingdom	–	–	–	12.6	1.7	–	14.3	14.3
United States	251.0	425.0	676.0		27.0	27.0	54.0	730.0
Total	430.6	531.8	926.4	195.8	98.4	32.9	277.1	1,239.5

Source: OECD, "The Food Situation in the Developing Countries," February, 1974 and U.S. Department Agriculture.

tions were beginning to make themselves felt in Liberia.

Ghana—The government had requested assistance from the U.S. because of increasing shortages, it was reported April 7. Export of cocoa, Ghana's main crop, had fallen off because of the drought, but high world market prices were helping to compensate for the drop in production.

Nigeria—It was reported April 30 that $75 million worth of livestock had perished in Nigeria's Northeastern State as a result of the drought. The report also said that Lake Chad, which bordered the state, had receded 20 miles in some areas, rendering hundreds of fishermen jobless.

The world's largest exporter of peanuts, Nigeria had stopped all peanut exports, it was reported April 7. The crop had dropped from 800,000 tons to an expected 300,000 tons in 1974 because of the drought.

Nigeria had told the U.S. State Department that it wanted no outside aid, according to an April 7 report.

Central African Republic—The country's cotton crop was suffering and the thinly populated eastern and northern portions were particularly affected, it was reported April 7. The government had sought assistance from the U.S. State Department to help determine the extent and effects of the drought.

Sudan—The FAO reported serious food shortages in Sudan's central provinces and said about 50,000 persons were receiving relief in the southwest, it was reported April 7, 1974.

Burundi—Government officials indicated March 22 that famine was creating problems in Burundi. The agriculture minister directed the population to take emergency measures to preserve food.

Kenya—About 70% of the country and an estimated 2 million people were affected by the drought, especially in the east and northeast regions, it was reported April 7. The government was distributing maize to some 60,000 people in 11 northern districts.

Masai tribesmen had been driven from their villages as 90% of their cattle perished in the drought, according to a May 5 report. About 250,000 head of cattle were reported to have perished.

Kenya had told the U.S. State Depart-

ment that it wanted no outside aid; the British weekly the Economist criticized the Kenyan government March 23 for refusing to declare a state of famine.

Tanzania—The government had rejected outside aid for the almost 50,000 people suffering from the food shortages that resulted from the drought spreading in northwestern Tanzania, it was reported April 7, 1974. As happened in Kenya, the cattle-raising Masai tribe was most seriously affected.

Bangla Desh & India

Bangla Desh famine feared. Secretary General Waldheim told the U.N. Security Council Jan. 1, 1973 that the chances for famine in Bangla Desh were "more serious and more threatening" than in 1972, when U.N. states raised nearly $1 billion to help overcome a food shortage there.

He said the situation had been worsened by a poor December 1972 grain harvest and by a 40% drop in monsoon rains during the growing months. Supplies of fertilizer were deficient, Waldheim declared, and agricultural pests had been more active than usual. He emphasized that "only member states interested in the lives of the people of Bangla Desh can provide the supplies and funds essential to deal with the situation."

Waldheim Jan. 5 made a new appeal for grain and transportation to assist Bangla Desh, saying the aid was needed to forestall a major crisis and "possibly a tragedy" in the new nation later in 1973.

Waldheim said 1,700,000 tons of grain were needed if widespread malnutrition and almost certain starvation were to be avoided. He also said $5 million was needed for inland transportation services. The U.S. and Canada were providing 200,-000 tons and 100,000 tons of grain, respectively, but other pledges of help were essential before the end of March, Waldheim asserted.

In an emergency action, the World Food Program, a joint undertaking by the U.N. and the Food and Agriculture Organization, was purchasing 100,000 tons of grain for Bangla Desh, it was reported Jan. 19. The price, $11.8 million, would be paid by Dacca.

Bangla Desh suffered serious food shortages because of insufficient monsoon rains in 1972, but rainstorms in 1973 and 1974 also damaged crops.

In 1974, at least 2,500 persons were killed following monsoon rains which had left 20,000 of Bangla Desh's 55,000 square miles under water. Property and crop damage was estimated at $2 billion. It was reported Aug. 12 that the floods were subsiding following two months of rainfall. Aircraft were dropping $2.5 million worth of food and 20 tons of medical supplies, including cholera vaccine, allocated by the United Nations, to those marooned. Cholera was reported widespread, with the problem in the cities aggravated by masses of people crowding in from flooded areas.

Gandhi reassures India. Prime Minister Indira Gandhi reassured Indians Aug. 9, 1973 that there was "no cause for panic" despite worsening economic conditions, which she called a "passing phase."

Soaring inflation had increased the price of food by 25% in the past six months and the country was further beset by food shortages and rising unemployment.

Rising prices and food shortages had caused riots in Bombay and other parts of the country. More than 1,000 persons were arrested in demonstrations in Madhya Pradesh State Aug. 4–6.

Birth control was being reduced because of a cut in the 1973–74 budget funds for the Ministry of Health and Family Planning, it was reported Aug. 5. The ministry had asked for $81.1 million, considerably lower than the previous year's budget of $104 million, but the government was only providing $75.1 million.

As a result of the economy campaign, the government was abandoning plans to build family planning and maternal care centers in rural areas and was sharply reducing mass vasectomies and birth control publicity in cities and villages.

India's population was increasing at about 13 million a year despite family planning efforts of recent years. The government had sought to reduce the birth rate from 41 per thousand population in 1968 to 25 by 1976. The target date was extended to 1980. The current birth rate was about 37 per thousand.

Soviet grain loan. India announced Sept. 28, 1973 that the Soviet Union had agreed to lend it two million tons of grain. The cost was not specified, but the price of two million tons of wheat in the current market amounted to at least $350 million.

Food Secretary G.C.L. Joneja said Soviet Communist party General Secretary Leonid I. Brezhnev had informed Prime Minister Indira Gandhi that he was offering the loan because of his government's "aspirations to develop friendly Soviet-Indian relations." Joneja said the loan would consist mostly of wheat and some rice.

U.S. Agriculture Secretary Earl Butz Oct. 5 denied what he said were rumors that the Soviet Union was diverting recently purchased U.S. grain to India. The Soviet wheat to India "will be their own wheat," he said. Butz said the Russians had recently assured Assistant Agriculture Secretary Carroll Brunthaver that "none of the United States grain they bought is being diverted to other destinations outside the bloc."

(Under a trade protocol made public Jan. 23, 1974, the U.S.S.R. agreed to provide India with an additional 325,000 tons of fertilizer.)

Food, price rise riots. Riots protesting food shortages and price rises broke out in three Indian states Sept. 12–15, 1973.

More than 8,000 persons were reported Sept. 13 to have been arrested in Tamil Nadu state in the previous two days in an unsuccessful attempt to smash plans for a general strike. The walkout, organized by the Communists, Dravidian party and other political groups, paralyzed transport Sept. 13 in five towns in the state and forced closure of factories and businesses.

Troops were called out Sept. 14 in Mysore and Manipur states after widespread violence. One person was killed in Maddur Sept. 14 when police fired on demonstrators, raising the death toll in

Mysore to four since the rioting began there Sept. 13. Two persons were killed Sept. 13 in Imphal, capital of Manipur. Rioting, arson and grain looting occurred in Maddur Sept. 15.

There were riots in January 1974 over food shortages and rising prices in the States of Maharashtra and Gujarat. The cost of basic items, especially food and fuel, had risen by 20% in the past six months, the greatest increase in India's cost of living in 26 years.

As violence mounted, seven people were killed and 25 wounded when police fired at participants in food riots in Bombay Feb. 22. Thousands of persons had marched in protest against rising food prices and shortages. The demonstrators burned shops, public buses and police vehicles and stoned police.

Crisis intensifies. As 1974 advanced, drought and severe power shortages were intensifying India's food crisis in September, with the New Delhi government seeking to increase food imports and end hoarding to stave off the spread of starvation in the northern and central sections of the country. Millions of persons in those areas were said to be moving into Calcutta and Bombay and into Bhubaneswar in eastern Orissa state.

The chief ministers of the two key food-producing states of Punjab and Haryana met with Prime Minister Indira Gandhi Sept. 24 to discuss ways of easing crop failures in their regions brought about by severe drought. The ministers urged Gandhi to order further electricity cuts in New Delhi and in nearby Rajasthan and Madhya Pradesh states to divert power to their states for irrigation. The government had already ordered such electricity cutbacks for several hours in New Delhi.

The crisis was pointed up by reports Sept. 23 of hunger and violence in Uttar Pradesh, West Bengal and Rajasthan states. A West Bengal minister said 15 million people in rural areas were either starving or living on one meal a day. Another report said more than 500 people had died of malnutrition in West Bengal. The newspaper Indian Express said: "Famine conditions, widespread destitution and starvation deaths are being reported from different parts of the country."

Prime Minister Gandhi had expressed confidence in a speech in Madras Sept. 9 that India would overcome the difficulties of inflation and hunger. She said "some of our shortages are due to the fact that many more people than we had imagined are asking for certain things—whether it was water for irrigation or fertilizer for high-yielding seeds." In an Oct 1 address, she said the food grain shortage would be met "provided that hoarded stocks are unearthed." The prime minister appealed for strict austerity, suggesting that "the relatively better-off section" of the country "voluntarily forgo a portion of their rations."

Indian sources reported Sept. 28 that the government had asked the Soviet Union to supply India with 2-4 million tons of food.

Violence broke out again. A general strike in Bihar State Oct. 5 protesting rising prices and food shortages resulted in clashes between police and demonstrators, leaving 12 dead.

A similar demonstration held in New Delhi Oct. 6 was peaceful as a crowd estimated at up to 50,000 tried to march on the residence of Prime Minister Gandhi. Police stopped the marchers but permitted a small delegation to visit Gandhi.

Meanwhile, reports continued of drought-caused food shortages and resulting starvation. A dispatch from New Delhi Oct. 4 told of widespread hunger in the states of Orissa, Gujarat, Rajasthan, Madhya Pradesh, West Bangal, Uttar Pradesh and Bihar. The inadequate diet was causing widespread blindness, especially among children. There were more than five million blind people in India and the number was said to be increasing by 60,000 a year.

A Rajasthan official said the "misery this year is going to be unprecedented." Virtually half the state of Madhya Pradesh was affected by the drought, with 70%-80% of the rice harvest lost. The Economic and Political Weekly asserted that government "management of the food economy is in a shambles."

The food situation was particularly critical in West Bengal State, according to a report published by the Washington Post Oct. 15. More than 1,000 persons were said to have starved to death in the past two months in the Cooch Behar district. An official of the ruling Congress Party placed the death toll at 3,000 in that period. Hundreds were said to be dying every day in Cooch Behar and three other districts in the state.

Food Minister Chidambaram Subramaniam had said Oct. 8 that the government would combat the food shortages through imports and the raising of emergency short-term crops in the areas not affected by the drought. This type of program already had been started in Andhra Pradesh, Tamil Nadu and Maharashtra States, where rains had been normal and water was available, the minister said.

Assam State legislators urged Prime Minister Gandhi to aid Assam and to provide their state with emergency food in view of mass hunger and starvation there. They said the total number of deaths from malnutrition and starvation might have reached 15,000, largely because of floods that had devastated crops. The food problem in Assam had worsened because of an influx of refugees from neighboring Bangla Desh, the legislators said.

(A World Bank report had asserted that India faced critical food shortages for years and would have to import at least two million tons of grain annually during the next five years.)

Food Supply & International Trade

U.S. action. The U.S. Agriculture Department (USDA) took further action Jan. 10-11, 1973 to increase food supplies in order to hold down retail food prices.

Actions taken included the rapid disposal of Commodity Credit Corp. grain stocks; termination of additional loans to farmers for grain crops harvested before 1972 and for 1972 wheat crops; expansion of grain and meat supplies by allowing production and grazing on 15 million acres set aside for conservation under the wheat program; and termination of remaining export subsidies.

President Nixon Jan. 11 terminated mandatory price and wage controls except in such "problem areas" as food.

Nixon also was creating a new advisory group "to give special attention to new ways of cutting costs and improving productivity at all points along the food chain," he said.

Treasury Secretary George P. Shultz said the government would sell its grain stocks. "We expect to empty the bins and put this on the market," he emphasized. The effort to restrain rising food prices "will be stepped up," he said.

Nixon discussed the problem at a closed meeting with the AFL-CIO executive council in Bal Harbour, Fla. Feb. 19.

White House Press Secretary Ronald Ziegler, who reported on the meeting, cited the Administration view that neither rationing nor price controls would solve the problem of increased food prices and that the problem primarily was one of supply and demand.

The President had noted at the meeting that the demand for meat was increasing in the U.S. and in the world, Ziegler said, and had referred "to certain steps such as lifting [import] quotas on meat which would help deal with the supply part of the problem."

Ziegler said the Administration would take a number of steps to increase the food supply. One step under consideration, he said, was an end to agricultural export subsidies.

As meat prices continued to rise, the Cost of Living Council (CLC) March 22 extended price controls to most meat packers, and Nixon March 29 ordered ceilings on the prices of beef, lamb and pork "for as long as necessary to do the job."

A nationwide consumers' boycott of meat took place April 1-7 but ended with meat prices holding firm at their previous high levels despite an estimated 50%-80% drop in retail meat sales during the week beginning April 1.

Spokesmen emphasized that their protest was aimed at public policy changes and noted that a prolonged boycott of meat could drive small farmers out of business, leaving consumers "at the mercy of agribusiness."

The Congressional Joint Economic Committee April 4 released a staff study on food costs.

According to the study, compiled in association with a Washington consulting firm headed by John Schnittker, undersecretary of agriculture in the Johnson Administration, "the overriding single cause of the recent sharp rise in the prices of agricultural commodities was a decline of 42 million tons in world grain production in 1972."

Because of declining grain and potato production in the Soviet Union, short grain crops throughout the world and a falloff in rice production in Southern Asia, "internal stocks have been drawn down to rock bottom levels in virtually all importing and exporting countries."

The report said that the USDA "did not appreciate the significance" of this or of the U.S. sale of grain to the U.S.S.R. in 1972.

The report cited several instances of "chaotic decision making" within the USDA that had contributed to the recent price spiral:

■ By continuing wheat subsidies at "buyer's market" levels until Sept. 22, 1972, the USDA wasted "some $300 million in public funds."

■ Two weeks after the Soviet Union began to purchase U.S. wheat, the USDA announced a "maximum acreage set-aside for the 1973 crop" and continued restrictions on barley acreage, which remained in effect until it was too late to expand the fall, 1972 planting of wheat.

■ On Dec. 11, 1972, the USDA announced a "feed grain program designed to divert some 25 million acres from production and to produce a 1973 corn crop of only 5.7 billion bushels." Modifications in the allotment system were not made until Jan. 31 and March 27.

■ Because the USDA allowed farmers to substitute corn for soybeans under a 1970 acreage allotment program, soybean production in 1971 and 1972 was reduced. The shortage contributed to the high prices of oil seed and protein meals, such as soybean meal used as feed for livestock and poultry.

The Wall Street Journal reported April 25 that losses resulting from severe rain and snow conditions during the spring totaled $1 billion to livestock and crops.

Crop curbs eased—The Agriculture Department (USDA) announced Jan. 31 that it was reducing the amount of land

farmers were required to leave idle under provisions of the livestock feed subsidy program.

The action was designed to increase corn and soybean production and reduce farm subsidy costs by $60 million. Instead of the 25 million acres now set aside under that program, only 16.5 million would go unused in 1973.

The Agriculture Department said March 26 that crop controls on corn and other grain would be lifted for spring planting.

Under the federal feed grain support program, farmers would be required to set aside only 10% of their lands, rather than the previous allotment of 25%. A total of 13.5 million acres, including 1.5 million–2.5 million acres of corn, would be released for production.

Nixon raises cheese quota. President Nixon April 25 authorized a 50% increase in cheese imports through July 1973 in an effort to lift supplies and lower prices for consumers who had been substituting cheese for higher priced meat. Per capita consumption of cheese had risen 9% in 1972 while its price had increased 5%–10% since June 1972.

An additional 64 million pounds of cheese could be imported above the 128 million pounds permitted to enter the country annually.

U.S. food habits change. The Agriculture Department released a report Aug. 17 detailing the nation's eating habits in the 1952–1972 period. According to the study, meat consumption increased steadily, totaling 116 pounds per person in 1972, 54 pounds above the 1952 level. Consumers also indicated an increasing propensity for processed and frozen foods, chicken and cheese. Per capita food consumption in 1972 totaled 1,448 pounds.

According to another report issued Aug. 22, consumers spent $116.2 billion on farm produce in 1972, an increase of $5.5 billion over the previous year. Middlemen collected 66% of the total, but farmers received 66% of the increase.

Bakers see $1 a loaf for bread. The American Bakers Association warned Jan. 9 that a spring wheat shortage could force prices up to $8–$12 a bushel and cause retail bread costs to climb to $1 per 1.5 pound loaf. (Wheat prices reached a new high of $5.93 a bushel in trading Jan. 9 on the Chicago commodities market. Large-sized loaves of bread currently were selling for an average 50¢.)

Bill O. Mead, chairman of the association, urged the Administration to set export controls because wheat already contracted for sale abroad could cause a deficit in U.S. supplies before the 1974 wheat crop became available in July.

Assistant Agriculture Secretary Carroll G. Brunthaver termed the bakers' fears "irrational" but he conceded that the government was seeking to delay grain export shipments and that negotiations were under way with Canada to increase U.S. wheat purchases. (The Agriculture Department announced Jan. 11 that the Soviet Union had agreed to a delay in delivery of 18.4 million bushels of wheat until after the start of the summer harvest. The U.S. was still obligated to deliver 38.7 million bushels to the U.S.S.R. by June 30.)

Brunthaver accused the bakers of alarming the public with "scare tactics" but Mead said at his news conference that the warnings were issued directly to consumers because the Agriculture Department had ignored its requests for export controls.

U.S.S.R.'s food needs for '73. The Soviet Union was expected to spend $1.05 billion in purchases of 14 million tons of grain on the world market during the 1973-4 crop years, the U.S. Agriculture Department reported April 10, 1973.

The predictions of reduced grain purchases by the Soviet Union was based on new estimates of improved Soviet crops as well as reports from Europe that the Soviet had arranged ship charters to transport 9 million tons of grain within an 18–20 month period.

Canadian officials announced April 9 that the Soviet Union had concluded a $200 million deal for 1.5 million tons of wheat and 500,000 tons of barley.

The Associated Press reported data released by the Agriculture Department July 11 showing that the Soviet Union had already ordered more than 7.85 million metric tons of U.S. grain for delivery by next summer.

The figures showed that China had ordered 2.7 million metric tons of U.S. wheat, corn and soybeans for 1973-74, after importing 1.5 million tons in 1972.

The New York Times reported July 13 that Agriculture Department specialists had disputed the AP report. The Times quoted the specialists as stating that the Soviet Union had sharply curtailed its purchases of U.S. grain.

The sale to Russia of 200,000 tons of surplus butter at sharply reduced prices was approved by the EEC Commission, it was officially announced April 9. The sale would effectively halve the EEC's 400,-000-ton butter surplus.

An EEC spokesman said the Soviet government would pay 35 units of account (UA—each unit representing $1 U.S. prior to the 1971 devaluation) per 100 kilos of butter, one UA per kilo more than the Russians had originally offered. This compared with the 186 UA per 100 kilos that the community had paid its farmers as the minimum guaranteed price for the butter. The export rebate for the Russian sale was set at 151 UA per 100 kilos.

The Commission came under heavy criticism for the sale terms, with opponents arguing the community was subsidizing cheap butter for the Russians. The Commission countered that the butter otherwise would have to be stored or destroyed, resulting in further financial loss to the community.

U.S. grain data accord set—The Soviet Union agreed to begin in 1974 to supply regular information to the U.S. on crop prospects, to ease world market disruptions in the future, it was reported Nov. 16.

Emergency farm measures—The Soviet Communist Party's Central Committee May 3, 1973 announced several emergency measures to prevent a repetition of recent crop failures, including plans to conscript workers for harvesting, if needed.

Office and factory workers and students would be drafted by the Council of Ministers of the republic involved and would be paid farm wages plus 50% of their former salaries.

The Central Committee ordered a speedup in delivery of farm equipment and repair of silos. Pools of spare parts and wages would be established, and trucks and drivers mobilized for around-the-clock farm work at bonus pay.

Grain and sugar harvesters would receive 20% bonuses for good work, with double bonuses in Siberia and the Urals, and permanent state farm workers could buy up to 10% of fruit and vegetable production at discount prices. The government had already decided to increase fertilizer production to 9.5 million tons a year.

Poor harvests and other problems had caused widespread shortages and rationing in many regions over the winter in a variety of goods including meats, poultry and dairy products.

Early optimistic crop reports proved to be inaccurate. The Supreme Soviet was told Dec. 12 that the 1973 grain harvest was a record 220 million tons, 52 million tons above the poor 1972 harvest and above planned targets. The Central Statistical Board Jan. 25, 1974 put the figure at 222.5 million tons.

Deputy Premier Nikolai Baibakov, chairman of the State Planning Committee, said agriculture would continue to receive a high capital influx, a quarter of all investment in 1974.

But in a speech at a closed Central Committee meeting in December 1973, General Secretary Leonid Brezhnev acknowledged that "due to the shortage of storage place, packing materials, transport, and undeveloped capacity for processing produce," the 1973 grain harvest provided a much smaller yield of usable grain than reported.

The verbatim excerpts of Brezhnev's speech were reported by Western newspapers March 5, 1974.

Western specialists had projected that the claimed 222.5 million ton yield should be revised downward to about 165 million tons because waste and rain-drenched grain had been included in the quoted figure, according to the New York Times March 6.

U.S. fertilizer arrangement—Officials of the Soviet government and the Occidential Petroleum Corp. signed a multi-billion dollar barter arrangement in Moscow April 12, 1973.

Although the Soviet news agency Tass put the value of the deal at $8 billion, Dr. Armand Hammer, chairman of Occidential, said the figure was lower.

Under terms of the deal, Occidental would ship to the Soviet Union large quantities of superphosporic acid to be used in production of phosphate fertilizers. With the Bechtel Corp. of San Francisco, Occidental would help with construction of a fertilizer complex at Kuibyshev, 500 miles southeast of Moscow. It would receive as repayment liquid ammonia and urea from the Kuibyshev plant and potash from other parts of the country.

The Soviet minister of chemical industry was reported Jan. 21 to have claimed that the U.S.S.R. had become the world leader in chemical fertilizer output.

By surpassing U.S. production totals, the Soviet Union hoped to prevent sharp fluctuations in future annual harvest yields.

New farm program—Leonid Brezhnev announced March 15, 1974 that the party's Central Committee had approved a $45 billion agricultural project for the 1976–1980 five-year plan. The program, reminiscent of the late Nikita Khrushchev's once-denounced virgin lands project, accounted for more than 33% of the plan's total agricultural allotment.

To be implemented over 15 years, the project called for development of the Soviet Union's non-black soil zone, comprising 125 million acres of marginal land extending across European Russia from the Baltic Sea into Siberia. In keeping with Moscow's aim of improving the livestock sector of the economy in order to enrich the Soviet diet, the project was intended primarily to foster the growth of cattle farming. It would entail, for the most part, reclamation of crop and grazing land already under cultivation and would seek not only to increase production but also to improve the distribution scheme.

(An Argentine economic mission in Moscow Sept. 20 signed an agreement under which Argentina would sell 90,000 tons of meat to the Soviet Union over the next three years.)

Higher U.S.S.R. shipping rate set with U.S. The U.S. Commerce Department said June 5, 1973 that a new shipping agreement with the U.S.S.R. called for higher Soviet payments to U.S. ships carrying grain to the Soviet Union after June 30.

Under the old agreement the Soviet Union paid a fixed rate of $10.34 per ton, supplemented by U.S. government subsidies to shippers of an additional $11 per ton. The new rate would fluctuate according to world market conditions, and would be $16.94 in the first week of the agreement. Most of the 19.5 million tons of grain sold by the U.S. to the Soviet Union in 1972 was covered by the earlier shipping contract.

Chinese program. China was reported March 10, 1973 to have launched a new campaign to prevent a recurrence of the 1972 drop in grain production.

The government, directing its appeal to the rural areas, was urging more effective measures to cope with natural disasters, which had contributed to the previous year's fall in grain output, and also was calling for improved production through expenditure of more local funds.

An editorial published the previous week by the Communist party newspaper Jenmin Jih Pao said because natural disasters were not uncommon to China, the country must establish the basis for good harvests, demonstrating that "man can master nature."

The first sale of fertilizer by a U.S. firm to China was reported by the Journal of Commerce April 2. Agricultural & Industrial Corp. of New York City had sold 14,000 tons of diammonium phosphate valued at nearly $2 million.

China announced Dec. 23 that its 1973 grain harvest exceeded the 1971 record of 250 million tons but gave no exact figures. (Western estimates later put China's 1973 grain harvest at 240 million tons, but the Chinese reiterated Sept. 26, 1974 that the total exceeded 250 million.)

The statement said the 1973 harvest had increased by more than the annual average growth rate since 1949, officially placed at about 4%.

The Chinese press agency Hsinhua had reported Dec. 18 that China had achieved self-sufficiency in food supplies and had "solved the problem of feeding its population by self-reliance." It said the 1973 grain production would be "more than double the country's output" in 1949. The Chinese were now assured of adequate food supply even if some areas had lean harvests, Hsinhua said.

Hsinhua then reported July 23, 1974 that China had a record summer wheat harvest despite severe drought conditions in some areas, but no specific figures were given.

The report said production in 10 key areas "hit an all-time high" and "total output rose by a big margin over that of last summer." Farmers reaped one-half to three-fourths of a ton of wheat per 2.2 acres, Hsinhua said, but it did not list the total number of acres set aside for wheat.

Hsinhua said Sept. 26 that in the 25 years of Communist rule, China's cereal production had doubled and that every person now received 100 kilograms (about 220 pounds) more grain a year than in 1949.

China, however, continued to import food during 1973 and 1974. The U.S. Agriculture Department had said July 1, 1973 that it expected Chinese purchases of U.S. crops to exceed 1972 levels.

Soybean sales to the Chinese already reported totaled at least 500,000 tons (about 1.8 million bushels) valued at $12–$15 million, according to the Agriculture Department.

Canada said Oct. 5 that China had agreed to a three-year purchase of 179–224 million bushels of wheat, at a potential price of over $1 billion.

Otto Lang, the minister responsible for the Canadian Wheat Board, said a contract had been signed for the first 37 million bushels, to be delivered between January and June, 1974, at a price of about $200 million.

Australia then announced Oct. 11, 1973 the conclusion of a three-year wheat agreement with China worth more than $A600 million ($US893 million). The accord, involving 4.7 million tons of wheat, was the first long-term wheat agreement between Australia and China.

The first contract under the three-year pact was recently signed by an Australian Wheat Board delegation in Peking, board Chairman John P. Cass announced Oct. 22. It provided for the sale of 600,000 tons of Australian wheat worth $A80 million during the first six months of 1974.

China and Argentina signed an agreement Dec. 14 under which China would buy three million tons of Argentine wheat and maize over the next three years. It was the first grain agreement between the two countries since 1966.

Farm prices soar. The Agriculture Department reported May 31, 1973 that the prices paid to farmers for raw agricultural products climbed 4% in the 30-day period ending May 15. The price level was 33% higher than in May 1972. Using 100 as a base reflecting farm prices in 1967, the index was at 163 in May.

Leading the USDA list were record price increases for soybeans. Soybean futures (July delivery date) on the Chicago Board of Trade June 4 were at a record $12.12 a bushel. A year earlier, a bushel of soybeans had sold for $3.275 on the commodities market.

The extraordinary price increase resulted from poor spring weather which ruined the crop in Illinois, where most of the nation's supply of soybeans was produced. Other factors were: depleted stockpiles caused by large grain sales in 1972 to the Soviet Union; a severe shortage of the railroad cars needed to distribute the grain, also caused by the strain imposed on the nation's transportation system by the Soviet purchases; and a sharp decline in the anchovy catch off Peruvian waters.

Anchovy meal and soybeans comprised the principal source of protein in livestock feed.

Drought in Cyprus. Cyprus was suffering its worst drought in a century, the New York Times reported Aug. 7, 1973. The rainfall was less than a third of the normal annual rate of 20 inches, with some areas dry for nearly 18 months. The government estimated a loss of more than 95% of the nation's cereals, 100% of fodder, more than 95% of the tobacco crop, and heavy losses of olives, almonds and citrus fruits, the Times reported. Drought-related losses were estimated by the government at $90 million.

Producers Curb Food Exports

Soybean & feed-grain export curbed. The U.S. imposed export controls on soybeans, cottonseed and their oil and meal byproducts June 27, 1973 in an effort to avert a livestock feed grain shortage. An embargo on all shipments was in effect until July 2, when rules for the export program were announced. (Soybean and cottonseed oil controls were lifted at that time. But the U.S. July 5 imposed export controls on 41 more farm commodities in the categories of lifestock feeds, edible oils and animal fats.)

The action, announced jointly by Commerce Secretary Frederick B. Dent and Agriculture Secretary Earl L. Butz, was to supplement a 60-day price freeze that the Administration announced June 13. Dairy farmers and poultry and cattle producers had been warning the Cost of Living Council (CLC) and the public that the nation faced an imminent food supply crisis because costs for feed grains, already skyrocketing, were not limited by price restrictions; food processors, however, were subject to price ceilings.

The limit on food grain shipments abroad would remain in effect until new crops were harvested in September. The brief embargo was replaced by a system of export licenses allowing exporters to ship 50% of soybean orders on hand by June 15 and 40% of their orders for soybean meal.

Cottonseed and cottonseed oil exports were also subject to licensing restrictions, but all orders on hand before June 13 were permitted to be shipped.

The export level was selected to provide the U.S. grain processing industry with sufficient stocks to keep production at full capacity, according to Carroll G. Brunthaver, assistant secretary of agriculture.

U.S. export controls were expected to have international repercussions. Japan relied heavily on U.S. soybean, importing 98% of its supplies from the U.S. European livestock producers were also dependent on U.S. supplies of feed grains.

MAJOR IRRIGATING COUNTRIES (based on amount of irrigated area)[1]

Country	Year[2]	Cultivated area[3]	Irrigated area	Percentage irrigated Percent
		---- 1,000 hectares ----		
China (PRC)	1967 (1960)	110,300	75,980	68.9
India	1968	164,610	27,520	16.7
United States	1969	192,318	15,832	8.2
Pakistan	1969	19,235	12,505	65.0
USSR	1970	232,809	11,100	4.8
Indonesia	1969	18,000	6,800	37.8
Iran	1971	16,727	5,251	31.4
Mexico	1960 (1964)	23,817	4,200	17.6
Iraq	1970 (1963)	10,163	3,675	36.2
Egypt	1971	2,852	2,852	100.0
Japan	1970	5,510	2,836	51.5
Italy	1971 (1960)	12,409	2,444	19.7
Spain	1970	20,626	2,435	11.8
Thailand	1965 (1969)	11,415	1,830	16.0
Argentina	1968 (1959)	26,028	1,555	6.0
Turkey	1970 (1967)	27,378	1,549	5.7
Australia	1969	44,610	1,476	3.3
Chile	1965 (1964)	4,632	1,091	23.6
Peru	1971	2,979	1,116	37.5
Bulgaria	1971	4,516	1,021	22.6
Total[4]		1,457,000	203,600	14.0

[1] Includes individual countries having irrigated areas exceeding 1 million hectares. [2] Year refers to year for which data on cultivated area apply; year in parentheses refers to year for irrigation data when different from year for cultivated area. [3] Cultivated area is arable land plus land under permanent crops. [4] Total and numerical values should be regarded as approximate because of incomparability of data between countries and different years of data collection.

Source: FAO, *Production Yearbook*, 1971, and earlier years.

(Soybeans were the U.S.' second largest cash crop and second largest export crop. The cash value of the U.S.' 1973 crops were $13.4 billion for corn, $8.8 billion for soybeans and $6.5 billion for wheat.)

Assistant Agriculture Secretary Carroll G. Brunthaver told the American Soybean Association Aug. 21 that controls on grain exports would not be extended because the restrictions could damage the U.S. dollar value and balance of payments position.

In an effort to increase production, Agriculture Secretary Earl L. Butz lifted all planting restrictions on wheat Aug. 16.

Japanese criticism—Japanese Foreign Minister Masayoshi Ohira, in a keynote address July 16 to the annual conference of the Joint Japan-United States Committee on Trade and Economic Affairs, urged the U.S. "to exercise an increasing degree of discipline in managing its own economy" and to continue to provide a "stable supply" of certain key commodities to Japan.

Japan's concern at recent U.S. restrictions on the export of soybeans was strongly expressed at the talks, held in Tokyo.

A joint communique issued July 17 at the end of two days of talks pledged the U.S. to its "best efforts" to continue to supply soybeans, wheat, feed grains, timber and scrap iron and steel to Japan.

(Brazil signed an agreement to sell Japan 2.5 million tons of soybeans in 1974 for a total of $1 billion, it was reported Aug. 18. The sale would push soybeans ahead of coffee as Brazil's principal export-cash earner. Farmers reportedly were substituting soybeans for the traditional coffee, wheat, corn and other crops to take advantage of the soybean prices on the international market.)

Canada acts—Canada's Industry, Trade and Commerce Minister Alastair W. Gillespie announced June 29 that export of oilseeds and protein for animal feed would be put under new controls, to meet a tight supply situation.

Under the curbs, licenses would be needed for export of soybeans, rapeseed, flaxseed, linseed and derivatives, and fishmeal. Export levels would depend in part on U.S. allocations for Canada under recent U.S. export curbs.

The government estimated that there was still a three- or four-week supply of protein feed for livestock and poultry, but officials said higher feed prices could cause farmers to reduce the protein content of animal diets, reducing supplies and driving up prices of pork, eggs and poultry.

EEC curb—In an attempt to avert depletion of European Economic Community stocks, the EEC Commission introduced export taxes on soft wheat, maize and barley, effective Aug. 14-15. The taxes would be adjusted regularly to reflect changes in world market prices. The tax on soft wheat exports would replace an export ban imposed Aug. 7. But an export ban on hard wheat, used principally for Italian pasta, would remain.

The Commission Aug. 29 banned exports of hard wheat flour, groats and meal, effective immediately. The measure was aimed at preventing EEC exporters from transforming wheat into flour and other products and then exporting them. World market prices for wheat were slightly more than double the EEC's price, currently 132 units of account (one unit of account equaled $US1 prior to the 1971 devaluation).

Exports of Italian pasta products to non-EEC nations were banned by the Commission Sept. 8, it was disclosed Sept. 13. The ban was introduced at the request of Italy.

(A record 1973 European Economic Community grain harvest of 106.4 million tons, 4% higher than in 1972, was reported Nov. 13. New highs were set for barley [34.6 million tons], maize [16.3 million] and rice [840,000 tons], in addition to a record 67.7 million tons for sugar beet. The 1973 wheat crop totaled 41.2 million tons, down slightly from the 41.5 million tons harvested in 1972.)

U.S. rejects retaliation re Arab oil—The U.S. had no plans for the present to retaliate against Arab nations for their oil embargo against the U.S., Administration officials said Nov. 19.

Secretary of Agriculture Earl L. Butz told a news conference that proposals had been received from "many quarters" for a halt to U.S. grain shipments to Arab nations in reprisal for the oil ban. Butz said that such action "would simply

WORLD PRODUCTION, CONSUMPTION
& EXPORTS OF 6 MAJOR GRAINS[1]

Year	Production	Consumption	Exports	Beginning stocks[2]
		million metric tons		
1969/70	826	839	102	191
1970/71	824	856	109	169
1971/72	911	893	111	131
1972/73	888	925	142	149
1973/74	970	960	151	108
1974/75[3]	916	931	137	108

[1]Wheat, rye, barley, oats, corn, and sorghum. [2]Selected countries; Total adjusted for estimated annual changes in the USSR. [3]Preliminary.

Source: Foreign Agricultural Service and Economic Research Service, *Grain Data Base,* Nov. 1974.

WORLD NET GRAIN EXPORTS & IMPORTS

Country	1969/70-1971/72 average	1971/72	1972/73	1973/74
		million metric tons		
Developed countries	31.9	41.9	62.4	58.4
United States	39.8	42.8	73.1	72.5
Canada	14.8	18.3	18.8	13.1
Australia & New Zealand	10.6	10.8	5.8	9.9
South Africa	2.5	3.7	.4	4.0
EC-9	-16.6	-14.0	-13.4	-13.0
Other West Europe	-4.8	-4.3	-5.3	-8.9
Japan	-14.4	-15.4	-17.0	-19.2
Central plan countries	-6.8	-13.0	-32.2	-15.9
East Europe	-7.6	-9.2	-8.0	-4.8
USSR	3.9	-1.3	-19.6	-4.4
PRC	-3.1	-2.5	-4.6	-6.7
Developing countries	-19.1	-26.9	-23.2	-30.3
North Africa & Middle East	-9.2	-11.9	-8.1	-14.9
South Asia	-5.7	-5.4	-4.5	-7.0
Southeast Asia	3.2	3.3	1.2	2.5
East Asia	-8.4	-9.2	-10.4	-10.2
Latin America	3.2	-2.0	--	.7
Central Africa	-1.9	-2.0	-2.0	-2.1
East Africa	-.3	.3	.6	.7
Other	-.2	-.2	-.3	-.3
World total exports	107.6	111.2	141.8	151.0

Source: Foreign Agricultural Service and Economic Research Service, *Grain Data Base,* Nov. 1974.

irritate the situation, make negotiations more difficult and would not put any pressure on the Arab countries."

Butz said American grain exports to the Arab states were "not high enough to be significant, and in view of the fact that the Russian nation has a much easier grain situation than a year ago they could very easily make up the deficit of anything we cut off."

Wheat export supplies down. In its monthly wheat review released Aug. 14, Statistics Canada said that wheat available for export by the four major wheat export producers dropped 43% to 964.3 million bushels from the 1.7 billion bushels available in 1971–72.

The report said that Canada, Australia and the U.S. had shorter supplies than in 1972. Only Argentina had supplies left for export 11 months into the 1972–73 accounting year for crops.

The decline in export wheat supplies reflected the steadily rising international demand for wheat, the report said.

Fertilizer prices decontrolled. The U.S. Cost of Living Council (CLC) Oct. 25, 1973 lifted price controls on the fertilizer industry. CLC Director John T. Dunlop conceded there would be substantial increases in the cost of fertilizers, but he said they would be offset by higher crop production needed to stabilize food costs in 1974.

Other steps were being taken to increase fertilizer supplies according to Dunlop. Nearly 40 fertilizer companies had promised to divert exports to the domestic market, a move that was expected to raise supplies by 10%.

Wheat quota suspended. President Nixon Jan. 25, 1974 lifted the U.S. import quota on wheat for five months to provide a "stabilizing effect" on domestic wheat prices, which were at record levels.

A White House spokesman denied that the action signaled an impending grain shortage, although he conceded that some "regional dislocations" were possible in the spring because of dwindling wheat supplies.

The American Bakers Association had warned that the country faced large increases in the price of bread and a possible grain shortage before the 1974 wheat harvest was marketed in July because of excessive exports throughout 1972 and 1973. Agriculture Department officials had scoffed at the warning, insisting that supplies were adequate but admitting that negotiations were under way with Canada to increase wheat sales to the U.S. President Nixon's action suspending import restrictions came after the Tariff Commission urged a relaxation in the trade curbs.

(New Agriculture Department figures released Jan. 30 showed that 714 million bushels of wheat were exported during the last six months of 1973. Their record value was $2.62 billion, more than triple the value of exports during the same period of 1972. China was the largest single purchaser within the six-month period, buying 95 million bushels worth $272.4 million.)

In its report Jan. 24, the commission stated that the 1973 wheat crop, which totaled 1.7 billion bushels, and supplemental carry over supplies would be nearly exhausted by June because of the combination of domestic consumption and a record export total of 1.2 billion bushels. According to the Agriculture Department, less than 200 million bushels of wheat—equivalent to a seven-week domestic and export supply—would remain from the 1973 crop when the 1974 harvest was ready for market. It would be the lowest carry over level since 1946, officials said. (As of Jan. 1, only 934 million bushels were on hand—the smallest amount in storage on that date since 1952.)

The U.S. had set wheat import levels at 800,000 bushels annually but the quota had not been met since 1965 when the U.S. support price was higher than the world price. Since July 1, 1973, less than 100,000 bushels had been imported.

(A White House spokesman said June 26 that President Nixon had lifted wheat and wheat product import quotas indefinitely. Since the quota had been suspended Jan. 25, only small amounts of Canadian wheat were imported. They had little effect on domestic prices. The quota would have been automatically reimposed June 30 if Nixon had not acted.)

FOOD PRICES IN THE OECD CONSUMER PRICE INDEX

Country	Weight of food in CPI	1972 to 1973		March 1973 to March 1974	
		Changes in food prices	Weighted contribution to rise of total CPI	Changes in food prices	Weighted contribution to rise of total CPI
		percent			
Canada	30.8	12.5	51.3	15.3	45.3
United States	22.2	14.5	51.6	18.3	39.8
Japan	43.1	12.4	45.3	25.8	46.3
Australia	36.6	15.3	62.1	19.8	56.2
France	40.2	9.7	53.4	12.5	41.2
Germany	33.3	7.6	36.2	5.1	23.6
Italy	43.3	12.0	48.1	14.4	39.0
United Kingdom	41.6	11.5	52.2	14.4	44.4
Belgium	30.0	8.0	34.3	7.8	24.9
Denmark	36.9	10.8	43.0	13.0	34.8
Ireland	48.1	16.5	69.3	11.1	39.5
Netherlands	35.1	7.3	32.5	7.1	27.1
Austria	39.2	7.5	38.2	7.2	31.4
Finland	39.8	11.2	39.5	9.4	21.1
Norway	35.9	7.2	33.3	7.4	29.1
Portugal	53.8	9.0	37.2	25.2	47.2
Spain	55.2	12.6	61.4	15.2	53.4
Sweden	33.3	6.8	34.3	7.2	22.2
Switzerland	36.0	6.1	25.3	6.4	24.0

Source: OECD, *Economic Survey*, 1974.

Australian wheat output. The Australian Bureau of Statistics reported July 5, 1974 that Australia's wheat output in the financial year ended June 30 was the third highest on record, with output rising about 86% to almost 12 million tons. A Wheat Board spokesman said a 21% increase in the area sown to wheat in 1973 was in response to rising world demand.

But Wheat Board Chairman John P. Cass, in an interview published in the New York Times Aug. 8, expressed doubt that Australia would raise wheat production to meet the needs of Asian countries.

Although Australia had the potential for a sharp increase in wheat production, Cass noted that prevailing factors discouraged any major expansion of farming areas allocated for the growing of wheat.

Cass disclosed that the Wheat Board had received an increasing number of requests for supplies, but that it could not meet all demands and would have insufficient wheat in 1975 "to meet all of the sales opportunities that could be presented to us."

Price spiral. The Agriculture Department reported Jan. 24, 1974 that the U.S. food market basket index rose 1% in December. By the end of 1973, the annual retail food costs for a theoretical household of 3.2 persons were $1,650, slightly below the year's record level of $1,653 set in August 1973.

The index rose 23.3% or $312 over a 12-month period, with the average 1973 market basket costing $1,537. The increase over the average 1972 figure was 17.2%, the highest one-year rise in 25 years.

In its index of farm prices published Jan. 31, the Agriculture Department announced that prices received by farmers climbed 9% from mid-December to mid-January, reaching a figure exactly double the level of 1967 prices.

U.S. intervenes, bolsters beef prices— Agriculture Secretary Earl L. Butz announced March 27, 1974 that the U.S. Commodity Credit Corp. would move to bolster sagging beef prices by buying $45 million worth of hamburger made from prime, grain-fed cattle for use in the 1974-75 school lunch program.

That figure did not represent a significant increase over similar purchases made for the 1973-74 year, which totaled $43.4 million, but officials hoped their action would have an impact on market conditions because the purchases were made far ahead of schedule and involved a much better grade of meat than was usually bought.

Cattle prices had slumped to $40-$42 per hundredweight from the year's record high of $50.50 per hundredweight, set in January. Chaotic supply conditions were resulting from the immediate oversupply of animals ready for slaughter: in protest against the low prices, cattle feeders were withholding fattened livestock from market and choosing to sell their grain rather than use it to feed young animals.

The various price indexes indicated that a curious pattern was developing with food prices—significant declines were apparent at the farm level but these large price drops were not being passed along to consumers. In a roundup of regional supermarket prices June 17, the Wall Street Journal reported that wholesale choice beef prices were down 28% from their February high, but consumers were paying only 10% less. In other Journal comparisons, wholesale pork prices were down 27% but retail prices fell only 19%; frying chickens were down nearly 58% from Jan. 1 wholesale levels but supermarket customers were paying only 46% less; similar price relationships were noted for other commodities.

Most of the pricing controversy centered on livestock, which had plummeted in price, and meat, which had shown considerably smaller declines at the retail price level.

A meeting for cattlemen, meat packers and supermarket officials was held at the White House June 17 to discuss the price squeeze threatening cattle feeders, who faced soaring grain prices and falling livestock prices. (Prices in Midwest markets fell $30-$35 in one week for an average 1,100 pound prime steer, the Washington Post reported June 13.)

Following the meeting, food chain executives promised to spur consumer demand by reducing meat prices and promoting sales for the glutted meat market.

In subsequent developments, it was announced June 18 that the government would increase its purchases of beef and pork for the school lunch program. Of-

AVERAGE ANNUAL PRICES RECEIVED BY U.S. FARMERS FOR MAJOR COMMODITIES

Year	Wheat $/bu.	Corn $/bu.	Hay $/ton	Rice $/100 lb.	Soybeans $/bu.	Peanuts $/100 lb.	Beef $/100 lb.	Poultry $/lb.	Sugarbeets $/ton
1945	1.49	1.23	19.45	3.98	2.08	8.27	12.10	.30	12.82
1946	1.90	1.53	20.64	5.00	2.57	9.10	14.50	.33	13.65
1947	2.29	2.16	22.13	5.97	3.33	10.10	18.40	.32	14.44
1948	1.98	1.28	23.55	4.88	2.27	10.50	22.20	.36	12.94
1949	1.88	1.24	21.38	4.10	2.16	10.40	19.80	.28	13.41
1950	2.00	1.52	21.56	5.09	2.47	10.90	23.30	.27	13.70
1951	2.11	1.66	23.05	4.82	2.73	10.40	38.70	.29	14.13
1952	2.09	1.52	24.52	5.87	2.72	10.90	24.30	.29	14.48
1953	2.04	1.48	22.07	5.19	2.72	11.10	16.30	.27	13.91
1954	2.12	1.43	22.18	4.57	2.46	12.20	16.00	.23	13.22
1955	1.98	1.35	20.98	4.69	2.22	11.70	15.60	.25	13.51
1956	1.97	1.29	21.30	4.86	2.18	11.20	14.90	.20	14.32
1957	1.93	1.11	18.62	5.11	2.07	10.40	17.20	.19	13.58
1958	1.75	1.12	18.16	4.68	2.00	10.60	21.90	.19	14.09
1959	1.76	1.05	20.62	4.59	1.96	9.56	22.60	.16	13.54
1960	1.74	1.00	20.41	4.55	2.13	10.00	20.40	.17	13.97
1961	1.83	1.10	20.42	5.14	2.28	10.90	20.20	.14	13.54
1962	2.04	1.12	21.18	5.04	2.34	11.00	20.20	.15	15.24
1963	1.85	1.11	21.44	5.01	2.51	11.20	21.30	.15	14.34
1964	1.37	1.17	23.48	4.90	2.62	11.20	19.90	.14	14.04
1965	1.35	1.16	23.42	4.93	2.54	11.40	18.00	.15	14.21
1966	1.63	1.24	24.11	4.95	2.75	11.30	19.90	.15	15.10
1967	1.39	1.03	23.04	4.97	2.49	11.40	22.20	.13	15.88
1968	1.24	1.08	22.75	5.00	2.43	11.90	22.30	.14	15.91
1969	1.25	1.16	23.57	4.95	2.35	12.30	23.40	.15	14.96
1970	1.33	1.33	24.20	5.17	2.85	12.80	26.20	.14	17.06
1971	1.34	1.08	26.28	5.34	3.03	13.60	27.10	.14	17.47
1972	1.76	1.57	31.93	6.73	4.37	14.50	29.00	.14	18.12
1973	4.00	2.38	42.84	13.80	5.57	16.20	33.50	.24	25.12

ficials said that up to $100 million would be set aside for immediate purchases while meat prices were cheap, the market glutted and cattlemen were threatening further dislocations in the market by withholding livestock from slaughter until price conditions improved.

Wisconsin members of the National Farmers Organization (NFO) Oct. 15 slaughtered more than 650 calves and buried them in trenches to protest high feed costs and low prices received for farm products.

Although President Ford criticized the action as "shocking and wasteful" in remarks made Oct. 16 during a campaign trip to South Dakota, and despite a loud outcry from the public, the killings continued.

By Oct. 28, the NFO had arranged the slaughter of about 1,000 animals. Because of adverse public reaction to their protest, the farmers decided to send the meat to hurricane victims in Honduras and unspecified U.S. charities after the Dubuque Packing Co. agreed to absorb the cost of dressing the livestock for shipment.

Ford discussed the situation Oct. 31 during a campaign visit to Sioux City, Ia.

Ford said he had made three policy decisions that day: he would invoke the meat import law if the level of imports reached or threatened to reach that point, and then would "either impose quotas or negotiate voluntary export restraint agreements with foreign suppliers;" he would not change the dairy import quotas "without a thorough review of market conditions and full opportunity for our dairy producers to be heard;" and he said "the Administration is not going to permit foreign dairy producers to compete against American dairymen in the U.S. market with subsidized products." "If the Europeans reinstate their export subsidies of dairy products directed at this market," he said, "I will impose countervailing duties on these products."

As a further step, Ford said, he had asked that an effort be made to increase government purchase of beef for the national school lunch program.

'74 U.S. crop harmed. Early frost in the Midwest causing widespread damage to the U.S. corn crop forced the Agricul-

ture Department (USDA) Oct. 10 to revise its estimates of the 1974 harvest. The corn crop was expected to total 4.72 billion bushels, spokesmen said, off 16% from the previous year's yield. Soybean production was also affected by adverse weather conditions. Forecasts showed a drop of 19% (compared with the 1973 harvest) to 1.26 billion bushels.

The wheat crop was expected to total a record 1.78 billion bushels (4% above the 1973 level), but the crop was far smaller than originally anticipated.

In another USDA report Oct. 11, it was announced that the nation's grain reserves would be at their lowest level in 25 years by the time new crops were harvested in mid-1975. Reserves of wheat on July 1, 1975 were expected to total 218 million bushels, compared with 249 million available on July 1, 1974 because of greater domestic and export demands. The 1974 reserve figure was 43% below the previous year's and the lowest level in 26 years.

The department announced Oct. 24 that the nation's corn reserves totaled 481 million bushels on Oct. 1, its lowest level since 1948. Corn stocks were 32% lower than in 1973. The reduction was attributed to heavy domestic and international demand. The figures did not include the 1974 harvest.

At a meeting on inflation Sept. 12, Agriculture Secretary Earl L. Butz had minimized the effect of previously reported Midwest drought and crop failures on prices paid by U.S. consumers, noting, "We've just produced the largest wheat crop we've ever had. The corn crop has been hurt somewhat by the drought, but it's going to be the fourth largest we've ever produced, the largest since 1970."

However, in remarks Sept. 4 before a U.S. group studying world food problems, Butz had warned that disappointing crops had limited the nation's ability to aid food-starved nations in Asia and Africa. "Our ability to deliver is limited this year," Butz said, although he added, "We're not going to permit starvation in any part of the world so far as it is in our power to prevent it."

Butz described speculation about a world food shortage as "apocalyptic nonsense." More time should be spent talking about how to increase food production and less time in discussion about how to manage food stockpiles, he said.

Butz had said Aug. 26 that there is "absolutely no basis for panic" among U.S. consumers about the adequacy of food supplies. Total U.S. crop production was expected to decline about 6% in 1974 from the previous year's level, causing the volume of U.S. agricultural exports to drop as well, Butz said. Because of higher prices, however, the dollar value of the reduced exports was expected to be the same as in 1973—about $21 billion. The Agriculture Department announced Nov. 28 that the federal price support program for soybeans was being eliminated in 1975, although supports would be continued for wheat and feed grain crops. Officials said the free market price for soybeans was 2-3 times the government-supported price.

U.S. urged to avoid waste. In his anti-inflation program, presented Oct. 8, 1974, President Gerald R. Ford urged Americans to waste less food.

"To help increase food and lower prices, grow more, waste less," Ford said. "If you can't spare a penny from your food budget, surely you can cut the food you waste by 5%."

The President promised new efforts to reduce prices by increasing supplies. Congress would be asked to remove all remaining acreage limits on rice, peanuts and cotton. Farmers were promised all the fuel allocations required to produce at full capacity. Ford said he would ask for authority to allocate the needed fertilizer supplies.

He also directed the Council on Wage and Price Stability to "find and expose all restrictive practices, public or private, which raise food prices." The Administration also would "monitor" food production, margins, pricing and exports.

U.S. halts grain to U.S.S.R., curbs exports. Officials of two major U.S. grain exporting firms agreed Oct. 5, 1974 to cancel Soviet orders for corn and wheat valued at $500 million. They acted after meeting with President Gerald Ford, Treasury Secretary William E. Simon and Agriculture Secretary Earl L. Butz.

In a statement issued later that day, the White House said that at the meeting with representatives of Continental Grain Co. and Cook Industries Inc., Ford had "expressed his strong concern about the potential domestic impact that such sales could have at a time when the U.S. is experiencing a disappointing harvest of feed grains."

Although Butz told reporters that the Soviet shipments had been halted voluntarily by the exporting firms, the White House had indicated its displeasure with the sales Oct. 4 when Simon announced that the shipments were "being held in abeyance" until grain officials could meet with the President the next day. The announcement was made only hours after the Agriculture Department released reports of contracts signed by Continental and Cook to supply the Soviet Union with 2.4 million tons of corn and 1 million tons of wheat.

Although spokesmen for the Agriculture Department denied that Simon's action constituted an "embargo" on grain exports, Simon said he was also issuing a directive from Ford that "all major exporting companies be informed that for the time being he expects no large contracts for grain will be signed in the future without specific prior approval by the White House."

President Ford attempted to defuse the political impact of the new Soviet grain order when a "modified form of control over grain exports" was outlined for the Administration Oct. 7 by Secretary Butz.

Although he described the plan as "voluntary," Butz added, "It's no use kidding ourselves; this is a modified form of controls."

Butz said the voluntary system would apply to exports of wheat, corn, sorghum, soybeans and soybean flour. Exporters would be required to obtain advance approval from the Agriculture Department for sales involving more than 50,000 tons of a particular commodity in a single day "for shipment to any one country of destination" or when cumulative sales of any commodity to a single destination exceeded 100,000 tons in a week. Advance approval was also necessary when changes in export destinations under existing contracts (including the category of "unknown" destinations) affected more than

30,000 tons of one commodity in a single day or over 100,000 tons during a week.

The aim of the voluntary plan, Butz said, was the "freest possible flow of supplies." He attempted to reassure Japan and other nations, which had traditionally relied on U.S. grain exports to supplement their food supplies, that U.S. shipments were not being curtailed by the new program, although he admitted that if the voluntary system failed, mandatory export curbs would have to be imposed.

(It was reported Oct. 14 that barley and oats had been added to the Agriculture Department's list of grain commodities requiring Administration approval before, being sold abroad.)

Continental said Oct. 7 that it had informed the Agriculture Department Sept. 30 that the Soviet Union was making purchase inquiries about corn. After consultation with government officials, Continental said the sale was limited to about 1 million tons (38 million bushels). The Agriculture Department was informed that the deal had been completed Oct. 3. Cook also announced Oct. 7 that it had reported a corn sale totaling 1.4 million tons and a 1 million ton sale of wheat to the department Oct. 4. Notification of the contracts prompted Ford to issue his order Oct. 5 delaying the sales.

At his news conference Oct. 7, Butz accepted some of the blame for the "very embarrassing" cancellation of the Soviet efforts to conclude the grain deal. Butz conceded that he had not been "firm enough" in warning Soviet officials and U.S. exporters that the Administration would not permit repetition of the massive 1972 grain purchases in light of poor 1974 harvests and reduced reserves. "Errors were made on a number of fronts," Butz said.

Butz's handling of the Soviet contracts was criticized by Secretary of State Henry Kissinger at a news conference Oct. 7. He said there was a "strong possibility that we may have misled the Soviet Union as to what we thought we could deliver over a period of time."

White House Press Secretary Ron Nessen said Oct. 7 that the Administration regarded the Soviet Union as a "valuable customer" and that objections to the sale were largely related to the timing of the shipments.

The New York Times reported Oct. 5 that sources on the Kansas City Board of Trade, a major commodity market, were "puzzled" by the Administration's unexpected decision to halt sales to the Soviet Union. Since July 1, more than 1 million tons of wheat (49 million bushels) had been shipped to China. "Not a word came from Washington about the sale to China, so we're as puzzled as everybody else about why the Russian sale was suddenly halted," the sources said.

The Soviet attempt to buy so much grain was reported to have surprised U.S. officials, who had not expected Moscow to seek such large and sudden purchases, the New York Times reported Oct. 9.

Soviet Communist Party General Secretary Leonid Brezhnev had said Sept. 8 that the U.S.S.R.'s 205.6 million ton wheat target would be reached, and the U.S. Agriculture Department had issued its own predictions Sept. 11 that the Soviet harvest would total 210 million tons. U.S. officials had also speculated Sept. 27 that world grain prices were unattractively high for Moscow. The bid led U.S. specialists to suggest that the Soviet grain harvest had failed to attain the projected target.

Hearings probe grain sale halt—The Senate Permanent Investigations Subcommittee held hearings Oct. 8 to study the circumstances surrounding Soviet efforts to purchase 3.4 million tons of U.S. grain and Administration actions to block the sale.

Officials of the two U.S. grain exporting companies involved in the transactions, Cook Industries Inc. and Continental Grain Co., testified that Agriculture Secretary Earl Butz had been informed of the Soviet intentions Sept. 25 but that he took no actions opposing the sales.

Bernard Steinweg of Continental testified that Butz had specifically approved the sale of 1 million tons of corn Oct. 1, three days before final negotiations were abruptly halted by the Administration. Butz confirmed the account in later testimony, saying he assumed the Soviets would buy no more grain. Butz said he told Continental Oct. 2 not to sell 2 million tons of wheat to the Soviets, and that it was not apparent to him until Oct. 4 that the Soviets intended to purchase up to 6 million tons of grain.

Butz said Soviet Ambassador Anatoly F. Dobrynin had told him Sept. 26 that Soviet grain purchases would be "modest." Dobrynin would not provide actual figures, Butz added. Subcommittee chairman Henry Jackson (D, Wash.) responded, "If they don't tell us, I don't think they should be allowed into the marketplace."

Grain company officials recounted their talk at the White House Oct. 5 with President Ford and Administration officials. According to Edward W. Cook, Ford "said that there was a political problem with Congress and a political problem with the people, who would be irate at sales to Russia of this magnitude." Steinweg concurred with that account, and Butz admitted that political considerations surrounding the Soviet sale were discussed.

Cook and Steinweg differed on another point, however. Cook testified that he had been told by William D. Eberle, Ford's trade negotiator, that no future sales would be permitted to China, the Soviet Union or members of the Organization of Petroleum Exporting Countries. Because of this warning, Cook said he canceled a 400,000 ton wheat sale to Iran. Steinweg testified that he was not told of any ban, and that Continental had just sold Iran 160,000 tons of wheat.

U.S. allows limited Soviet grain purchases. Treasury Secretary William E. Simon announced Oct. 19 that the Soviet Union would be allowed to purchase up to 1.2 million metric tons of U.S. wheat and 1 million tons of corn, valued at an estimated $380 million, through June 30, 1975. The Soviets had agreed not to make any "further purchases in the U.S. market this crop year," Simon added.

According to arrangements for the new grain sale, which Simon negotiated, the Soviet Union also agreed that shipments would be made in phased intervals to further minimize the disruptive effects of the purchase on the U.S. market.

Simon's compromise plan also called for both nations to develop a supply and demand data system to facilitate a better matching of their grain capacities and needs. (There had been widespread U.S. criticism of the secrecy surrounding Soviet crop reporting and the conduct of import negotiations.)

Export wheat prices at record. Export wheat prices had reached a record $156 a ton as a result of high world demand, it was reported Nov. 6. In the past two weeks the Australian Wheat Board had announced contracts with the Soviet Union and Egypt totaling two million tons of wheat valued at about $A300 million. The board had sold or committed virtually all of the 8.5 million tons of the current wheat harvest expected to be available for export.

EEC to cut grain consumption. The European Commission Oct. 21, 1974 announced measures aimed at cutting consumption and exports of grain in anticipation of reduced cereal imports from the U.S.

Agriculture Commissioner Pierre Lardinois said the EEC would halt additional wheat exports to the Soviet Union and other developed nations in 1975, although existing contracts would be honored. He added that the community would send its surplus wheat to "our traditional buyers in the developing world, mainly in Africa and India." The community already had committed, as aid or sales, 4 million tons of grain to these areas in 1974.

The Commission, through its authority to issue licenses for trade transactions and set export taxes, had substantial powers to control grain exports. It had raised the export tax on grain the previous week by 25%.

In response to U.S. requests, the EEC had already pledged restraint in importing grains from America. According to EEC sources in an Oct. 22 New York Times report, the nine community members planned to reduce their U.S. soybean imports from 10 million tons in 1973 to seven million tons in 1974, with the difference to be supplied mainly by Brazil. The EEC wanted to import about 7.5 million tons of other feed grains, including corn, from the U.S., according to the report.

In a move designed to help reduce consumption of feed grains, the Commission also announced a reduction in export aid to pig and poultry producers.

Drought in Argentina. A persistent drought in the major grain producing areas threatened Argentina's agricultural production and its ability to help relieve' the world's acute food shortage, the New York Times reported Dec. 15, 1974.

Leading farmers' organizations said the drought had already cut the grain crop in southern Buenos Aires Province and La Pampa Province by one-third and the yield in Entre Rios Province by half. The three provinces produced more than half of Argentina's wheat, corn and sorghum.

The food situation was further complicated by extensive smuggling of grain into neighboring Bolivia, Chile and Paraguay, where merchants offered higher prices than the Argentine National Grain Board, the only authorized buyer of crops in Argentina.

Fishing Limits & Agreements

During 1973 and 1974 there was increasing agreement on the right of nations to protect their fisheries by barring foreign fishermen from waters that stretched an increasingly greater distance from their coasts.

200-mile waters limit endorsed. The Inter-American Juridical Committee (IJC) of the Organization of American States, meeting in Rio de Janeiro Feb. 11, 1973, endorsed decisions by some Latin American countries to extend their territorial waters to 200 miles offshore.

The IJC distinguished, however, between two zones: the first up to 12 miles offshore, and the second from that limit up to 200 miles. In the second zone the maritime state had exclusive rights to exploit, explore, investigate or conserve the natural resources in the sea and on or under the seabed, while other states had free navigation and overflying rights.

The delegates from Brazil, Colombia and Peru—among the strongest defenders of the 200-mile limit—opposed the division of territorial waters into two zones. The representatives of Argentina and Trinidad and Tobago abstained from the formal vote.

A conference of nonaligned nations was held in Algiers Sept. 5–9, with leaders of 76 Asian, African and Latin American member nations and nine observer nations calling for joint action to win economic concessions from the affluent industrial powers.

The conference approved a resolution calling on developing nations to form "producer associations" for each of the major raw material products they sell to the industrialized world, "in order to halt the degradation of their terms of trade, to eliminate unhealthy competition, to prevent harmful activities by multinational companies and to reinforce their negotiating power."

The resolution said each country, exercising control of its own resources, had the right to set the amount of compensation for seized foreign property, with reference only to its own laws and without international adjudication. The members said they would support all efforts by developing countries to regain control of their resources and defeat "the structures of imperialist and neocolonialist exploitation," including the efforts of underdeveloped countries to control sea resources up to 200 miles from their coastlines. The members agreed to work toward a common position for the upcoming conference on the international seabed.

Argentina President Alejandro Lanusse's signature of a bill banning foreign trawlers from fishing within 200 miles of the Argentine coast had been reported Feb. 16. This followed Argentina's decision Jan. 19 not to ratify a 1967 agreement with Brazil which allowed both countries' vessels to fish in each other's territorial waters up to six miles from the coast without paying duty. Argentina had arrested four Brazilian fishing boats Jan. 13 and another one Jan. 15 for allegedly violating Argentine territorial waters.

Pakistani President Zulfikar Ali Bhutto had issued a proclamation extending Pakistan's sea zone from the current 12 nautical miles to 50 miles, it was reported March 24. The action followed recent complaints by Rawalpindi to the Soviet Union that its fishing trawlers off Pakistan were depriving Pakistani fishermen of their livelihood.

Mexican President Luis Echeverria reiterated his announced intention to extend Mexico's 12-mile offshore territorial limits to 200 miles, it was reported June 29. Seafood industry officials in the U.S. said the move would cost the in-

U.S. COMMERCIAL FISH CATCH

Landings by states (1971 & 1972)[1]

State	1971 Thousand pounds	1971 Thousand dollars	1972 Thousand pounds	1972 Thousand dollars	Record landings Year	Record landings Thousand pounds
Alabama	[1] 36,727	[2] 14,141	[2] 39,564	[2] 18,326	1972	39,564
Alaska	449,089	84,504	390,137	80,733	1936	932,341
Arkansas	9,428	1,950	[3]	[3]	-----	[4]
California	585,484	87,172	639,764	91,898	1936	1,760,183
Connecticut	7,261	1,775	4,911	1,498	1930	88,012
Delaware	9,031	1,490	10,648	1,869	1953	367,500
Florida	173,904	45,154	176,271	55,711	1938	241,443
Georgia	18,409	7,478	17,544	6,802	1927	47,067
Hawaii	17,177	5,159	14,686	5,097	1954	20,610
Idaho	1,329	317	1,400	336	-----	[4]
Illinois	[2] 5,172	[2] 715	[2] 5,701	[2] 686	-----	[4]
Indiana	[2] 1,034	[2] 155	[2] 858	[2] 181	-----	[4]
Iowa	3,369	348	3,518	352	-----	[4]
Kansas	40	12	36	10	-----	[4]
Kentucky	[3]	[3]	[3]	[3]	-----	[4]
Louisiana	[2] 1,396,214	[2] 72,630	[2] 1,070,597	[2] 71,916	1971	1,396,214
Maine	142,619	31,068	149,271	34,819	1950	356,266
Maryland	72,680	18,441	67,636	18,261	1890	141,607
Massachusetts	273,064	45,970	248,035	48,052	1948	649,696
Michigan	19,137	2,671	14,213	2,985	1930	35,580
Minnesota	[2] 12,011	[2] 1,367	[2] 11,583	[2] 981	-----	[4]
Mississippi	[2] 397,605	[2] 13,380	[2] 260,216	[2] 11,897	1971	397,605
Missouri	773	148	790	150	-----	[4]
Montana	705	110	718	108	-----	[4]
Nebraska	174	12	179	13	-----	[4]
New Hampshire	1,296	841	1,442	1,133	-----	[4]
New Jersey	114,416	12,025	190,517	14,423	1956	340,000
New York	36,617	18,676	37,377	22,123	1880	[2] 335,000
North Carolina	143,475	11,227	175,410	11,827	1959	342,612
North Dakota	364	39	395	40	-----	[4]
Ohio	[2] 9,045	[2] 1,225	[2] 7,939	[2] 1,026	1936	31,083
Oklahoma	[3]	[3]	[3]	[3]	-----	[4]
Oregon	75,770	16,226	92,923	24,024	1970	98,089
Pennsylvania	451	46	357	111	-----	[4]
Rhode Island	84,553	12,398	16,376	12,443	1889	128,056
South Carolina	24,642	8,373	22,365	7,961	1965	26,611
South Dakota	3,013	235	3,159	253	-----	[4]
Tennessee	[3]	[3]	[3]	[3]	-----	[4]
Texas	[2] 168,682	[2] 70,037	[2] 117,000	[2] 85,011	1960	237,684
Virginia	488,981	21,937	663,845	25,992	1972	663,845
Washington	130,449	30,238	120,458	38,496	1941	197,253
Wisconsin	[2] 42,875	[2] 2,352	[2] 43,661	[2] 2,521	-----	[4]
Wyoming	-----	-----	144	[5]	-----	[4]
	[6] 12,335	[6] 1,158	[6] 18,756	[6] 3,535		
Total	4,969,400	643,200	4,710,400	703,600		

[1] Statistics on landings are shown in round (live) weight of all items except univalve and bivalve mollusks such as clams, oysters, and scallops, which are shown in weight of meats, excluding the shell.
[2] Catch in interior waters estimated.
[3] Data not available.
[4] Not determined.
[5] Less than $500.
[6] Data by State not available.

Note: Does not include landings by U.S. flag vessels at Puerto Rico or other ports outside continental United States and Hawaii. Does not include production of artificially cultivated fish and shellfish. Data are preliminary.

dustry $35 million–$40 million a year, since it would place most of the rich shrimp beds off Mexico's southern coast off limits to foreign boats.

Malagasy extended territorial waters limits from 12 to 50 miles offshore, it was reported Oct. 25.

During a visit by Panama's military ruler, Brig. Gen. Omar Torrijos, to Peru, Torrijos Jan. 24, 1974 endorsed Peru's declared 200-mile offshore territorial limits. (As a by-product of Torrijos' visit, Peru and Panama agreed to establish a joint fishing company, it was reported Feb. 1.)

In the U.S. Congress, legislation to extend U.S. fishing limits to 200 nautical miles from the current 12-mile boundary was passed by the Senate Dec. 11, 1974, but the House took no action on it before adjournment. President Ford had opposed the bill in a letter to Congress Sept. 30 as an impediment to international negotiations on the issue.

Norway had announced a three-phase extension of its fisheries limits off northern Norway in 1975 to preserve fish stocks and avert collisons between trawlers and other types of fishing gear.

Under the plan, Norway would establish, effective Jan. 1, 1975, "pocket zones" outside the existing 12-mile fishing limit which would bar all trawlers, both domestic and foreign; Norway would then extend its fishing limits from 12 to 50 nautical miles after consultation with the countries affected; ultimately, the government sought a 200-mile economic zone for coastal states.

Guinea-Bissau Jan. 3, 1975 set the limit of its territorial waters at 150 nautical miles.

U.N. parley on sea law. The 3rd U.N. Conference on the Law of the Sea opened a 10-week work session in Caracas, Venezuela June 20, 1974 with some 5,000 delegates and observers from 148 nations attending. It adjourned Aug. 29 after failing to agree on any of the more than 100 issues discussed.

U.N. Secretary General Kurt Waldheim opened the conference with an appeal to delegates to avoid replacing "old quarrels on land with new quarrels at sea." He called for a "new balance" in negotiations to enable mankind to "exploit the riches of the sea while preserving the interests of all."

Venezuelan President Carlos Andres Perez followed Waldheim with a welcoming speech to the delegations in which he noted that the U.N. and other international organizations traditionally had been "instruments of the strong rather than instruments at the service of humanity." This conference was "a challenge to the sincerity and future goals of the great powers," he asserted.

"We must create a new legal system for mankind, free of selfishness, national hegemony or imperialist aims, by applying the lessons of many centuries of betrayal and humiliations imposed by the powerful nations on the weak ones, in sum, by the developed countries on the developing countries, which are burdened by privileges claimed in the name of a science and technology which, like the oceans, must be the heritage of all mankind," Perez said.

Venezuela, he continued, supported the right of landlocked countries to share the wealth of the sea and, in particular, the claim of Bolivia to an outlet to the Pacific Ocean.

Perez said his country and a majority of nations sought establishment of a 200-mile "patrimonial" limit within which maritime states would control fisheries, mineral deposits and oil off their shores. This was "undoubtedly the ideal solution for what could be—if not solved—an unending source of conflict," he asserted.

A consensus seemed to be developing at the conference to establish a 200-mile patrimonial limit and to extend from three to 12 miles the territorial limits of maritime states. The U.S. delegation chief said June 20 that the U.S would agree to a patrimonial limit—although he did not say of what area—and the Soviet delegation June 29 backed the 200-mile proposal. However, both nations made it clear before the conference that acceptance of any treaty would depend on guarantees of free transit for their vessels through international straits.

The patrimonial limit was opposed by Japan and Peru, among other nations. Japan stood to lose substantial fish catches if the limit was approved, according to a report June 29.

During the 10-week Caracas session, delegates had confined themselves to stating and restating their countries' general positions, and had not even begun hard negotiations on the issues, the Wall Street Journal reported Aug. 27. "Progress has been made not in bringing the sides closer together, but in clearly defining where they are farthest apart," a Sri Lanka delegate told the Journal.

Although delegates from most nations said publicly that they had not expected the Caracas session to produce a new international treaty, many privately expressed disappointment with the session's lack of achievement. The head of the Ecuadorean delegation, Luis Valencia Rodriguez, blamed the session's failure on "the stubbornness of the, superpowers which have insisted on maintaining their privileges and the practice of sacking the riches of the seas next to other states," it was reported Aug. 24.

Delegates from many smaller countries, never having participated in sea law debates before, found the complex issues difficult to understand and negotiate, the Wall Street Journal reported Aug. 27. Some hired experts from the U.S. and Europe to assist them.

The U.N. Conference on the Law of the Sea met again in Geneva March 17–May 9, 1975 and worked out its first draft of a treaty governing the use of the seas.

The draft treaty provided for a 200-mile economic zone in which coastal states would have control over both fisheries and mineral resources, a 12-mile zone over which such states would have full sovereignty and an international authority to deal with the remaining waters.

John R. Stevenson, head of the U.S. delegation to the conference, said May 9 the "sharpest disagreement" had been over uses of the seabed. He implied criticism of the treaty by warning that the U.S. was unprepared to "give ultimate powers of exclusive exploitation to a single new international entity."

The president of the conference, Hamilton S. Amerasinghe of Sri Lanka, issued a "fervent appeal" May 9 to all coastal states not to extend their sovereignty beyond the 12-mile limit before work on the treaty could be completed.

80 countries in wildlife pact. Representatives of 80 countries meeting in Washington March 2, 1973 to prohibit commercial trade in 375 species of wildlife in danger of extinction.

The pact would ban the sale of products made from the species, and would prevent fishermen from bringing endangered sea life into national waters. A second category of 239 species would require trading permits from both importing and exporting countries. Countries could bar export of any other animal it considered endangered.

In October 1973 the International Conference for North Atlantic Fisheries concluded a three-year agreement establishing national quotas for catches in the North Atlantic. The overall quota for 1974 was set at 923,900 metric tons and the 1975 catch at 830,000, compared with 1,200,000 tons taken annually in 1972–73. The Soviet and East German quotas were reduced 30% each from 1973, and Poland's quota was cut 20%, but the U.S. quota was increased.

'Cod war' ends. The Icelandic Parliament, by 54–6 vote Nov. 13, 1973, approved an interim accord with Great Britain to end the territorial fishing dispute between the two nations. Later that day, both governments exchanged notes ratifying the accord, which became effective immediately.

The approval by the Icelandic Parliament followed the reversal Nov. 8 by the government's Communist partner, the People's Union, of its earlier rejection of the accord.

According to the terms of the settlement announced by British Prime Minister Edward Heath in the House of Commons Nov. 12, the 'Cod War' agreement was based on an annual British catch of 130,000 tons within the disputed 50-mile territorial water zone around Iceland, but did not actually introduce a catch limit; the figure was 54,000 tons less than Britain's recent annual catch. The fleet of "fresher" trawlers would be limited to 68 of the largest fishing boats and 71 of the smaller ones, a 15-trawler cut from each of the two groupings. Freezer and factory trawlers were excluded from the disputed 50-mile area, and British boats were barred from one-sixth of this area at any one time.

The International Court of Justice (the World Court) at The Hague Feb. 2 had declared itself competent to rule in the fishing dispute between Iceland and Great Britain and West Germany. In separate cases brought by both the London and Bonn governments, the court voted 14–1 that it could decide on the legality of Iceland's unilateral extension of its fishing limits from 12 to 50 nautical miles.

In announcing the ruling, Court President Sir Muhammad Zafrullah Khan criticized the Icelandic government for refusing to argue its case before the court. Iceland said it would continue its boycott of the court decisions on the ground that the court had no jurisdiction.

Britain's case was argued before the court Jan. 5 by Attorney General Sir Peter Rawlinson, who accused Iceland of embarking on a dangerous course of harassment and of deliberately flouting the court's provisional ruling that the fishing limit extension should not be enforced.

Continuing their harassment tactics of fishing boats within the 50-mile limit, Icelandic patrol vessels cut the trawling wires of five British fishing boats Jan. 7–15 and of two German boats Jan. 6 and Jan. 21. The British government sent an unarmed ocean-going tug to defend British trawlers within the disputed territorial waters Jan. 19. The government said the tug would help trawlers ward off net-cutting "and other aggressive actions." The measure was a concession to British trawler captains, who had demanded navy protection.

As the dispute continued, an Icelandic gunboat fired two shots across the bow of a British tug March 18, the first such incident involving live shots in the current "cod war."

The Icelandic coast guard said it fired after the tug tried to ram the gunboat. The British denied the ramming charges.

Live shots were also reported to have been fired at British ships March 25 and April 3. The most serious incident was said to have occurred April 24 when Icelandic sailors aboard a coast guard vessel fired live rifle shells at trawlers, while a trawler was reported to have rammed and seriously damaged a patrol boat. Previous news reports had alleged attempted rammings, but this was said to be the first time a boat was actually rammed.

Meanwhile, Icelandic gunboats continued to cut the trawling wires of a number of British fishing ships in March-May and of a lesser number of West German trawlers in March-April.

An Icelandic gunboat fired at a British trawler and damaged it May 26, just a week after British navy warships were sent into the zone to protect fishing boats harassed by the Icelandic coast guard.

The British government had sent three naval frigates into the disputed fishing grounds off Iceland's coast for the first time May 19, following the abrupt pullout May 17 of 40 British trawlers from the area because they had not been given the naval protection they demanded against Icelandic harassment. British warships had been previously standing outside the 50-mile zone.

Iceland reacted sharply to the British action. Premier Olafur Johannesson banned all British military planes from landing at the North Atlantic Treaty Organization (NATO) airfield at Keflavik May 20 on the grounds that U.K. reconnaissance planes refueling at Keflavik were allegedly employed in "aggression" against Iceland, mainly to monitor the trawlers. Both Iceland and Britain were NATO members.

The Icelandic government announced May 21 it was recalling its ambassador, Niels Sigurdsson, from London for "consultations."

Several thousand Icelandic demonstrators, mainly youths, smashed all the windows of the British embassy in Reykjavik May 24 to protest the presence of the warships inside the 50-mile zone. The demonstrators had marched on the embassy from a mass meeting organized by the Icelandic Labor Federation. Iceland apologized for the attack the following day and promised to pay for all damages.

The sharpest retaliation against dispatch of the warships came with the shelling of a British trawler May 26. The Icelandic coast guard said its gunboat Aegir had fired blank warning shots at the 884-ton trawler Everton fishing within the claimed 50-mile territorial water limit, but that the Everton ignored orders to stop and steamed away instead. An hour-long chase followed, the coast guard said, before the Aegir opened fire with live ammunition. Two or three shells smashed the Everton's bow, seriously damaging but failing to stop it. The Aegir eventually abandoned the chase.

Premier Johannesson warned May 27 that Iceland would engage in "more similar actions" until the warships were withdrawn.

Britain and Iceland sent angry notes to the president of the United Nations Security Council May 29. Britain accused Iceland of violating international law by following "a consistent policy of forceful action against British vessels" which had taken "increasingly dangerous forms."

In its letter, Iceland accused Britain of invading Icelandic waters by sending the three naval frigates into the disputed zone.

Iceland also turned to the NATO Council May 29, asking it to intervene immediately to secure the withdrawal of the British warships. The NATO Council responded with a request to Secretary General Joseph M.A.H. Luns to "mediate and intervene" in the dispute to secure a peaceful solution.

However, Icelandic Foreign Minister Einar Agustsson later May 29 rejected NATO mediation. He said, "We have not referred the fishing dispute to NATO, but have asked it only to arrange for the withdrawal of British warships."

The Icelandic government May 30 expelled a member of the British Foreign Office news department, Michael Elliott, on charges that he had divulged secret information on the movements of Icelandic gunboats in the 50-mile offshore territorial zone.

Britain and Iceland exchanged charges of ramming and endangering each other's fishing and naval vessels off Iceland's southeast coast June 1. An Icelandic spokesman said British trawlers had rammed an Icelandic coast guard vessel, the Arvakur, three times. A British spokesman, however, blamed harassment tactics by the Arvakur for collisions with British vessels. Britain denied the Icelandic charge that the Arvakur had been in danger of sinking as a result of the collision.

After the incident, Icelandic Premier Olafur Johannesson renewed his govern-ment's demand that NATO order Britain to withdraw its warships from the 50-mile claimed zone and warned that "if NATO is not capable of maintaining peace in the North Atlantic, there is nothing for us in the alliance."

A British warship and an Icelandic coast guard vessel collided for the first time in the dispute June 7. A British spokesman claimed that the gunboat had "deliberately rammed" the warship, while the Icelandic government counterclaimed that the warship had "behaved unlawfully" and had caused the collision. Both ships were said to be only slightly damaged.

The defense ministers of Norway and Denmark, Johan Kleppe and Kjeld Olesen respectively, urged Britain June 7 "in the interests of NATO" to withdraw its warships from the disputed 50-mile fishing zone. The request was made in Brussels at the semiannual meeting of NATO's defense planning committee.

British warships had been given permission to return fire against Icelandic gunboats harassing trawlers fishing in Iceland's 50-mile zone, the British navy announced July 3.

The International Court of Justice at The Hague July 12 extended its injunction of 1972 authorizing Britain and West Germany to fish within Iceland's unilaterally declared 50-mile fishing limit, pending a final court decision. The vote was 11–3.

Iceland's Cabinet unanimously declared Sept. 11 that it would break diplomatic ties with Britain if British vessels "continue ramming Icelandic ships."

The Cabinet, accepting the proposal offered by Premier Olafur Johannesson, rejected the sharper demand from Fisheries Minister Ludvik Josefsson calling for an immediate and unconditional break with the British government.

The warning to Britain followed a collision between a British frigate and an Icelandic coast guard vessel Sept. 10, the 12th such incident. As in the previous incidents, each side blamed the other for the collision.

While most of the "Cod War" incidents in June-September occurred between Icelandic and British vessels, a few were with West German trawlers fishing within Iceland's self-proclaimed 50-mile territorial water limit. An Icelandic gunboat fired across the bows of West German trawlers June 28 and July 2 and 8, and cut the trawler wires of another German ship July 7. West German and Icelandic officials met in Reykjavik June 29 and in Bonn Sept. 6–7 in an attempt to settle their fishing dispute.

The British regime agreed Oct. 2 to withdraw its warships and tugboats from Iceland's unilaterally proclaimed 50-mile territorial waters zone, one day before expiration of an ultimatum issued by Iceland Sept. 27 that it would break diplomatic relations with Britain if the ships were not withdrawn.

British Prime Minister Edward Heath announced his government's decision in a note to Icelandic Premier Olafur Johannesson, whom he invited to Britain for discussions on the fishing dispute. Heath said withdrawal of the frigates was based on the assumption that Icelandic cutters would not harass British trawlers. Heath dropped the government's previous insistence that Iceland pledge in advance not to harass the fishing boats.

Johannesson immediately accepted Heath's invitation to visit London, but stopped short of a pledge that the coast guard would cease its harassment tactics.

Heath's concession was thought to stem from pressure by Western allies who feared for the future of the U.S.-run North Atlantic Treaty Organization (NATO) base on Iceland.

Icelandic gunboats had cut the nets of 68 British trawlers, during the past year, and had collided with British vessels on 13 separate occasions, according to unidentified officials cited by the New York Times Oct. 2.

Johanneson and Heath agreed in London Oct. 15–16 on an interim settlement of the dispute.

The International Court of Justice July 25, 1974 ruled, 10–4, that Iceland's unilateral decision in 1972 to extend its fishing limits from 12 to 50 nautical miles could not apply to Britain or West Germany. In separate decisions the court said British and West German fishing vessels could not be excluded by unilateral action from the disputed area. Iceland, which had maintained the court had no jurisdiction and refused to plead its case, rejected the ruling.

In arguing its case in March, Britain claimed it had been fishing off Icelandic coasts for centuries and therefore was entitled to traditional fishing rights. West Germany had argued in April that it depended on distant-water fishing for 70% of its catch.

Premier Johanneson told the Icelandic Parliament Aug. 29 that his government planned to extend Iceland's fishing limits from the current 50 nautical miles to 200 "not later than 1975."

Norway fishing accord—Iceland and Norway concluded an agreement authorizing a limited number of Norwegian ships to fish in the disputed 50-mile zone, Le Monde of Paris had reported July 12, 1973. Forty-five Norwegian trawlers would be permitted inside the 50-mile zone, but only 30 would be authorized to fish at one time.

Peru & Ecuador seize U.S. boats. Peru seized 22 U.S.-owned tuna boats Jan. 10–25, 1973 for fishing inside its declared 200-mile offshore territorial limits. The boats were fined according to weight, forced to buy Peruvian fishing licenses and then released. The penalties were said to average $30,000 a boat, but one vessel, a California boat seized Jan. 20, reportedly paid $100,000 in fines and license fees.

A U.S. State Department spokesman said Jan. 19 that the U.S. had formally protested the seizures and put military sales to Peru under review. The U.S. recognized only a 12-mile territorial limit, and reimbursed boat owners who were fined for fishing within the 200-mile limit.

U.S. Rep. John M. Murphy (D, N.Y.) charged Jan. 18 that Peru had seized some of the tuna boats with destroyers and other ships leased from the U.S. Navy, and said he was introducing legislation in Congress directing the U.S. to take back ships used by foreign nations to seize other U.S. vessels. Ecuador used converted U.S. patrol boats to seize U.S. tuna vessels, Murphy charged.

Peruvian Fisheries Minister Javier Tantalean denied Jan. 20 that U.S.-leased ships were used to capture tuna boats. He said Murphy's proposed legislation reflected the thought of "a person who still believes in the 'big stick' policy." He added that 21 foreign vessels, including ones from Canada, the U.S., Ecuador, Japan and France, had voluntarily bought Peruvian fishing licenses in January.

Ecuador seized three U.S. tuna boats Feb. 9–10. It released them after levying fines and license fees totaling $224,000, the American Tunaboat Association (ATA) said Feb. 17.

The ATA said Feb. 5 that a disabled U.S. tuna boat had been seized by an Ecuadorean gunboat while being towed to the Galapagos Islands for repairs. Ecuador said the boat had been seized at the islands Jan. 13 and forced to pay fines and fees totaling $78,800. Ecuadorean officials said repairs could not be made in the islands, which were Ecuadorean possessions.

Meanwhile, the Soviet Fisheries Minister, in Lima to discuss cooperation on technical questions, had asserted the Soviet Union would always respect Peru's territorial waters, the newsletter Latin America reported Feb. 2. The pledge was considered important because the U.S.S.R. had normally joined the U.S. in defending the 12-mile limit, according to the newsletter.

Ecuador seized four U.S. trawlers Jan. 26, 1975 for unlicensed fishing within 200 miles of Ecuador's coasts. They were fined a total of $464,000, and their catch, worth more than $800,000, was confiscated.

A fifth U.S. trawler was reported taken Jan. 28, and another two were reported captured Jan. 31. The captains of all the seized vessels later asked for Ecuadorean fishing licenses in what amounted to recognition of the 200-mile limit, it was reported Feb. 6.

The seizures angered officials in San Diego, Calif., where the boats were based. Rep. Lionel Van Deerlin (D, Calif.), who represented a portion of the city in Congress, called for an end to U.S. military aid to Ecuador Jan. 29. Mayor Pete Wilson asked President Ford Feb. 5 to cut off all aid to Ecuador.

One Ecuadorean newspaper reported that the crew of one seized vessel said it had been authorized by the U.S. government to fish in Ecuadorean waters, according to the London newsletter Latin America Feb. 7.

Etiel Rodriguez, Ecuador's fishing undersecretary, asserted Jan. 29 that Ecuador would continue to "defend its natural resources and the ichthyological wealth in its 200-mile territorial waters."

Peru nationalizes fishing. The Peruvian government May 7, 1973 created a state monopoly, Pescaperu, to take control of the major portion of the ailing fishing industry.

Production of fishmeal and fish oil, the country's major source of export revenue, was nationalized, but the relatively minor food fishing sector was not.

The nationalized sectors involved some 90 private companies employing 27,000 fishermen and plant workers and operating 1,486 boats and 105 factories. Included among them were subsidiaries of such U.S. firms as International Proteins Corp., which listed its Peruvian assets at $11 million; Cargill Inc., with $7.3 million; and General Mills Inc., with about $1 million.

A government decree published May 8 said owners of expropriated property would receive 10% of the value in cash and 90% in nontransferable bonds, redeemable in 10 years at 6% interest.

In announcing the nationalization, Fisheries Minister Javier Tantalean said the move was the only solution to the fishing industry's current indebtedness and to the crisis brought on by the disappearance of anchoveta from Peru's coastal waters in 1972.

Privately owned fishing and processing firms owed state banks the equivalent of $200 million, Tantalean asserted. He agreed with other officials that the industry's basic problem was overexpansion, and that it could get along with fewer fishmeal plants and only half as many fishing boats.

Exports of fish meal and oil earned $322 million in 1972 despite the drop in production caused by the disappearance of anchovy shoals, it was reported March 2.

Anchovy fishing was reported resumed March 9, but only from Monday to Friday and with a temporary catch limit of 50,000 tons for the entire fleet.

The government was using a Dutch credit of $13 million to build a pilot plant for experimenting with the processing of anchoveta, the anchovy found off the Peruvian coast, in a form suitable for human consumption, the newsletter Latin America reported Feb. 2. Anchoveta currently was used only to produce fishmeal. The government hoped tinned anchoveta might compete on world markets with sardines.

A new tuna fishing company with participation of both private and state capital had been set up to operate from the northern port of Zorritos, Latin America reported March 23.

The following year, on March 5, 1975, the government authorized the netting of a 500,000-ton catch, very small by old standards. Private and state-owned Peruvian fishmeal companies also were involved in surveying and trial fishing off the coasts of Panama and Mexico's Baja California in joint ventures with the Panamanian and Mexican governments, it was reported March 15.

Mexican program. The Mexican government was reported Jan. 4, 1974 to have planned an ambitious program to increase fish catches by as much as 200,000 tons a year by 1976. It planned to purchase 355 new vessels for the fishing fleet. Fishing exports earned $100 million in 1973, with 85% going to the U.S., it was reported Jan. 11.

The Inter-American Development Bank announced approval March 7 of a $43 million loan to help finance the government's $85 million fisheries development program.

U.S.-Soviet accords. U.S. and Soviet negotiators Feb. 21, 1973 signed three agreements regulating fishing off the U.S. Pacific coast and establishing fisheries review boards in each other's capitals.

The accords, resulting from talks begun Jan. 29 in Moscow, were signed for the U.S. by Donald L. McKernan, a State Department special assistant for fisheries, and for the Soviet Union by Vladimir M. Kamentsev, deputy fisheries minister.

One agreement limited the Soviet catch of king crab and tanner crab in the eastern Bering Sea and obliged the Russians to use traps, instead of nets, which had often become tangled with U.S. floating gear. The second accord restricted Soviet catch of Pacific hake and flatfish, including yellow-tail flounder. Under terms of this agreement Russian fishermen were forbidden to go for rockfish, flounder and sole off the coasts of Washington, Oregon and California but were to be given port access at Seattle, Portland and Honolulu equivalent to that extended the Soviet merchant marine

fleet. The third pact, affecting crab fishing off Kodiak Island, increased the area closed to Soviet vessels during the U.S. fishing season.

American and Soviet representatives signed an agreement to control Atlantic coast fising from Cape Cod to Cape Hatteras, it was reported June 22.

The Soviet Union agreed to reduce certain types of fishing by 50% to 75% over the next two years, in return for easier Soviet access to East Coast ports for refueling and maintenance. U.S. inspectors would have the right to board Soviet vessels to examine catches.

In early 1975 the Soviet government issued what a Soviet official described as "a permanent order" to Soviet fishing trawlers to remain out of areas designated for U.S. lobstermen in the Georges Bank waters off Newport, Rhode Island, it was reported Jan. 28. Newport fishermen had charged that they suffered more than $150,000 damage during the preceding week when Soviet trawlers cut through the area.

In another action, the U.S.S.R. agreed to pay damages totaling $11,400 to a U.S. fishing boat operator who claimed that his equipment had been damaged in 1971 by Soviet trawlers dragging their gear through lobster traps off Rhode Island. The settlement, reached at a meeting of the U.S.-U.S.S.R. Fisheries Claim Board, was the largest claim thus far resolved between the two countries, according to the Journal of Commerce Jan. 9.

U.S. seizes 2 vessels. U.S. Coast Guardsmen boarded and seized a 270-foot Bulgarian fishing trawler with its 79-man crew and a mackerel catch Jan. 26, 1973 in international waters off New Jersey. A Coast Guard cutter had chased the trawler for three miles. The captain at first denied fishing within the U.S.' 12-mile fishing limits. But he later pleaded guilty and was fined $20,000 Feb. 2.

The U.S. Coast Guard seized a Rumanian trawler off the North Carolina Coast March 26, and the Rumanian government May 7 paid a maximum $100,000 fine.

Finns halt Soviet ships. Soviet trawlers were intercepted March 24, 1973 by a Finnish coast guard ship in the northern

'HUNGER COUNTIES'

State	Failure-To-Feed Counties (A)	Poverty Counties (B)	Hunger Counties 1973 (C)	Total of columns A, B, C (D)	Total number of counties [1] (E)	Hunger Counties 1968 (F)
Alabama	1	43	3	47	67	17
Alaska	0	0	0	0	[2] 1	0
Arizona	7	1	0	8	10	1
Arkansas	12	31	28	71	75	6
California	6	0	0	6	56	0
Colorado	31	6	0	37	63	2
Connecticut	0	0	0	0	[3] 10	0
Delaware	0	0	0	0	3	0
District of Columbia	0	0	0	0	1	0
Florida	19	17	9	45	64	9
Georgia	21	86	15	122	159	50
Hawaii	0	0	0	0	4	0
Idaho	22	0	1	23	39	0
Illinois	55	3	2	60	102	2
Indiana	54	0	0	54	92	0
Iowa	74	0	0	74	99	0
Kansas	99	0	2	101	105	0
Kentucky	20	61	14	95	120	13
Louisiana	2	43	4	49	64	11
Maine	1	0	0	1	16	0
Maryland	9	1	1	11	[4] 24	1
Massachusetts	3	0	0	3	14	0
Michigan	1	3	0	4	83	0
Minnesota	47	3	2	52	85	0
Mississippi	3	73	3	79	81	38
Missouri	28	31	3	62	[4] 115	2
Montana	25	0	1	26	41	1
Nebraska	73	1	13	87	93	0
Nevada	10	0	0	10	[4] 17	0
New Hampshire	0	0	0	0	10	0
New Jersey	1	0	0	1	21	0
New Mexico	0	18	2	20	32	7
New York	9	0	0	9	62	0
North Carolina	41	24	30	95	100	28
North Dakota	23	0	4	27	43	1
Ohio	30	3	0	33	88	0
Oklahoma	17	33	1	51	77	5
Oregon	4	0	0	4	36	0
Pennsylvania	19	0	0	19	67	0
Rhode Island	0	0	0	0	[5] 2	0
South Carolina	5	27	1	33	46	18
South Dakota	25	1	9	35	47	7
Tennessee	24	36	16	76	95	11
Texas	94	67	67	228	254	35
Utah	20	1	0	21	29	0
Vermont	0	0	0	0	[3] 12	0
Virginia	65	13	32	110	[6] 133	14
Washington	4	0	0	4	39	0
West Virginia	0	32	0	32	55	0
Wisconsin	42	1	0	43	70	1
Wyoming	16	0	0	16	21	0
Total: All States	1,062	659	263	1,984	[7] 3,042	280

[1] Does not include counties with large Indian reservation populations.
[2] For Food Program purposes.
[3] Welfare districts.
[4] Includes one independent city.
[5] Public assistance districts.
[6] Includes 37 independent cities.
[7] Includes 40 independent cities.

Baltic Sea, allegedly for fishing in Finland's territorial waters. The trawlers were released after receiving a warning. It was reportedly the fourth time in 1973 that Soviet fishing boats penetrated Finnish waters.

Morocco waters dispute. An exchange of gunfire between Spanish and Moroccan navy ships in January 1973 was reported Jan. 31, when it was disclosed in Madrid that Morocco had decided to extend its territorial waters from 12 to 70 miles.

The naval incident, in which several injuries and possibly some deaths occured, followed the seizure by a Moroccan gunboat of a Spanish fishing vessel. A three-year fishing accord between the two nations had expired Dec. 31, 1972. Even while the accord was in effect some 160 Spanish ships had been seized, partly because, Morocco charged, the dimensions of their nets violated the accord.

The new territorial limit, which Morocco officially proclaimed in March, came within six miles of the Spanish coast between Cadiz and Malaga, and would surround the Spanish island of Alboran.

Fishing vessels were seized by both sides during March and April, and a Spanish seaplane exchanged gunfire with a Moroccan navy launch April 2.

The dispute ended Jan. 2, 1974 after the two nations signed an agreement under which they were to create a jointly owned bi-national fishing company to include up to 200 Spanish ships. The agreement did not constitute recognition of Morocco's 70-mile fishing limit, but Spain was expected to begin diversion of a major part of its fishing fleet to more distant waters.

In 1972, Morocco and the Soviet Union had signed a bilateral protocol of cooperation June 13 to provide Morocco with technical and educational assistance in the fishing industry, and to build fish processing facilities in Morocco to serve Soviet and international markets.

Hunger in the U.S.

Lag in food aid. A U.S. Senate study released May 6, 1973 found that of the 25–30 million poor eligible for federal food assistance programs, only 15 million were participating and that none of the programs assured nutritional adequacy.

The report, prepared by the staff of the Select Committee on Nutrition and Human Needs, concluded that food programs enacted by Congress in the 1960s might have become unsuited to present conditions, especially the rapid increases in food prices. Some federal programs had been unable to buy meat, fruit and dairy products during March and April because of high prices, the study noted.

Nationwide, the committee's survey identified 263 "hunger counties" compared with 280 mostly different counties in 1968 and an increase from 5.4 million to 15 million recipients of food stamps, food aid in schools, day care and surplus food, at a total annual cost of $4 billion. Despite the overall deficiencies in the programs, the study found significant improvement in food assistance in Southern states in the same period. Midwestern states, however, continued to lag.

The report noted that the food stamp program provided less than $1 per person per day for a family of four, an amount which failed to provide even the nationally-averaged foods on which the plan was based for recipients in high-cost urban areas. Recipients depending on surplus commodities distribution were provided food valued at 23¢ per person daily.

The Department of Agriculture was held responsible for many of the deficiencies of the programs, including poor administration and failure to increase benefits in line with changing conditions.

In 1972 the department used $30 million of an available $50 million appropriation for summer lunches for an estimated 1.4 million children in locally sponsored recreation programs.

FAMILY FOOD COSTS

(U.S. Agriculture Department's "market basket"
of farm foods for "typical" 4-member family)

Period	Retail	Farm value	Farm-retail spread
2d quarter 1971	$1,244.76	$474.16	$770.60
3d quarter 1971	1,260.90	482.30	778.60
4th quarter 1971	1,260.09	486.17	773.96
1st quarter 1972	1,291.36	506.86	784.50
2d quarter 1972	1,297.85	510.29	787.56
3d quarter 1972	1,323.42	534.15	789.27
4th quarter 1972	1,330.63	534.23	796.40
1st quarter 1973	1,413.83	614.46	799.37
2d quarter 1973	1,497.05	665.19	831.86
3d quarter 1973	1,603.92	762.29	841.62
January 1973	1,374.98	587.86	787.12
February 1973	1,409.47	607.13	802.34
March 1973	1,458.11	651.13	806.98
April 1973	1,481.32	654.48	826.84
May 1973	1,493.78	652.38	841.40
June 1973	1,517.55	686.74	830.81
July 1973	1,529.28	698.47	830.81
August 1973	1,653.76	838.84	814.92
September 1973	1,626.73	747.59	879.14
October 1973	1,620.20	723.19	897.01
November 1973	1,634.07	707.27	926.80
December 1973	1,650.00	710.00	940.00

PRICE & WAGE TRENDS

(In relation to food price trends)

	December 1971	December 1972	December 1973
Consumer Price Index			
(1967=100.0)	123.1	127.3	138.5
Food at home	120.3	126.0	151.5
Wholesale Price Index			
(1967=100.0)	115.4	122.9	145.3
Farm food	115.8	137.5	187.2
Processed foods	115.9	129.4	155.7
Average hourly earnings:			
Food processing	$3.52	$3.72	$3.97
Food retailing	3.07	3.24	3.43
Meat products	3.71	3.93	4.10

	December 1971	December 1972	December 1973
All manufacturing	3.69	3.95	4.21
Total private economy	3.52	3.74	4.01

	Percent change		
	1971 to 1972	1972 to 1973	1971 to 1973
Consumer Price Index	3.4	8.8	12.5
Food at home	4.7	20.2	25.9
Wholesale Price Index	6.5	18.2	25.9
Farm food	18.7	36.1	61.7
Processed foods	11.6	20.3	34.3
Average hourly earnings:			
Food processing	5.7	6.7	12.8
Food retailing	5.5	5.9	11.7
Meat products	5.9	4.3	10.5
All manufacturing	7.0	6.6	14.1
Total private economy	6.2	7.2	13.9

Source: Bureau of Labor Statistics.

Hunger, poverty found worsening. The Senate Select Committee on Nutrition and Human Needs was told during hearings June 19–21, 1974 that the needy were getting hungrier and poorer and that government programs dealing with hunger were ineffective.

A report prepared for the committee by a panel of outside experts cited steeply rising food costs and inequities in federal food programs, particularly food stamps, as the major problems.

The panel noted that between December 1970 and March 1974, food stamp benefits for a family of four had increased 34% while the cost of foods in the Agriculture Department's "economy" food plan—the basis for food stamp allocations—had increased a total of 42%.

With the cheapest foods undergoing the sharpest price increases during that period (124% for rice, 256% for dried beans), the poor did not have the "spending down" option available to higher-income groups.

The report said only about 15 million of an estimated 37–50 million eligible persons were buying food stamps, and that many were not even aware of their eligibility. There were basic flaws in the program, according to the report, including an unfairly large monthly amount needed to purchase the stamps, the time-consuming "and frequently degrading" process of application and periodic recertification, and the exclusion of persons without kitchen facilities.

Among the report's recommendations were: easing of income-eligibility requirements and increased availability of free stamps; changes in the Agriculture Department's food classification system; and allowing the elderly, disabled and persons without kitchen facilities to use food stamps for restaurant or take-out meals.

A separate outside panel on nutrition and the consumer recommended that all food policy programs be centralized in one federal agency covering production, programs for the poor, safety and nutrition standards, and labeling and advertising.

Court orders stamp fund released. Judge Miles Lord of federal district court in Minneapolis Oct. 13, 1974 ordered the Agriculture Department to spend $278 million remaining in 1973 funds for the food stamp program rather than return the money to the Treasury Department.

A suit brought on behalf of the National Welfare Rights Organization and three Minnesota plaintiffs accused the department and Agriculture Secretary Earl Butz of inadequately administering the $2.5 billion food stamp funds allocated by Congress for the 1973 fiscal year. Judge Lord agreed with the charge, ruling that the department and Butz had violated the law in refusing to spend money to implement the Food Stamp Act's "outreach" program. The program was designed to inform low income persons of their rights to food stamps. According to a plaintiff's lawyer, an estimated 37-million persons were eligible for assistance, but only 14 million persons were receiving food stamps. Suits recently filed in 17 states also charged state officials with failing to implement outreach programs.

Food stamp benefits for a low income family of four would be increased $4 a month to $150 a month beginning Jan. 1, 1975, the Agriculture Department announced Oct. 14. The adjustment was based on new calculations of food costs for an "economy" menu, showing it cost $35.40 a week to feed a family of four, including two school age children.

International Action

Food Situation Called Worse

As evidence mounted that the world food-population situation was getting worse, there were renewed efforts at international cooperation to solve the problem. A U.N. World Population Conference was held in Bucharest in Aug. 1974 to discuss action on population control, and a U.N. World Food Conference took place in Rome in November to seek ways of averting hunger and famine.

The problem of food shortages was considered increasingly serious. "The fight for food is intensifying," David Bird reported in an annual review in the New York Times Jan. 26, 1975. "An increasingly hungry world was harassed [in 1974] . . . by spreading scarcities and rising prices. On top of skimpy harvests and enormous demand came the soaring cost of petroleum needed to make fertilizer and run agricultural machines. . . ."

The same issue of the Times reported that some nations, "after arguing long and loudly over the problem of population pressure, are now doing something about it. . . . Several countries, in a momentous change of attitude, have adopted a policy of controlling their population growth by encouraging family planning. . . . Other countries insist that population growth is not the answer They want to ease the plight of teeming multitudes by accelerating economic development. . . ."

Observers say that the hungry multitudes owe their deprivation both to (a) to the runaway growth of population in the developing countries and (b) to increased consumption by the developed countries. Rep.

Edward I. Koch (D., N.Y.) noted Dec. 9, 1974 that "while population generates 70% of the increased demand for food each year, increased affluence, largely in the United States, the Soviet Union, Japan and Western Europe, accounts for 30% of the [increased] demand for food. . . . The Soviet Union and Eastern Europe accounted for 5.5% of the world's grain imports in 1966. In 1973 they accounted for 29%." Sen. Mark O. Hatfield (R., Ore.) had told the Senate July 16 that "the amount of food and protein consumed by the diets of . . . all 210 million Americans could feed 1.5 billion Africans and Indians on a stable though vastly different diet."

Prof. Carl Schramm of Johns Hopkins University, in the March-April 1975 issue of Challenge, gave the following data for per capita cereal consumption (in pounds) by developing and various developed countries:

	1964–66 average	1972–74 average	Percent increase
United States	1,600	1,850	16
U.S.S.R.	1,105	1,435	30
European Community	[1]900	[1]1,000	17
Japan	[1]530	[1]620	17
China	420	430	2
Developing countries (excluding China)	[2]370	395	[2]7

[1] Figures for the cereal consumption of the European Community, and to a lesser extent of Japan, are reduced somewhat by the extensive use of noncereal grains for livestock feeding. Japan's figure is also reduced by the fact of extensive direct imports of meat, thus cutting the livestock consumption of cereals.

[2] The 1964–66 figure was depressed in the averages by India's 2 bad crop years in that period. The percent increase to 1972–74 thus exaggerates an increase that was in fact minimal.

Source: U.S. Department of Agriculture.

'Child emergency.' The U.N. Children's Fund (UNICEF) May 24, 1974 declared a "world child emergency" to call international attention to the plight of millions of famine-stricken children in the poor countries.

"For years we have known that some 10 million children under five in developing countries were slowly starving to death," UNICEF reported. It warned that this situation "is giving way to the grim prospect of hunger on a scale so staggering that the mind can hardly grasp it. Now 400 to 500 million children live in the 60 poorest countries..., confronted with starvation...."

Food for Peace cut. The fiscal 1975 U.S. budget, submitted by President Nixon Feb. 4, 1974, proposed a reduction in P.L. 480 (Food for Peace) funding.

The Food for Peace program was budgeted at $742 million, a $54 million cut "because of commodity shortages and increased food prices," according to the budget. Requests for Indochina rehabilitation, including South Vietnam, Laos and Cambodia, totaled $648 million. North Vietnam was not included.

More foreign trade problems forecast. In his second annual international economic report to Congress, President Nixon warned Feb. 7 that the U.S. "has moved from an era of near self-sufficiency to one of rising dependence on foreign resources with a concomitant need to earn more foreign exchange to pay for these imports."

But, Nixon added, it was unlikely that nations producing these vital raw materials could exploit their advantageous trade position by forming a cartel or "monopoly" similar to the Arab's control of the petroleum market.

The report was ambivalent in its analysis of the current worldwide food shortage. "There is considerable disagreement as to whether the current food gap is permanent or whether we will soon be faced with a food glut," the report stated.

In a mixed conclusion, the report added, "Most agricultural experts now believe that the situation that has characterized the past several decades will continue for the foreseeable future—that is, generally adequate supplies with occasional shortages."

U.S. disaster aid. A bill authorizing $150 million in foreign disaster aid was passed by the Senate June 21, 1974 and House June 26 and signed by President Nixon July 8. The funds, already appropriated by Congress in the fiscal 1974 foreign aid appropriations bill, were earmarked for assistance to victims of floods in Pakistan, the 1972 earthquake in Nicaragua and drought and famine in Ethiopia and the nations of the Sahel. The breakdown was $65 million for Pakistan and Nicaragua and $85 million for Africa.

Declaration on Food & Population

The U.N. World Food Conference held in November 1974 had been proposed by Henry A. Kissinger Sept. 24, 1973 in an address to the U.N. General Assembly. (The speech was Kissinger's first major address as U.S. secretary of state.) The conference was held after numerous groups had submitted proposals on the action the conferees should take.

Prominent citizens urge action. The adoption of a world food plan by the forthcoming U.N. World Food Conference was urged in a "Declaration on Food & Population" presented to U.N. Secretary General Kurt Waldheim April 25, 1974. The document, signed by some 1,000 prominent citizens of about 100 countries, warned that "tens of millions of lives are suspended in the delicate balance between world population and world food supplies." It called for the formulation of population as well as food policies. The declaration, presented by British author C. P. Snow, was signed by Nobel Prize winners, scientists, authors, scholars and world leaders. The signers included 51 U.S. Congress members, Dean Rusk, William Rogers, Arthur Goldberg, Jonas Salk, Lon Nol and Mrs. Martin Luther King Jr.

Text of the declaration:

To governments, organizations and to men and women everywhere we, the undersigned, address this Declaration on Food and Population.

No link unites the family of man more than his need for food. For food is an essential condition of life, common to all people; wherever they are, whatever they do, they share alike in this need.

The stark truth is that man's ability to produce food is not keeping pace with his need. Despite efforts by governments and the international community to solve world food problems, more people are hungry today than ever before.

Hundreds of millions of the world's peoples are undernourished. Population growth is adding 75 to 80 million more people each year, 200,000 each day. Within the next 25 years or, so our present numbers of nearly 4 billion will be nearly 7 billion. They must all be fed.

The world food situation took a sharp turn for the worse in 1972 and 1973:

1. Stocks of grain have hit an all-time low since the end of World War II. Surplus stocks formerly held in reserve have nearly been exhausted and no longer offer security against widespread hunger and starvation.

2. Food prices have reached new highs. Last year, despite a record world harvest, escalating demand nearly doubled grain prices. The increasing cost of food threatens to cause serious hardship for many people already spending most of what they have on food.

3. Less of the cheaper protein foods, which normally supplement grain diets, is available. The world's fish catch and per capita production of protein-rich legumes, the staple diet in many countries, have declined.

4. Food shortages have created serious social unrest in many parts of the world and are particularly severe in countries where hunger and the diseases that thrive on undernourished bodies are prevalent. This scarcity has been aggravated by the consumption of more and more grain to produce meat, eggs, and milk.

5. Mounting fertilizer and energy shortages are reducing food production in certain areas and increasing food prices.

In this new and threatening situation, a bad monsoon in Asia (which could occur in any year), or a drought in North America (like those in the 1930's and 1950's), could mean severe malnutrition for hundreds of millions and death for many millions.

This dangerously unstable world food picture, when seen against an unprecedented population increase, has created an immediate sense of urgency. The dangers of food shortages could remain a threat for the rest of this century—even if, hopefully, bumper crops in some years create temporary surpluses and even if the trend toward reduced birth rates becomes general throughout the world.

World food production in the years ahead must rise at least 2 per cent a year to keep pace with the present rate of population growth. But it must rise a good deal more if the world's people are to be provided with an adequate diet. This required annual increase in food production is considerably greater than that which occurred during recent decades—and seems to be increasingly

harder to achieve each year. But unless there is this necessary and continuous increase in food production, there will be even more hunger and malnutrition and soaring food prices.

The need to seek solutions is pressing. The nature of the problem, the precarious state of world food production made critical by predicted expectations of continued population growth, calls for concerted action by the world community. There is only one cure for hunger and that is food. No palliatives or panaceas in the form of reports or resolutions can alleviate the pain of empty stomachs that must be filled. International resolutions, however high-minded, are a mockery if they do not have a tangible impact on the human condition.

The United Nations is now providing leadership on both these problems. In August the United Nations will convene the World Population Conference in Bucharest. In November it will convene the World Food Conference in Rome. These are the first occasions when governments have agreed to meet to consider these crucial questions and to consider taking action on them.

With these two conferences only a few months away, we urge governments, acting before, at and after these two global conferences, to consider realistic and purposeful measures such as the following:

1. Give high priority to programs in each country which will increase the production of grains, legumes and other staple food crops; ensure the availability of protein-rich foods, particularly to the more vulnerable population groups; expand the production of fertilizer; and improve the opportunities for small farmers to make a reasonable living. Develop a comprehensive and constructive World Food Plan for adoption at the World Food Conference.

2. Support sound population policies relevant to national needs which respect national sovereignty and the diversity of social, economic and cultural conditions; accept and assure the human right of each couple to decide for themselves the spacing and size of their families; [1] and recognize the corresponding responsibility of governments to provide their peoples the information and the means to exercise this right effectively.[2] Embody these policies in a World Population Plan of Action to be agreed upon by governments at the World Population Conference.

3. Recognize that the interdependence of the world community creates an obligation to assist in the necessary funding of food and population programs by both developing and developed countries. This calls for the elaboration and implementation of a global strategy by the United Nations and its family of agencies, including the Food and Agri-

---

[1] United Nations Teheran Declaration of Human Rights, 1968 (para. 16)

[2] Resolution 1672 (LII) of the United Nations Economic and Social Council, 1969

culture Organization of the United Nations and the United Nations Fund for Population Activities.

4. Establish sufficient food reserves through national and international efforts to provide continuing vital insurance against food shortages.

5. Recognize that, in our finite world where resources are limited, the family of man must one day, and hopefully fairly soon, bring birth rates into reasonable balance with the lowered death rates that have been achieved. Many governments see the need to guide national policy toward this objective. A solution to the present world food crisis must be found within the next few years. The social transformation which can lead to a reduction in the world rate of fertility, along with lowering the rate of mortality, will take decades to accomplish. But a start must be made now because the millions of people being born each year place a heavy burden on the resources available to many nations for education, health, employment and the maintenance of environmental quality. A reduction in population growth could help alleviate this burden. Effective measures toward resolving both the world food and population problems must come within a total strategy of development. Not only is social and economic development desirable in itself, but also it contributes to moderating population growth. All these measures are designed to improve the quality of life. In this Declaration, we focus on food because it is the most critical of the pressures on the world today. It is the greatest manifestation of world poverty, which has many aspects. The absolute number of desperately poor are far greater today than ever before in history. The need to eradicate acute poverty is being recognized more than ever as a collective responsibility. It is a task which global partnership and the demands of social justice make imperative.

We repeat, food is crucial because literally tens of millions of lives are suspended in the delicate balance between world population and world food supplies. Growing populations, denied sufficient food needed for survival, resist all efforts to secure a peaceful world. With increased production and more equitable distribution of food, the future could provide a prospect of less misery and more hope for countless people now deprived of the basic necessities that are their right. uniqûe opportunity. This opportunity must not be missed. Comprehensive international agreements must be reached to assure at least minimal food supplies, with sufficient annual carry-over stocks. Disastrous breakdowns in the world food supply can thus be avoided. All nations may then rest secure in the knowledge that this, the most critical of their immediate problems, is being attacked with wisdom, vigor and unity of purpose.

In the name of humanity we call upon all governments and peoples everywhere, rich and poor, regardless of political and social systems, to act—to act together—and to act in time.'

U.S. GRAIN YIELDS (1950–74)

Grain	1950-54 average	1955-59 average	1960-64 average	1965-69 average	1970-74 average
		metric tons per hectare			
Wheat	1.16	1.49	1.70	1.85	2.11
Corn	2.47	3.06	3.92	4.93	5.31
Grain sorghum	1.22	1.77	2.68	3.32	3.39
Barley	1.50	1.59	1.82	2.26	2.27
Oats	1.22	1.39	1.57	1.81	1.80

	1970	1971	1972	1973	1974[1]
Wheat	2.08	2.28	2.20	2.14	1.87
Corn	4.54	5.53	6.08	5.74	4.65
Grain sorghum	3.16	3.37	3.81	3.69	2.92
Barley	2.30	2.46	2.35	2.17	2.05
Oats	1.76	2.01	1.83	1.69	1.71

[1] Preliminary.

Source: Statistical Reporting Service, *Agricultural Statistics.*

Waldheim, on receiving the declaration, indicated his agreement with its proposals. Among his remarks:

I have recently described the times we are living in as being characterized by mass poverty, food shortages, an energy crisis, a continuing oppressive burden of military expenditure, inflation exacerbated by world monetary instability, and the prospect before us of a doubling of human numbers by the turn of the century.

The Declaration addresses itself primarily to the dramatic depletion of available food reserves and the shortfall in world food production. There is no more immediate task than that of rescuing the world from a situation which, for many, has always been precarious and is now even more hazardous. Short-term measures, while essential, must not be allowed to become palliatives, for the coming years will increase our vulnerability. Virtually in no other area is it more pressing than in the one to which your Declaration addresses itself: the need to assure that the men, women, and children in Africa, Asia, Europe and the Americas, whatever their origin, their religion, their political philosophy, their age, their social condition have the basic foods which are the one essential and undebatable pre-condition of a life of dignity and decency. Without an assured supply, all our other aspirations for peace, for social justice, for growth and creativity, both as individuals and as nations, lose their meaning and take on a hollow ring.

I cannot but be sharply and painfully conscious of the dangers posed by the Declaration, having recently returned from the Sahel. There, the suffering provoked by a six-year drought is resulting in premature death, disease and a dreadful sense of helplessness. The tragic spectacle of dying cattle and their owners fleeing the encroaching desert induces a sense of desperation into what should be the objective analysis of the world's food situation and prospects....

This is a year in which the international community, with some brutally abrupt reminders of what the future may hold, is facing up to the situation.

The unprecedented growth of the world's population is compounding man's difficulties in feeding himself. The time at our disposal is very short. You point out that the world's food production has barely kept pace with population increases. Our goal is not mere survival but a life of dignity and peace with hope for each new generation to improve the conditions of life for the billions of men, women and children who will inhabit the earth in the coming decades.

Whether or not we can increase food production depends, as the Declaration states, not on a torrent of words and resolutions, but on adopting new and tangible objectives, hammering out the global strategies needed and revitalizing the machinery to achieve them. In spite of its ideological complexity and the political and other constraints that must exist in any global body, the United Nations can and will respond.

Population Problem

Population conference. The U.N. World Population Conference was held in Bucharest, Rumania Aug. 19–30, 1974 with delegates from more than 130 nations attending. It adopted a vaguely worded "plan of action" to slow the pace of world population growth.

The 10-day parley, approved by the General Assembly in 1972, was aimed at producing a global consensus on the population problem and on the range of possible remedies, as well as agreement on a "plan of action" drafted by preparatory symposia to help nations develop their own population control programs.

Attainment of these goals was held unlikely because of serious disagreements between developed and underdeveloped countries. While industrial nations urged population control to alleviate hunger, poverty, environmental deterioration and shortages of raw materials, many developing countries viewed population growth as essential to economic development, and asserted only a greater sharing of wealth would ease global misery.

The world's population was increasing at an annual rate of 2%, or more than 70 million persons. At this pace the present population of four billion would double in 35 years.

U.N. Secretary General Kurt Waldheim opened the conference with an appeal to delegates to approve the draft action plan, which he described as "limited in scope" but "shaped by technical advice and political guidance" from U.N. member nations. Waldheim assured the delegates that the plan "emphatically recognizes the prerogatives of national sovereignty."

The draft recommended the broadest distribution of family planning information, establishment of minimum ages for marriage, abolition of child labor, full integration of women into social, economic and political life, and institution of social security and old age benefits throughout the world.

With such programs, the draft declared, "population growth in the less developed countries would decline from the present annual rate of 2.4% to about 2% by 1985." In the more developed countries, it stated, the growth rate would remain about the same at less than .9%, for a world growth rate decline from 2% to about 1.7%.

Waldheim linked excessive population growth to future scarcity of food, energy and raw materials as well as to poverty, and he said all of the problems were "leaping over" national boundaries.

Rumanian President Nicolae Ceausescu spoke after Waldheim and stressed that the population crisis could be eased through a redistribution of the world's wealth. He blamed the gap between rich and poor nations on "the imperialist, colonialist, and neo-colonialist exploitation and oppression of many peoples."

"The population question is closely linked to the setting up of a new international economic order, to establishing economic relations on the principle of mutual advantage, to attaining a correct ratio between the prices of industrial products and raw materials, favoring a more rapid development of the countries lagging behind," Ceausescu said.

Ceausescu made it clear that Rumania would pursue its policy of increasing its population from 20 million to 25 million by 1980, and he reaffirmed the "sovereign right" of each nation "to promote that demographic policy and those measures it considers most suitable, consonant with its national interests, without any outside interference."

Antonio Carrillo Flores of Mexico, the conference's secretary general and chief organizer, told the delegates that while nations comprising the majority of mankind had agreed they must reduce their demographic growth rates, "it is also understandable that several nations in Europe, Africa and Latin America, where the objectives and situations are different, look at the problem in a different way."

"The task of the international community," Carrillo Flores said, "is to promote research, the knowledge and interpretation of the demographic realities, its trends and prospects, and to provide cooperation to all peoples who might need that cooperation."

The finally accepted "plan of action" was approved by acclamation after extensive revisions sought mainly by underdeveloped countries led by Communist and Latin American nations. It failed to set national or international population goals, or to focus on the possibility that overpopulation would soon overtax the world's supplies of food and other resources.

The plan subordinated population control to economic and social development, seeing the latter as the key to solving population problems. Countries which considered their birth rates "detrimental to their national purposes" were "invited to consider setting quantitative goals and implementing policies that may lead to the attainment of such goals by 1985." However, "nothing herein should interfere with the sovereignty of any government to adopt such ... goals," the document stated.

The plan recognized that "per capita use of world resources is much higher in the more developed than in the developing countries," and urged industrial nations "to adopt appropriate policies in population, consumption and investment, bearing in mind the need for fundamental improvement in international equity."

It affirmed the basic right of couples to freely decide the number and spacing of their children, and to have the information, education and means to do so. Nations were asked to make these means and information available to their citizens, but no target date was set for compliance.

The plan also strongly recognized the right of women to contribute to economic development and to participate in all spheres of life on an equal basis with men. The improved status of women was described as essential in its own right and conducive to lower fertility.

"Governments should make a sustained effort to insure that legislation regarding the status of women complies with the principles spelled out in the Declaration on the Elimination of Discrimination Against Women and other United Nations documents, declarations, conventions and international instruments, to reduce the gap between law and practice through effective implementation, and to inform women at all socio-economic levels of their legal rights and responsibilities," the document declared.

In conference debates following the opening addresses and at a parallel, nongovernmental conference called the Population Tribune, most developing nations emphasized economic development measures over birth control programs. There were frequent references to "excessive consumption" in the U.S., according to the Washington Post Aug. 20.

The chief U.S. representative, Secretary of Health, Education and Welfare Caspar Weinberger, who headed an eight-person delegation, told the U.N. conference Aug. 20 that the draft action plan should be strengthened to provide a greater decrease in the world population growth rate. He introduced a proposal to include in the plan "national goals together with the world goal of replacement level of fertility by the year 2000"—i.e., average families of parents and only two children.

Weinberger noted that world food reserves had dropped "to about one month's supply," and he urged action not only on family planning but on increasing food production. He pledged continued U.S. support for U.N. population control and health aid projects and said the U.S. would join other nations willing to increase assistance to "bilateral and multilateral health and population programs in developing countries."

In an apparent reference to Arab oil exporting nations, Weinberger said if "newly rich" nations would provide "a steady increase" in contributions to the U.N. Fund for Population Activities, he would ask U.S. Congress for additional assistance to developing nations.

(Rafael Salas, executive director of the U.N. fund, called for $500 million in contributions in 1974-77. The fund operated about 900 projects in 90 developing countries, concentrating on six nations with which it had long-term agreements).

Weinberger asserted the conference action plan had struck a "sensible balance" between economic development and birth control measures.

His position was backed by the chief West German delegate, Interior Minister Werner Maihofer, but delegates from developing nations continued to emphasize redistribution of wealth over population control. Indian Health Minister Karan Singh urged industrialized nations to take

"a searching look at their own economies" and to reverse "the headlong flight toward limitless consumerism."

At the Population Tribune, Lester R. Brown, a U.S. expert, warned Aug. 20 that the world had food reserves for only 27 days, and that the 1974 world grain harvest would almost certainly fall below that of 1973, threatening a catastrophe.

He said the two areas most affected by poor yields were likely to be the world's main food-exporting regions—Asia, where energy shortages had resulted in a lack of fertilizer and fuel to run irrigation pumps, and North America, which had suffered bad weather.

Brown said the development of high-yield food grains in the international program called the Green Revolution had achieved all that could be expected, partly because fertilizers were now in such short supply and partly because population growth had outpaced even the highest food production rates.

(Dr. Norman E. Borlaug of the U.S, developer of the Green Revolution, had said he was dismayed to find little government concern over the shortage of fertilizers during a recent tour of Asia and Africa, the New York Times reported June 20.)

A report issued by the U.N. Food and Agriculture Organization June 2 had said developing nations would face severe grain shortages by 1985 that they would not be able to alleviate through imports if current population trends and food demand continued.

At the Population Tribune, John D. Rockefeller 3rd, chairman of the Rockefeller Foundation and an advocate of family planning for 40 years, delivered an address Aug. 26 in which he reversed his long-standing position and proposed a birth control policy within the context of general economic and social development.

"I have changed my mind," Rockefeller said. "The evidence has been mounting, particularly in the past decade, that family planning alone is not adequate."

Rockefeller endorsed a new approach which "recognizes that rapid population growth is only one among many problems facing most countries, that it is a multiplier and intensifier of other problems rather than the cause of them. And it recognizes that motivation for family planning is best stimulated by hope that living conditions and opportunities in general will improve."

He called for a reappraisal of all work done in the population field, and a revision of "our concept of economic growth so that it could be consciously and deliberately directed toward human goals." Modern development should give greater attention to an "equitable distribution of the fruits of progress," and industrial nations should "assist in broadening the choices available to the poorer nations," Rockefeller said.

Discussions at the conference were often interrupted by political digressions, notably attacks by China against the U.S. and the Soviet Union. Chinese chief delegate Huang Shu-tse devoted the major part of his address Aug. 21 to a denunciation of the two "superpowers" as the "chief culprits" of the poverty of underdeveloped countries.

Huang said the alleged alarm of the U.S. and Soviet Union over the population explosion was "utterly groundless and ... propagated with ulterior motives." "Each day the two superpowers talk about detente but they are continually creating tensions ... Now they are trying to shift the blame for global problems on the Third World," he asserted. He said China opposed any outside interference in a nation's population growth.

Lev Volodsky, Soviet deputy health minister, told the conference the same day that "imperialists and colonialists" were responsible for the plight of the Third World, and that economic development was the key to resolving the population crisis. Volodsky repeated the U.S.S.R.'s long-standing proposal for a 10% cut in the military budgets of all nations, saying such reductions could be diverted to help underdeveloped nations achieve "economic and social independence."

Delegates generally praised the U.N. conference and called the action plan a valuable initial step in approaching the world population problem, according to the New York Times Sept. 3. The chief U.S. delegate, Secretary of Health, Education and Welfare Caspar Weinberger, had lauded the plan Aug. 30 as a "landmark advance in international understanding and agreement on population matters." That "a population conference of 135 nations has been held at

all has been a great accomplishment," he said.

However, delegates from industrial nations and many population and food experts privately expressed disappointment that the conference did not emphasize the need for urgency in finding remedies for population growth and its attending problems, the Washington Post reported Sept. 1.

"It will be said that the conference was convened on the eve of greatest famine and the the conference failed to recognize it," said Rene Dumont, a French agricultural expert who addressed the Population Tribune.   •

Ford Pledges U.S. Food Aid

Gerald R. Ford was inaugurated as U.S. President Aug. 9, 1974 to succeed Richard M. Nixon. In a major address the following month, Ford promised to increase the amount of food the U.S. sends to the world's starving people.

U.S. food aid pledged. President Ford, addressing the 29th U.N. General Assembly in New York Sept. 18, 1974, promised increased U.S. food assistance to needy countries.

Ford urged all countries to join in a "global strategy for food and energy" and warned that "failure to cooperate on oil and food and inflation could spell disaster for every nation represented in this room."

Ford told the General Assembly that the U.S. "recognizes the special responsibilities we bear as the world's largest producer of food," but he said "it has not been our policy to use food as a political weapon despite the oil embargo and recent oil price and production decisions." He emphasized that "energy is required to produce food, and food to produce energy."

Ford challenged oil-exporting nations to "define their policies to meet growing needs" without "imposing unacceptable burdens on the international monetary and trade system." He said that by "confronting consumers with production restrictions, artificial pricing and the prospect of ultimate bankruptcy, producers will eventually become the victims of their own actions."

Ford pledged that the U.S. would "not only maintain the amount it spends for food shipments to nations in need, but it will increase this amount this year." He also promised a substantial increase in U.S. assistance to agriculture production programs in poor countries, and U.S. help in the establishment of an international system of food reserves.

He urged all nations to substantially increase food and energy production, and to hold prices at levels that consumers could afford. He noted that world population would double by the year 2000, requiring such production increases if living standards were to improve.

Among Ford's remarks:

Today, the economy of the world is under unprecedented stress. We need new approaches to international cooperation to respond effectively to the problems that we face. Developing and developed countries, market and nonmarket economies—we are all part of one international economic system.

The food and oil crises demonstrate the extent of our independence. Many developing nations need the food suplus of a few developed nations. And many industrialized nations need the oil production of a few developing nations.

Energy is required to produce food and food to produce energy—and both to provide a decent life for everyone. The problems of food and energy can be resolved on the basis of cooperation—or can, I should say, be made unmanageable on the basis of confrontation. Runaway inflation, propelled by food and oil price increases, is an early warning signal.

Let us not delude ourselves. Failure to cooperate on oil, food, and inflation could spell disaster for every nation represented in this room. The United Nations must not and need not allow this to occur. A global strategy for food and energy is urgently required.

The United States believes four principles should guide a global approach:

First, all nations must substantially increase production. Just to maintain the present standards of living the world must almost double its output of food and energy to match the expected increase in the world's population by the end of this century. To meet aspirations for a better life, production will have to expand at a significantly faster rate than population growth.

Second, all nations must seek to achieve a level of prices which not only provides an incentive to producers but which consumers can afford. It should now be clear that the developed nations are not the only countries which demand and receive an adequate return for their goods. But it should also be clear that by confronting consumers with production restrictions, artificial pricing, and the prospect of ultimate bankruptcy, producers will eventually become the victims of their own actions.

Third, all nations must avoid the abuse of man's fundamental needs for the sake of narrow or national bloc advantage. The attempt by any country to use one commodity for political purposes will inevitably tempt other countries to use their comodities for their own purposes.

Fourth, the nations of the world must assure that the poorest among us are not overwhelmed by rising prices of the imports necessary for their survival. The traditional aid donors and the increasingly wealthy oil producers must join in this effort.

The United States recognizes the special responsibility we bear as the world's largest producer of food. That is why Secretary Kissinger proposed from this podium last year a World Food Conference to define a global food policy. And that is one reason why we have removed domestic restrictions on food production in the United States. It has not been our policy to use food as a political weapon despite the oil embargo and recent oil price and production decisions.

It would be tempting for the United States—beset by inflation and soaring energy prices—to turn a deaf ear to external appeals for food assistance, or to respond with internal appeals for export controls. But however difficult our own economic situation, we recognize that the plight of others is worse.

Americans have always responded to human emergencies in the past and we respond again here today.

In response to Secretary General Waldheim's appeal and to help meet the long-term challenge in food, I reiterate:

To help developing nations realize their aspiration to grow more of their own food, the United States will substantially increase its assistance to agricultural production programs in other countries.

Next, to ensure that the survival of millions of our fellow men does not depend upon the vagaries of weather, the United States is prepared to join in a worldwide effort to negotiate, establish, and maintain an international system of food reserves. This system will work best if each nation is made responsible for managing the reserves that it will have available.

Finally, to make certain that the more immediate needs for food are met this year, the United States will not only maintain the amount it spends for food shipments to nations in need, but it will increase this amount.

Thus, the United States is striving to help define and contribute to a cooperative global policy to meet man's immediate and long-term need for food....

Now is the time for the oil producers to

define their conception of a global policy on energy to meet the growing need—and to do this without imposing unacceptable burdens on the international monetary and trade system.

A world of economic confrontation cannot be a world of political cooperation. If we fail to satisfy man's fundamental needs for energy and food, we face a threat not just to our aspirations for a better life for all our peoples, but to our hopes for a more stable and a more peaceful world. By working together to overcome our common problems, mankind can turn from fear towards hope.

From the time of the founding of the United Nations, America volunteered to help nations in need, frequently as the main benefactor. We were able to do it. We were glad to do it. But as new economic forces alter and reshape today's complex world, no nation can be expected to feed all the world's hungry peoples. Fortunately, however, many nations are increasingly able to help and I call on them to join with us as truly United Nations in the struggle to provide more food at lower prices for hungry and, in general, a better life for the needy of this world.

America will continue to do more than its share. But there are realistic limits to our capacities. There is no limit, however, to our determination to act in concert with other nations to fulfill the vision of the United Nations Charter: "to save succeeding generations from the scourge of war" and "to promote social progress and better standards, better standards of life in a larger freedom."

U.S. aid to India, Bangla Desh & Pakistan. U.S. State Secretary Henry L. Kissinger visited India, Bangla Desh and Pakistan in October 1974 and apparently promised food aid to all three countries.

The visit to India took place first, Oct. 27–30, and the subject of world food scarcity was discussed in a joint communique issued Oct. 29 after Kissinger had conferred with Prime Minister Indira Gandhi and other Indian officials.

Both sides expressed hope that the world food conference in Rome, which Kissinger was to address Nov. 6, would find "a way of conserving world food stocks and making them available to the most seriously affected developing nations on more favorable terms." The statement made no mention of U.S. food shipments to India, but New Delhi officials said India expected to receive at least one million tons of American grains before 1975 on easy terms.

The communique affirmed "there is no conflict of national interests" between New Delhi and Washington, but acknowledged there was "considerable scope for further strengthening of bilateral relations."

Kissinger had signed an agreement with Foreign Minister Y.B. Chavan Oct. 28 establishing an Indian-U.S. commission for economic, commercial, scientific, technological, educational and cultural cooperation. Chavan called the body "an important landmark" and a "concrete expression" of a desire by both nations to conduct "meaningful cooperation."

In a speech later Oct. 28, Kissinger said "higher oil prices directly affect food prices by increasing the cost of fertilizer, of operating agricultural machinery and of transporting food to deficit areas."

Kissinger flew to Dacca Oct. 30 and conferred with Bangla Desh Prime Minister Mujibur Rahman. After the discussions, Kissinger pledged that the U.S. would "do what is within our capacity to help" Bangla Desh cope with its domestic problems, but cautioned that Dacca must depend largely on its own economic development.

It was announced in Dacca that the U.S. was providing Bangla Desh with an additional 100,000 tons of food grains, for a 1974 total of 250,000 tons.

Kissinger continued his Asian tour with a one-day visit Oct. 31–Nov. 1 to Rawalpindi, where he conferred with Pakistani Prime Minister Zulfikar Ali Bhutto, conveying a message from President Ford that stressed the U.S.' commitment to Pakistan "would remain an important principle of American foreign policy."

According to a joint communique issued after completion of the official talks Oct. 31, the U.S. had agreed to provide Pakistan with about 100,000 tons of wheat at long-term, low-interest credit.

World Food Conference

Rome session adopts program. The U.N. World Food Conference was held in Rome Nov. 5–16, 1974 with more than 1,000 government and private delegates from 130 countries attending. It approved the broad outlines of a program to "end the scourge of hunger and malnutrition" but took no concrete action to provide immediate relief for the millions of people threatened with starvation. The conferees decided to set up a new U.N. agency to supervise food programs.

A final conference declaration asked "all governments able" to substantially increase their agricultural aid, and urged all to "reduce to a minimum the waste of food and of agricultural resources."

The new agency, called the World Food Council, would be established by the U.N. General Assembly and would report to the Assembly through the U.N. Economic and Social Council (ECOSOC). The food council would be composed of officials at ministerial or plenipotentiary level, who would meet at various times a year to coordinate existing and new policies concerning food production, nutrition, food security and food aid. (The creation of two subcommittees was recommended: a world food security council and a food aid committee.) It would have a full-time secretariat in Rome, whose staff would be drawn from the U.N.'s Food and Agricultural Organization (FAO), which sponsored the World Food Conference.

The formula establishing the council represented a compromise between the developed nations, who wanted ECOSOC to create and control the coordinating body, and the developing nations, who favored establishment and control of the body by the General Assembly, where each nation had one vote and the developing countries had numerical superiority.

The conference Nov. 16 approved several new programs to be supervised by the projected council. Details and machinery would be formulated later. They included:

An international agricultural development fund, originally proposed by Arab nations, including major oil producers, to channel investment toward improvement of agriculture in the developing countries, with voluntary contributions to come from traditional donors and from new wealthy developing nations, mainly the oil producers; a fertilizer-aid program to provide increased supplies to developing nations and to help them build new and improved plants; a pesticide-aid program; an irrigation, drainage and flood control program; a nu-

trition-aid program; and a call for "achievement of a desirable balance between population and the food supply."

Earlier, the conference pledged to create an internationally coordinated system of nationally-held grain reserves, a 10-million-ton a year food aid program for poor nations, and an early-warning system of data-sharing to disseminate information about climatic or other threats to food supplies or sudden increases in demand. (The Soviet Union, which was not a member of the FAO, initially expressed strong reservations on the last proposal.)

Edwin M. Martin, deputy chairman of the U.S. delegation, praised the conference results Nov. 16, declaring that the meeting "was not called to get food to people tomorrow but to lay out a plan of action to prevent the crisis that we have now from recurring." His comment was an apparent allusion to President Ford's refusal Nov. 15 to pledge a million-ton increase in U.S. emergency food aid. He added that "we will probably be giving that much" in additional food aid, but said "It would not be useful to announce a figure."

Sayed Ahmed Marei of Egypt, secretary general of the conference, said Nov. 17 that he was "absolutely certain" the Arabs would contribute "millions, no hundreds of millions of dollars" to the proposed agricultural development fund.

Reflecting pressures on oil-producing nations at the conference, Iranian Interior Minister Jamshid Amouzegar said Nov. 17 that his nation was "prepared to give— and give more—provided we do not replace the traditional donors' contributions." He stressed that the oil countries were not responsible for the food crisis, which, he said, "has its roots in unfair policies of the developed countries, the enormous grain purchases of the Soviet Union and the population explosion."

Pope Paul VI had received more than 2,000 conference delegates at the Vatican Nov. 9. In calling for immediate action to deal with starvation, the pope ruled out population control as a valid measure. "It is inadmissible that those who have control of the wealth and resources of mankind should try to resolve the problems of hunger by forbidding the poor to be born," he said.

Secretary General Waldheim had opened the conference Nov. 5 with a call for

PRODUCTION, CONSUMPTION & NET TRADE IN FERTILIZER

(For the three major fertilizers: nitrogen, phosphate and potash)

Item	1962/63	1966/67	1970/71	1971/72	Rates of growth	
					1962-71	1967-71
	---- million metric tons ----				---- percent ----	
Production						
Developed countries	32.5	49.4	64.0	67.7	8.5	6.5
Developing countries[1]	1.5	2.8	5.3	6.0	16.7	16.5
Asian planned countries	[2]0.5	1.4	2.2	3.0	22.2	16.5
Total	34.5	53.6	71.5	76.7	9.3	7.5
Consumption						
Developed countries	29.5	42.9	56.2	58.9	8.0	6.5
Developing countries[1]	3.2	5.4	9.1	10.1	13.6	13.3
Asian planned countries	[2]1.0	2.5	4.1	4.6	18.5	13.0
Total	33.7	50.8	69.4	73.6		
Net imports						
Developed countries[3]	-3.0	-6.5	-7.8	-8.8	12.7	6.3
Developing countries	1.7	2.6	3.8	4.1	10.3	9.5
Asian planned countries	[2]0.5	1.1	1.9	1.6	13.8	7.8

[1]Excludes Asian planned economies. [2]Estimated. [3]Includes stock changes and losses.

Source: FAO *Annual Fertilizer Review.*

urgent measures to increase food production in the developing countries "in magnitudes never before undertaken or even planned." He also emphasized that sufficient food stocks must be established on an international basis to meet emergencies such as the spreading famine and starvation in parts of South Asia and the sub-Sahara region of Africa.

Kissinger proposes doubling food output. U.S. Secretary of State Henry A. Kissinger addressed the conference Nov. 5.

U.S. Secretary of State Henry Kissinger also addressed the conference Nov. 5, calling for concerted worldwide action to conquer the "eternal problem" of hunger and famine. He said, "We must act now and we must act together to regain control over our shared destiny. If we do not act boldly, disaster will result from a failure of will."

He set as the objective of the conference that "within a decade no child will go to bed hungry, that no family will fear for its next day's bread, and that no human being's future and capacities will be stunted by malnutrition." This objective would require at least a minimum doubling of food production in the next 25 years, and improvement of its quality, he said.

To accomplish this goal, Kissinger proposed international cooperative action in five areas: increasing production of traditional food exporters; accelerating production in developing countries; improving means of food distribution and financing; enhancing the quality of food; and insuring security against food emergencies by establishing a reserve system, coupled with an early warning information system.

Kissinger called on the conference to organize a reserves coordinating group, composed of all major exporters and importers, to negotiate an international system of nationally held grain reserves. He said such a system, which would determine the size of necessary global reserves to assure food security, should entail international agreements on each nation's responsibilities for reserves, and said guidelines should be set for their management. An information system to share data on reserves, working stocks

and crop prospects, should be established, he said. Kissinger also proposed preference for nations that contributed in the distribution of reserves, and sanctions against those refusing to cooperate.

"A worldwide reserve of as much as 60 million tons of food above present carry-over levels may be needed to assure food security," Kissinger said.

The secretary offered no figures on the prospective size of increased U.S. food aid, although he said the Ford Administration was asking Congress for a $350 million increase in development assistance. He also said the U.S. was prepared to contribute $65 million for nutrition research and special nutrition aid proposals.

He also proposed creation of two other groups: an exporters planning group and a food production and investment coordinating group. The latter would assemble representatives from traditional donors and new financial powers and from multilateral agencies and developing countries. He urged this group to create a subcommittee to finance transfer of food to deficit developing nations. Kissinger emphasized the "special responsibility" of prosperous oil exporting nations to extend aid to poor nations hardest hit by soaring petroleum prices over the last year.

Aid, Kissinger said, should be focused in such strategic areas as developing fertilizer industries and improving storage facilities, transport and pest control in the developing countries.

Noting a 2.5% gap between production and need in developing nations, Kissinger said by 1985 their needed food imports would rise from 25 million tons to 85 million tons. To help meet this need, exporting nations should make an all-out food production effort. Technical assistance could help developing nations boost their food production growth rate from 2.5% annually to 3.5%, which would halve the estimated food deficit, Kissinger said.

He also proposed establishment of a "global nutrition surveillance system" by the World Health Organization, the Food and Agriculture Organization and the U.N. Children's Fund.

Among Kissinger's remarks:

We must act now and we must act together to regain control over our shared destiny. Catastrophe when it cannot be foreseen can be blamed on a failure of vision or on forces beyond our control. But the current trend is obvious and the remedy is within our power. If we do not act boldly, disaster will result from a failure of will; moral culpability will be inherent in our foreknowledge.

The political challenge is straightforward: Will the nations of the world cooperate to confront a crisis which is both self-evident and global in nature? Or will each nation or region or bloc see its special advantages as a weapon instead of as a contribution? Will we pool our strengths and progress together, or test our strengths and sink together?

President Ford has instructed me to declare on behalf of the United States: We regard our good fortune and strength in the field of food as a global trust. We recognize the responsibilities we bear by virtue of our technology, and our tradition of assistance. That is why we proposed this conference. That is why a Secretary of State is giving this address. The United States will make a major effort to match its capacity to the magnitude of the challenge....

We must begin here with the challenge of food. No social system, ideology, or principle of justice can tolerate a world in which the spiritual and physical potential of hundreds of millions is stunted from elemental hunger or inadequate nutrition. National pride or regional suspicions lose any moral and practical justification if they prevent us from overcoming this scourge.

A generation ago many farmers were self-sufficient; today fuel, fertilizer, capital, and technology are essential for their economic survival. A generation ago many nations were self-sufficient; today a good many exporters provide the margin between life and death for many millions.

Thus, food has become a central element of the international economy. A world of energy shortages, rampant inflation, and a weakening trade and monetary system will be a world of food shortages as well. And food shortages in turn sabotage growth and accelerate inflation.

The food problem has two levels: First, coping with food emergency, and second, assuring long-term supplies and an adequate standard of nutrition for our growing populations.

During the 1950's and 1960's global food production grew with great consistency. Per capita output expanded even in the food-deficit nations; the world's total output increased by more than half. But at the precise moment when growing populations and rising expectations made a continuation of this trend essential, a dramatic change occurred: During the past 3 years, world cereal production has fallen; reserves have dropped to the point where significant crop failure can spell a major disaster.

The longer term picture is, if anything, starker still. Even today hundreds of millions of people do not eat enough for decent and productive lives. Since increases in production are not evenly distributed, the absolute number of malnourished people are, in fact, probably greater today than ever before except in times of famine. In many parts of the world 30 to 50 percent of the children die before the age of five, millions of them from malnutrition. Many survive only with permanent damage to their intellectual and physical capacities.

World population is projected to double by the end of the century. It is clear that we must meet the food need that this entails. But it is equally clear that population cannot continue indefinitely to double every generation. At some point we will inevitably exceed the Earth's capacity to sustain human life. The near as well as the long-term challenges of food have three components:

There is the problem of production in the face of population trends. Maintaining even current inadequate levels of nutrition and food security will require that we produce twice as much food by the end of this century. Adequate nutrition would require 150 percent more food, or a total annual output of 3 billion tons of grain.

There is the problem of distribution. Secretary General Marei [Sayed A. Marei of Egypt, Secretary General of the World Food Conference] estimates that at the present rate of growth of 2½ percent a year the gap between what the developing countries produce themselves and what they need will rise from 25 million to 85 million tons a year by 1985. For the foreseeable future, food will have to be transferred on a substantial scale from where it is in surplus to where it is in shortage.

There is the problem of reserves. Protection against the vagaries of weather and disaster urgently requires a food reserve. Our estimate is that as much as 60 million tons over current carryover levels may be required.

In short, we are convinced that the world faces a challenge new in its severity, its pervasiveness, and its global dimension. Our minimum objective of the next quarter century must be to more than double world food production and to improve its quality. To meet this objective the United States proposes to this conference a comprehensive program of urgent, cooperative worldwide action on five fronts.

Increasing the production of food exporters;

Accelerating the production in developing countries;

Improving means of food distribution and financing;

Enhancing food quality; and

Insuring security against food emergencies.

A handful of countries, through good fortune and technology, can produce more than they need and thus are able to export. Reliance on this production is certain to grow through the next decade and perhaps beyond. Unless we are to doom the world to chronic famine, the major exporting nations must rapidly expand their potential and seek to insure the dependable long-term growth of their supplies. . . .

The United States has taken sweeping steps to expand its output to the maximum. It already has 167 million acres under grain production alone, an increase of 23 million acres from 2 years ago. In an address to the Congress last month, President Ford asked for a greater effort still. He called upon every American farmer to produce to full capacity; he directed the elimination of all restrictive practices which raise food prices; he assured farmers that he will use present authority and seek additional authority to allocate the fuel and fertilizer they require; and he urged the removal of remaining acreage limitations.

These efforts should be matched by all exporting countries. Maximum production will require a substantial increase in investment. The best land, the most accessible water, and the most obvious improvements are already in use. Last year the United States raised its investment in agriculture by $2.5 billion. . . .

A comparable effort by other nations is essential. The United States believes that cooperative action among exporting countries is required to stimulate rational planning and the necessary increases in output. We are prepared to join with other major exporters in a common commitment to raise production, to make the necessary investment, and to begin rebuilding reserves for food security. Immediately following the conclusion of this conference, the United States proposes to convene a group of major exporters—an export planning group—to shape a concrete and coordinated program to achieve these goals.

The food exporting nations alone will simply not be able to meet the world's basic needs. Ironically, but fortunately, it is the nations with the most rapidly growing food deficits which also possess the greatest capacity for increased production. They have the largest amounts of unused land and water. While they now have 35 percent more land in grain production than the developed nations, they produce 20 percent less on this land. In short, the largest growth in world food production can—and must—take place in the chronic deficit countries. . . .

International and national research programs must be concentrated on the special needs of the chronic food deficit nations, and they must be intensified. New technologies must be developed to increase yields and reduce costs, making use of the special features of their labor-intensive, capital-short, economies. . . .

The United States is gratified by the progress of two initiatives which we proposed at the Sixth Special Session of the U.N. General Assembly last April: the International Fertilizer Development Center and the study of the impact of climate change on food supply. The Fertilizer Center opened its doors last month in the United States with funds provided by Canada and the United States; we invite wider participation and pledge its resources to the needs of the developing nations. And the important study on climate and food supply has been taken on by the United Nations World Meteorological Organization (WMO). . . .

The events of the past few years have brought home the grave vulnerability of mankind to food emergencies caused by crop failures, floods, wars, and other disasters. The world has come to depend on a few exporting countries, and particularly the United States, to maintain the necessary reserves. But reserves no longer exist, despite the fact that the United States has removed virtually all of its restrictions on production and our farmers have made an all-out effort to maximize output. A worldwide reserve of as much as 60 million tons of food above present carryover levels may be needed to assure adequate food security.

It is neither prudent nor practical for one or even a few countries to be the world's sole holder of reserves. Nations with a history of radical fluctuations in import requirements have an obligation, both to their own people and to the world community, to participate in a system which shares that responsibility more widely. And exporting countries can no longer afford to be caught by surprise. They must have advance information to plan production and exports.

We commend FAO Director General Boerma for his initiative in the area of reserves. The United States shares his view that a cooperative multilateral system is essential for greater equity and efficiency. We therefore propose that this conference organize a Reserves Coordinating Group to negotiate a detailed agreement on an international system of nationally held grain reserves at the earliest possible time. It should include all the major exporters as well as those whose import needs are likely to be greatest. . . .

Butz addresses session—U.S. Agriculture Secretary Earl Butz, in his address to the conference Nov. 6, stressed that the profit motive was the key to greater food security through increased production.

Implicitly calling into question Kissinger's proposals for world food reserves, Butz said no grains currently existed for "an internationally coordinated" food stockpile, unless citizens of developed nations paid more to eat less. However he held out hopes of "substantially larger production" as a result of the opportunity for the farmer "to gain increased returns from the market."

He expressed opposition to locking away "a part of current short food supplies" for reserve because this would call for "less consumption this year, higher food prices and more inflation." Although he indicated willingness to accept a future reserves system, he said he opposed reserves of such a size that they would depress prices, destroy farmer incentives and mask deficiencies in national production efforts.

Butz, as well as Kissinger, ran into considerable opposition from other members of the U.S. delegation, who, according to news reports, wanted the U.S. to make a firm commitment on additional food aid. The Ford Administration wanted to avoid specific figures, according to a senior member of the delegation, because it would drive up commercial grain prices in the U.S.

In another dispute, Sen. Mark O. Hatfield (R, Ore.), one of the Congressional advisers, was reported to have said at a delegation strategy session Nov. 6 that Americans should reduce their consumption of food, particularly meat, to help make more available for starving persons around the world. Butz countered that reducing U.S. meat consumption would not effectively divert grain to developing nations. Animal forage was not edible for humans, Butz said, and even if it were, it could not be transferred immediately because someone would have to pay for it.

(Lester R. Brown, a senior fellow of the Overseas Development Council in Washington, asserted that eight pounds of grain were required to produce one pound of meat, it was reported Nov. 6. He estimated that a 5% reduction in meat consumption in the U.S. would free 6 million tons of grain, equivalent to 60% of the present food shortage in the part of the world faced with mass starvation.)

Other speakers—Canada's secretary of state for external affairs, Allan J. MacEachen, pledged to the conference Nov. 6 that his government would increase its food aid to developing nations by 20% in the next three years, raising total Canadian aid to a million tons a year.

Indian Agriculture Minister Jagjivan Ram called Nov. 6 for creation of a food security council with "stature and authority to evolve a world food policy and oversee and guide its implementation." Kissinger had deleted a similar suggestion from an earlier draft of his address.

Immediate relief discussed—A. H. Boerma, director general of the FAO, organized a private meeting Nov. 6 with principal grain producing nations, including the U.S., Soviet Union and China, and major importers, including India, to tackle the problem of short-term food relief. Boerma produced an FAO paper which estimated the grain shortage in South Asia and sub-Sahara Africa, as of Oct. 15, at 7 million–11 million tons, which at current prices would cost about $2 billion, and in 20 other countries, mainly in Africa, at 1.3 million tons. The neediest countries were India 3.4 million–7.4 million tons; Bangla Desh 1.9 million; Sri Lanka 200,000; Tanzania 500,000; and Pakistan 1 million.

A similar meeting was held Nov. 13, at which the U.S. reportedly questioned the accuracy of the FAO figures, estimating instead that the crop need of the five most threatened nations was 10.5 million tons, of which six million had been met and the rest was "in sight" if financing were found. The Soviet Union was absent from the meeting.

The Saudi Arabian spokesman said Nov. 6 that his nation was mistakenly considered rich and asserted it suffered, along with other oil-producing nations, from many social and economic problems. Saudi Arabia had done more than its share to help developing countries, he insisted.

Alberto Vignes, Argentine foreign minister, said Nov. 6 that the U.S. had exploited developing nations and should pay food in reparation. Algerian President Houari Boumedienne expressed a similar view the same day charging that a "policy of domination" combined with "world inflation, caused and maintained by industrialized countries," had brought developing nations to the verge of famine and disaster.

(A group of 25 internationally known experts, including anthropologist Margaret Mead and Nobel prize-winning crop expert Norman Borlaug, had called Nov. 4 for immediate worldwide expenditures of up to $5 billion to avert mass starvation, estimating the shortage in food grains in 1974–75 at about 20 million tons, and that of fertilizer at one million tons.

(Borlaug was quoted by the New York Times Dec. 11 as saying in Santiago, Chile that the conference "was nonsense.... Nothing tangible was done.... I spent three days ... to help draw up general suggestions.... I left before the conference began because I knew what was going to happen." He warned that millions of people would die in the next eight to nine months in such countries as India and Bangla Desh, where "the deaths ... are going to make the fatalities from starvation caused by drought in the Sahara lands over the last couple of years look like very small numbers.")

*U.S. rejects food increase request—*President Ford Nov. 15 rejected a request by the U.S. delegation at the World Food Conference to announce an immediate doubling of U.S. humanitarian food aid in fiscal 1975 to 2 million tons, valued at $350 million, for nations facing famine.

Announcing the decision in Rome, U.S. Agriculture Secretary Earl Butz, chief of the U.S. delegation, said the increase "would have a bullish effect on the market." He cited budget constraints, tight supplies and pressure on already inflated U.S. consumer food prices.

The Administration decision was in response to a cablegram sent Nov. 8 by the U.S. delegation to Ford. Butz acknowledged signing the cable, but said he was merely passing along the request by three Democratic senators in the delegation. (According to copies of the cable reported in news stories, the proposal appeared to be the sense of the U.S. delegation.) Sen. Mark Hatfield (R, Ore.) had joined the Democrats in persuading Butz to send the cable.

Butz charged that the Democratic senators—Hubert Humphrey (Minn.), Dick Clark (Iowa) and George McGovern (S. D.)—had acted "for partisan political gain" and had embarrassed the U.S. delegation by their pressure. "These things have placed the United States in a position of seeming reluctant to go along with food aid," Butz said. "Nothing could be further from the truth." He noted that the U.S. had given 46% of all food aid to developing nations since 1962.

White House Press Secretary Ron Nessen said Nov. 15 it would be inaccurate to say Ford had "turned down" the request for increased U.S. food aid. He

said the U.S. would honor Secretary of State Henry Kissinger's commitment of increased contributions in the current fiscal year. But Nessen then added that the Administration would await information about crop levels before giving a more specific statement.

(The U.S. had budgeted nearly $1 billion for food aid programs in fiscal 1975, of which 20% had been allotted for the neediest nations, with the bulk used as a prop for U.S. foreign policy. South Vietnam and Cambodia had received much of this aid in the past, and in 1974 substantial shares were planned for Chile, Jordan, Syria and Egypt. Only $175 million was for humanitarian assistance, or outright food donations; the major share was distributed in long-term, low-interest loans with which nations could buy U.S. food.)

U.S. aid record defended. On his return to Washington from the World Food Conference, U.S. Agriculture Secretary Earl Butz Nov. 18 defended the U.S.' food aid record by releasing the following summary of such U.S. assistance since the enactment of Public Law 480 (the Food-for-Peace law) in 1954:

U.S. FOOD AID

In eight years 1965–72, provided 84 percent of all food aid contributions of developed countries (both bilateral and multilateral aid).

46 percent of all World Food Program aid since beginning in 1962. (Canada second with 13 percent)

$25 billion in donations and concessional sales since beginning of P.L. 480 in 1954.

143 million tons of wheat, rice, and other grains since 1954.

Current year: Higher spending level on P.L. 480 than a year ago. More wheat and rice in physical quantities in P.L. 480 programs this year than a year ago.

AID TO BANGLADESH

U.S. has contributed a third of all food aid to Bangladesh since its independence (1972).

Current year U.S. is already programming 250,000 tons of wheat and rice to Bangladesh (Title I).

We are watching food situation closely in Bangladesh.

AID TO INDIA

U.S. leading provider of economic development since India's independence.

Last year, U.S. sent outright donations of $67 million (far more Title II-type programs then any other country).

New shipments of food grains expected soon, inaddition to Title II donations.

AID TO SAHEL

U.S. made direct donations of over a half million tons of grain in FY 1973 and FY 1974. This year, additional donation of 100,000 tons are now moving to the Sahel.

U.S. donated $3.3-million to UN Sahelian Trust Fund through FAO for assuring delivery of food in drought relief programs.

U.S. has donated $29 million for aid supplies including medicine, vitamins, tools and equipment.

U.S. supplied aircraft to assist in delivery.

U.S. is providing technical assistance to improve production in the Sahel.

FERTILIZER DEVELOPMENT AID

in FY 1975, U.S. will provide 329,000 tons of fertilizer valued at $164,000,000.

This could increase substantially during year.

⅔ or more of the amount will be purchased offshore.

DEVELOPMENT AID AND TECHNICAL ASSISTANCE

U.S. has provided more than $1½ billion in last 10 years (much of it for agricultural development).

Current year: FY 1975 budget requested a doubling of FY 1974 development aid with 60 percent earmarked for agriculture.

TRAINING PROVIDED FOR FOREIGN NATIONALS IN U.S.

For 22 years, have averaged over 1000 a year.

OVERSEAS TECHNICAL ASSISTANCE SINCE 1966

An average of 300 USDA people serve overseas in any given year.

Land Grant Colleges have provided more than 1,000 man years since 1960.

P.L. 480 RESEARCH GRANTS

Since 1954, P.L. 480 counterpart funds have provided 1500 research grants in 32 countries.

DIRECT GRANTS TO OVERSEAS RESEARCH CENTERS

USDA provides one-fourth of the budgets for 10 research centers around the world, including IRRI (Philippines) and the Center for maize and wheat improvement in Mexico.

By 1978, these contributions will double.

P.L. 480 PROCEEDS FOR ECONOMIC DEVELOPMENT

In 20 years, $11 billion has been generated by P.L. 480 for development use by foreign countries.

U.S. Action

Food aid cut in '76 budget. President Ford Feb. 3, 1975 submitted a fiscal 1976 budget that proposed an increase in overall foreign aid (from $3.9 billion in fiscal

1975 to $4.1 billion in fiscal 1976) but recommended a cut in food aid.

The budget for the Agency for International Development was set at $1.1 billion for fiscal 1976, about $95 million more than in the prior year.

The foreign food aid expenditures under Public Law 480 were planned at $1.1 billion for fiscal 1976, a decrease of $273 million. The Administration planned a substantial increase in total obligational authority for the program of $1.34 billion in fiscal 1976, a rise from fiscal 1975's authorization of $778 million. This presumably would result in expanded future expenditures.

Ford budgeted less money for direct payments to farmers and for food programs. The latter, including food stamps and child nutrition programs, were allocated $5.4 billion in fiscal 1976, a $411 million drop from the previous year. A proposed increase in the cost of food stamps to the poor was designed to save the government $215 million in fiscal 1975 and, combined with tightened eligibility rules, $650 million in fiscal 1976. Expenditures for the program were budgeted at $3.7 billion for fiscal 1975 and $3.6 billion in fiscal 1976.

Direct federal payments to farmers were budgeted at $401 million, a $605 million decline from fiscal 1975. No payments under the "target price" program for major crops were scheduled for fiscal 1976 because of the anticipation that prices would remain above the price-support trigger.

President Ford March 26, 1975 signed legislation appropriating $3.7 billion in foreign aid for fiscal 1975. (Programs, which otherwise would have been shut down for lack of funding, had been kept running by a series of emergency appropriations resolutions while Congress completed action.)

Ford said he was signing the bill, which was $2.3 billion less than requested, despite "considerable misgivings" about reductions in overseas assistance programs.

Approved March 24 in the Senate by voice vote without debate, the bill faced opposition in the House, where it passed March 24 by a narrow margin of 193-185. Opponents of the bill argued that the money could be better used in the U.S. to help fight the current recession and to help lower the projected federal spending deficit.

The bill contained funds for developmental assistance, postwar reconstruction of Indochina, military aid grants and credit sales, international banks, refugee and disaster aid and United Nations development programs.

Besides drastically cutting Administration requests for postwar Indochina reconstruction aid and for military assistance, Congress appropriated $300 million for food and nutrition, $246 million less than asked.

U.S. grain to India. The U.S. agreed to send India 800,000 tons of wheat valued at $128 million, U.S. officials announced March 20, 1974. The agreement, under negotiations for months, called for the new shipments to be completed by June 30. They would increase total U.S. wheat sales to India to an estimated 5.4 million metric tons in the 1974–75 season, ending June 30. The accord provided for Indian repayment in dollars over 40 years

Congress freezes cost of food stamps. An administrative proposal by President Ford to increase the cost of food stamps March 1 was overwhelmingly rejected by Congress. The House Feb. 4 approved by 374–38 vote a bill blocking food stamp price increases for the remainder of 1975. The Senate followed suit Feb. 5, passing an identical bill 76–8.

The Administration had proposed the increase as part of its effort to stem the rapid growth in the cost of social programs. Under the proposal, the cost of a month's allocation of food stamps would have increased from an average of 23% of recipient families' net income to 30%.

Congressional opponents of the increase argued that it would worsen the plight of the poor and elderly during a time of recession and inflation.

In testimony before the House Agriculture Committee Jan. 30, Edward Hekman, administrator of the Food and Nutrition Service of the Agriculture Department, had defended the proposed increase. Calling it a means of slowing the growth rate of federal expenditures, Hekman asserted the increase would make the program more equitable because "everybody would pay the same thing for food." Hekman, who claimed to have suggested the increase, also said that poor people paid

a lower percentage of income for food than the rest of the population.

Food stamp allotments raised. The Agriculture Department announced April 8 that food stamp allotments would rise 5.2% effective July 1. A family of four that currently paid $25 for $154 worth of stamps would receive $162 in stamps for the same amount of money

Department officials said that because of increased benefits and the quantum leap in the number of persons qualifying, the total cost of the program would be $5 billion in the fiscal year ending June 30 and $6 billion in fiscal 1976.

Meanwhile, the department reported March 31 that the number of persons receiving stamps had increased by 500,000 in February, bringing current total enrollment to 18.4 million persons.

China & U.S.S.R. Halt Wheat from U.S.

China cancels U.S. wheat orders. China canceled contracts to purchase 601,000 tons of U.S. wheat, Cook Industries, Inc. announced Jan. 27, 1975. The firm, a trading company based in Memphis, Tenn., was to have delivered the grain between February and September. The shipment accounted for about 60% of the 991,000 tons of U.S. wheat that was to have been sent to China between then and June 30, 1976, according to U.S. Agriculture Department records.

Peking's cancellation of the wheat order was attributed by diplomatic sources in Washington Jan. 28 to concern over its foreign exchange drain and debts abroad.

China canceled an order for another 382,000 metric tons of U.S. wheat, the U.S. Agriculture Department announced Feb. 27. This order and the previously canceled one covered all the wheat that China had contracted to receive from U.S. exporters during 1975.

Canada sold China 42 million bushels of wheat valued at about $175 million, it was reported April 7. The wheat would be shipped monthly from May 1975 through March 1976. As in previous sales, terms of the contract called for payment of 25% cash when each shipment was loaded in western Canada, with the balance plus interest payable in 18 months.

Moscow cancels wheat purchase. The Soviet Union had cancelled orders for 3.7 million bushels (100,000 tons) of U.S. wheat and was negotiating for the cancellation of a further 7.5 million bushels ordered in 1974, it was disclosed Jan. 29.

The cancellations would represent about a third of the remaining Soviet wheat orders from the 1974 crop. The original purchase had been reduced by the U.S. government in October 1974.

It was reported that the Soviet cancellation had been arranged weeks earlier by executives of Cook Industries, Inc., one of two major U.S. sellers involved in the controversial 1974 grain sale.

The Agriculture Department Feb. 4 approved the sale of 100,000 tons of corn to the Soviet Union, Cook Industries, Inc. said. Moscow had asked to make the corn purchase in place of the canceled wheat shipment, Agriculture officials confirmed.

According to Feb. 4 reports, the trade developments came as revised data was released on 1974 Soviet grain crops, showing that wheat production had fallen sharply from the 1973 level and was well below December 1974 forecasts.

The reported crop failure suggested, according to the New York Times Feb. 4, that the Soviet wheat purchase cancellation had stemmed partly from temporary congestion at some ports. It was also noted that wheat prices had dropped since the Soviet Union had made its purchases in 1974 and that the cancellation indicated Moscow's unwillingness to take a loss if forced to resell the wheat.

U.S. grain export curbs eased. U.S. Agriculture Secretary Earl Butz announced Jan. 29, 1975 that export curbs on wheat and soybeans would be eased. The restrictions had been set in October 1974 because of soaring food prices and fears of domestic shortages, prompted in part by a controversial Soviet grain purchase.

Butz said the action "returns the export trade in wheat and soybeans virtually to a free basis, following a period in which tight supplies forced us into a program where the possibility of export controls was to a degree implicit." The new regulations doubled to 100,000 tons the quantity

of wheat or soybeans that an exporter could sell to any one destination in a single day without government approval and to 200,000 tons the quantity permitted sold to a single destination in a week. Butz noted that U.S. supplies of wheat and soybeans had increased and that it therefore was unnecessary to keep so close a watch on export sales.

However, the 50,000-ton-a-day and 100,000-ton-a-week regulations would be maintained on corn and feed grains until the supply situation became clearer.

(The Agriculture Department reported Jan. 24 that supplies of wheat in storage were 19% higher than a year earlier; storage supplies of livestock feed grains— corn, oats, barley and sorghum—were down 22%. The department reported Jan. 25 that at the beginning of 1975 the nation's supplies of feed grains on hand totaled 114 million tons. The nation's 1974 corn crop was 18% smaller than the previous year's harvest. The crop totaled 4.65 billion bushels and yield per acre was down sharply. The total 1974 production of all crops declined 8% from 1973's record level to a level 110% of the 1967 average.)

Butz had commented Jan. 28 on the Chinese cancellation of a 601,000-ton wheat purchase, saying it would have no appreciable effect on U.S. consumers. The cancellation, he stated, confirmed that China had "a better food production year in 1974" and "signifies that Chinese foreign exchange is not as strong as before."

Meat Surplus & Import Curbs

While developing countries continued to suffer serious shortages of grain and other basic food supplies during 1974–75, the major livestock producing countries had an oversupply of meat animals. Many of them took action to protect the local markets of domestic producers by imposing curbs on the import of meat and livestock.

Canada curbs meat imports. The Canadian government announced regulations, effective April 9, 1974, to limit the importation of meat and livestock. Temporary beef subsidies of 7¢ a pound had been instituted March 15 in another move to protect and assist the depressed national cattle market.

The new import rules, disclosed by Agriculture Minister Eugene Whelan, required certification by the federal authorities of the exporting country that the animals involved had not been given the growth-stimulating hormone, diethylstilbesterol, known as DES. The drug's use as a livestock feed additive was illegal in Canada.

Whelan described the move as a "protection for the consumer" rather than an "embargo," but he admitted that consumer prices might rise. Price drops had been predicted, but did not occur, following establishment of the March 15 subsidy.

Canadian cattle industry spokesmen were critical of both the subsidy and certification programs, which they regarded as stop-gap efforts applied without sufficient consultation with the industry. Whelan had announced March 6 that the government was "seriously considering" the demands by Canadian cattlemen for interim tariffs and a long-term quota system to protect them against rising imports. (U.S. cattle imports had risen 14-fold in the past year, depressing the price of Canadian livestock. The all-time high prices reported in August 1973 had plummeted about 25% to $43 a hundredweight.)

U.S. exports totaling more than $150 million annually were immediately effected by the import restrictions.

The Canadian government later lifted its ban on U.S. meat imports Aug. 2, announcing that Ottawa and Washington had agreed on a certification system that would assure that no cattle fed with DES would enter Canada.

At the same time, Canada also imposed cattle and beef import quotas and set up a price support program to protect the domestic market. Removal of the import ban was expected to bring lower meat prices in Canada.

U.S. President Ford Nov. 16 ordered quotas on importation of beef and pork from Canada, charging that Ottawa had erected "unjustifiable import restrictions" against U.S. products.

Ford contended that the Canadian meat restrictions "violate the commitments of Canada made to the U.S.,... oppress the commerce of the U.S. and prevent the expansion of trade on a mutually advantageous basis." Secretary of Agriculture Earl Butz said Nov. 18 that Washington was willing to drop its new quotas if Canada eliminated the restrictions on U.S. imports.

Prime Minister Pierre Elliott Trudeau told the Canadian Parliament Nov. 18 that his government was "most urgently" studying the U.S. action which, it was estimated, could cost Canada more than $100 million.

The White House set the following 12-month quotas, retroactive to Aug. 12: 17,-000 head of cattle; 50,000 head of swine; and 17 million pounds of fresh, chilled, frozen, prepared or preserved beef and veal. These quotas compared with the Canadian quotas of 82,000 head of cattle and 17.9 million pounds of beef and veal.

Previously, Canadian Agriculture Minister Eugene Whelan had announced May 8 that imports of U.S. eggs and turkeys would be limited to amounts equal to average imports during the last five years. The move was aimed at stopping the imports from undercutting the prices to Canadian producers.

(U.S. farmers, faced with falling prices in the domestic market, had been taking advantage of higher selling prices in Canada and selling heavily there; Canadian egg and turkey production was controlled by national marketing agencies which kept prices up by disposing of surplus eggs and turkey meat.)

Whelan had said May 2 that the egg industry was "in utter chaos and nearly broke" as a result of the influx of U.S. eggs. Canadian eggs and turkeys were being marketed below production cost and 50 million eggs had gone into storage because of the cheaper U.S. prices.

Canada announced a $20 million-to-$25 million subsidy program Dec. 13 to help cattlemen cope with the current slump in the beef industry. It also set plans to buy $10 million of low-grade beef for food aid.

Farmers had been attempting to relieve a glut in the cattle market—with 15 million head, 6.1% higher than in 1973—by selling cows in the hope that prices would rise when the cattle population dropped. The government program would set a support price of 23.21¢ a pound on low-grade beef sold between Nov. 16 and April 30, 1975.

EEC suspends beef imports. Agriculture ministers of the European Economic Community (EEC) July 16, 1974 approved a ban on most imports of beef from nonmember countries until Nov. 1. The action, designed to reduce the community's estimated 133,000-ton beef surplus, would replace the current program under which beef importers had to match purchases from abroad with purchases from EEC stockpiles.

The ministers, meeting in Brussels, also approved other measures, including sales of beef to poor persons at cut-rate prices; special premiums on a monthly rising scale to farmers for delaying slaughter of their cattle until February, when supply was normally lowest. (The payments between November–February 1974 would be financed mainly out of EEC funds, while national governments would pay the bill until November.)

The ban on beef imports excluded a 34,000-ton annual quota protected under rules of the General Agreement on Tariffs and Trade. France and Ireland had pressed for the import ban, while Britain had demanded the delayed slaughter premiums.

U.S. State Department spokesman Robert Anderson said July 18 that the U.S. "deeply regrets" the European measures. U.S. officials feared that the ban could cause beef producing nations to divert exports from the EEC to the U.S.

Argentina and Uruguay, beef exporters to the EEC, had sent protest notes to the community over the action, the French newspaper Le Monde reported July 28. (The EEC Commission had announced July 1 an increase of about 25% on export rebates for most beef products in an attempt to encourage overseas sales, and the agriculture ministers in Luxembourg June 4 had authorized overseas sales of 17,000 tons of surplus frozen beef at cut-rate prices.

The surplus crisis had been created after the EEC sharply raised guaranteed beef prices in early 1973 to stimulate a switch from milk to beef production. This caused a 15%–20% increase in production and sharply lower prices.

Farmers' protests—The agricultural ministers' decisions came after mounting demonstrations by cattle raisers and farmers in France and Belgium to press demands for aid to bolster their sagging incomes. Aside from the import of cheap agricultural products, the farmers were protesting the restriction on prices for their own goods under anti-inflation programs, coupled with soaring production costs, particularly sharp increases in the cost of farm machinery.

Belgian livestock producers and farmers blocked roads with tractors and other agricultural machinery in the Ardennes area of Belgium July 15–16. The protests continued around Liege July 17, with the farmers arguing that the action by the EEC ministers the day before failed to help other livestock producers or crop farmers.

French farmers and livestock producers, who had begun their demonstrations in early July, accelerated their protests July 10–16. Participating in the protests were the cattle and pig breeders in the west, the vegetable producers in the north and fruit growers in the southwest and Provence. Among their actions: they loosed pigs in the streets, distributed free meat to canteens and schools, dumped farmyard manure in town centers and blocked highways with farm machinery. On July 14–15, peasants drove cows on the Deauville beaches frequented by prominent society; dumped shiploads of Argentine meat into the harbor at Le Havre; discarded a cargo of British meat in the northeast and a truckload of Belgian pigs near Lille and dumped tons of peaches in front of the prefecture in Valence.

France, Belgium act—In the face of the continuing wave of farmers' unrest, France and Belgium took separate government actions to aid their agricultural sectors after the EEC ministerial decisions July 16.

The French Cabinet approved an "immediate salvage plan" July 17, which provided price support measures, including subsidies for livestock producers, storage aids for cheese farmers, grants to egg producers and credits to farmers hit by soaring production costs.

Violent demonstrations continued July 18, with French farmers placing nails on a highway south of Bordeaux so that the

Tour de France bicycle race had to be delayed. Another demonstration forced postponement of the inauguration of the Orleans-Tours highway.

(The French government July 12 had increased by 12% the threshold price for lamb and mutton imports, a move designed to halt cheap imports.)

French farmers, wine growers and fishermen staged further militant demonstrations Aug. 1-2.

In Belgium, amid continuing farmers' protests, the government July 31 approved a $40 million plan that would reduce farmers' taxes and provide direct government payments for meat producers and farmers in the poorer rural districts.

In the Netherlands, demonstrations were staged by farmers Aug. 1-2 in an apparent attempt to gain government financial support. The farmers blocked roads with tractors and farm machinery.

Soviet beef sale reported—The Soviet Union had purchased about 50,000 tons of beef from a French-led consortium of private companies, according to sources cited in July 26 reports. Delivery had reportedly begun in June.

The sources denied there were any special pricing arrangements, although they conceded that dealers were able to benefit from the EEC export rebates in offering a price of $830 a ton, compared with the world market price of nearly $1,-000 a ton.

The EEC spent nearly $118 million in subsidies in 1974 to dispose of beef, mostly to the U.S.S.R., according to EEC Commission sources cited in a London Times report Jan. 17, 1975. The EEC sold about 130,000 tons of beef abroad out of a surplus of 360,000 tons, the sources said.

About 85,000 tons were sold to the U.S.S.R., 70,000 tons of it from France. Other countries buying surplus EEC beef included Bulgaria, Iran, Israel and Greece.

The subsidies were needed to make the EEC's prices competitive with lower world market prices.

Uruguayan crisis—Uruguayan slaughtering had been curbed in 1974 because of difficulties in exporting beef to Uruguay's traditional market, the European Eco-

nomic Community, caused by high tariffs imposed by France and Italy, according to the Andean Times' Latin America Economic Report April 12, 1974.

Uruguay's storage facilities were completely filled, and some 15,000 tons of unsold meat were stored in Buenos Aires, the newsletter Latin America had reported March 22. Uruguayan cattle breeders had held finished steers off the market in 1973 in hopes of a rise in the world beef price, contributing to the current surplus.

U.S. livestock loans. President Nixon July 26, 1974 signed a bill providing $2 billion in government-backed emergency loans to livestock producers. Final action on the legislation came after the Senate gave voice vote approval to a conference report July 17. The House had passed the bill July 16 on a 210-204 vote divided along rural and urban lines.

The bill set a $2 billion ceiling on the credit extended to cattlemen and other livestock producers, set the maximum loan to any borrower at $250,000, and set loans for three years—renewable for an additional two. The loan program would run for one year, but could be extended another six months at the request of the secretary of agriculture. Interest levels would be at normal market rates.

Opponents of the bill, which was aimed primarily at benefiting the depressed cattle industry, labeled the measure a "great beefdoggle" that would provide little relief to consumers. Proponents argued that without federal credit, livestock producers would be forced out of business, thereby reducing the nation's available meat supplies and generating higher prices.

U.S.' 1975 beef import curbs. A compromise plan for U.S. beef imports in 1975 was announced by the Agriculture Department Dec. 31, 1974. The plan would limit imports to 1.15 billion pounds, an increase of 85 million pounds from the expected 1974 level of receipts, but voluntary restraint agreements would be negotiated with major exporting nations to keep the volume of imports from exceeding a "trigger level" that would require the government to set a formal import quota of 1.074 billion pounds.

Roncallo on cause of meat glut. Rep. Angelo D. Roncallo (R, N.Y.) discussed the causes of the meat oversupply March 14, 1975 in a statement printed in the Congressional Record. According to Roncallo:

The causes of the problem are many. The industry has been moving in recent years toward the present cyclical oversupply problem. Today there are simply too many cattle. In January 1974, there were 127.6 million head of cattle worth $321 per head, in this country. On January 1, 1975, there were 131.8 million head of cattle worth only $127 per head. The price per head is now 40 percent of that of 1 year ago. This cycle will most likely not peak for another 2 years.

The oversupply problem was compounded last year by a large rise in feed grain costs. For years, a policy of subsidized, cheap grain encouraged expansion of livestock production. Then, suddenly, changed world demand and export situations—in addition to an unexpectedly short crop due to drought conditions last summer throughout much of the Midwest, contributed to a devastating runup in feed costs. . . .

The magnitude of the problems facing producers today can only be understood in terms of how a crisis in this industry affects the overall economy. The beef cattle industry is the largest segment of American agriculture. Cattle sales in 1973 totaled $22.1 billion, or more than one-fourth of all cash receipts from farm marketing. This level becomes more understandable when it is compared with the steel mills, and their annual sales of $35.2 billion, or motor vehicles, and sales of $77.2 billion.

There are 1.9 million full- and part-time beef cattle operators across the country. . . .

A nation of 'beef-eaters.' The U.S. Labor Department April 16, 1975 issued a preliminary report of a survey of U.S. consumer spending and earnings. The study confirmed that the U.S. was a nation of "beef-eaters and gasoline consumers," according to Julius Shiskin, commissioner of labor statistics.

Among the survey's findings: the average family spend 15% of its home food budget on beef purchases, with the proportion rising as income increased; higher-income families spent more than one-third of their food budgets on eating

out; gasoline expenditures accounted for 50% of a family's direct energy purchases; the average family spend $30.32 for its entire weekly food budget.

The data were gathered from diaries kept by more than 10,000 families for two years beginning in mid-1972.

International Cooperation

Kissinger's proposals. At a meeting of the Organization for Economic Cooperation & Development (OECD) in Paris May 28, 1975, U.S. State Secretary Kissinger again sounded the theme of cooperation between the developing and industrial nations. Warning that "economic issues are turning into central political issues," the secretary said the economic well-being of the West "depends on a structure of international cooperation in which the developing nations are, and perceive themselves to be, participants." He added: "The new problems of our era—insuring adequate supplies of food, energy and raw materials—require a world economy that accommodates the interests of developing as well as developed countries."

The U.S., Kissinger said, was prepared to assist in providing long-term stability and growth in the export earnings of developing countries. He announced two specific decisions along this line: the contribution of $1 billion to increase food production in developing countries and American support of the creation of a special trust fund of up to $2 billion under the International Monetary Fund to financially assist the poorest countries.

The OECD ministers later issued a "declaration on relations with developing countries" pledging greater cooperative efforts, including the resumption of talks on energy matters that also would deal with the subject of food and other raw materials.

Latin agency proposed. The creation of the Latin American Economic System (SELA), a regional unit that would exclude the U.S., was formally proposed March 20, 1975 by Presidents Luis Echeverria of Mexico and Carlos Andres Perez of Venezuela.

The two leaders issued a joint communique in Mexico City, during a state visit by Perez, inviting the heads of state of 24 nations in Latin America and the Caribbean to appoint representatives to organize constituent meetings for SELA.

"Latin American nations must rely on their own, permanent system of consultation and economic cooperation . . . which should be capable of truly and effectively responding to their common needs and aspirations," the communique stated.

Among the "broad aims" of SELA cited in the communique:

■ To promote national and regional development projects and the creation of Latin American multinational companies.

■ To defend the prices of Latin American raw materials and manufactured goods, to insure foreign markets for them, and to guarantee their regular supply to Latin American nations.

■ To help improve food supplies to all countries in Latin America—particularly those of relatively lower economic development—and to create regional multinational schemes for the production and supply of fertilizers.

■ To promote the acquisition of capital goods and technology for the region, and to foster scientific and technical cooperation among Latin American nations and among world, inter-American and subregional organizations.

Venezuelan and Mexican representatives had traveled throughout Latin America and the Caribbean in late February and early March seeking support for SELA. Mexican National Patrimony Minister Francisco Javier Alejo, who visited a number of countries and conferred with their presidents, asserted March 12 that SELA was endorsed by all nations in the region, including Brazil.

Triage & 'lifeboat ethics.' According to many observers, the food crisis of the 1970s gives the rich, food producing nations the unhappy duty of deciding which starving people will be fed and which will be left to die. Two proposals as to how this decision should be made have been widely discussed under the labels "triage" and "lifeboat ethics."

"Triage," from the French word "trier" (to sort), is based on the World War I medical practice of dividing the wounded into three groups—(1) those who would

die regardless of treatment, (2) those who would live regardless of treatment and (3) those who would live only with medical care. Since medical manpower and supplies were limited, medical treatment was given only to the third group. In a book entitled "Famine—1975!" (published in 1967), William and Paul Paddock proposed a similar way of dealing with starving nations—sending food to nations whose people will live only if they receive such assistance but denying it to (a) those who would survive without help or (b) those who would not make it in the long run even if food were provided. The latter category was made up of "nations in which the population growth trend has already passed the agricultural potential," the Paddocks said. "This, combined with inadequate leadership and other divisive factors, makes catastrophic disasters inevitable. . . . To send food to them is to throw sand in the ocean."

A perhaps harsher proposal was advanced in the September 1974 issue of Psychology Today by Dr. Garrett Hardin, a University of California biologist and ecologist. In his article "Lifeboat Ethics: The Case Against Helping the Poor," Hardin compares the situation of the rich and poor nations to that of people (the rich) in a lifeboat while "in the ocean outside . . . swim the poor of the world." To allow all the swimmers into the boat would cause it to founder and doom all. To admit even a few would mean the loss of an essential "safety factor." Hardin suggests that the sharing of lifeboat room in such circumstances "is impossible" and that for the rich nations to share their food with the poor under current conditions would be similarly foolhardy.

The Paddock and Hardin "triage" and "lifeboat ethics" theories were widely attacked but also, although to a much lesser extent, defended. Sen. Mark O. Hatfield (R., Ore.), one of the most vehement critics of the proposals, asserted in a letter to Psychology Today that "the 'benign neglect' Dr. Hardin suggests will result in precisely what he wants to avoid. Refusal to feed the poor of the world will not stop their population growth—we have been refusing to do so for years and it has not done so—it will only put us in that 'lifeboat,' and I doubt that we could, even if we wanted to, defend our island of affluence in a hungry, impoverished world."

Documents

Malthus & the World Food Crisis

The U.S. House Agriculture Committee's Subcommittee on Department Operations, headed by Rep. Eligio (Kika) de la Garza (D, Tex.), held hearings July 23–25, 1974 on "the world food supply, demand, and population equation, world food reserves relative to the stocks on hand and the general policy question." The information and ideas developed at these hearings were summarized in a subcommittee report entitled "Malthus and America, A Report About Food and People." Major sections of this report are abridged below.

During the hearings, Dr. Don Paarlberg, Director of Agricultural Economics, U.S. Department of Agriculture, was asked about Thomas Malthus. He replied as follows:

Thomas Robert Malthus was a British clergyman and economist who lived about 200 years ago. He came up with the proposition that the food supply grows by arithmetic increments, two, four, six, eight, ten; but the population grows by a geometric ratio, two, four, eight, sixteen, thirty-two. And he came to the conclusion that inevitably, therefore, food supplies were going to be insufficient to provide for the population and that hunger and want and starvation were the natural lot of men. He did this writing about 200 years ago.

Shortly after he wrote, there came some striking developments, there came the advance of technology and the opening up of the New World, and in the Western World for quite a time, contrary to Malthus, the food supply ran ahead of the population growth. Meanwhile, in much of Asia, the Malthusian principle was operating.

Now in modern times with the success of medicine and the reduction of the death rate, there is a revival of concern about the ability of the world to feed its people.

123

Population & the Demand for Food

The earth's population is growing at such a fantastic rate that all of us are going to be drastically affected by that phenomenon. A quick look at how fast our world's population is growing tells us that.

From the time man-creatures first stood erect until the year 1830 there were less than one billion people in the world.

In the *next 100 years* a second billion souls appeared.

In the *next 30 years* (by 1960) a third billion was present and accounted for.

In the *next 15 years* (by 1975) the fourth billion will be here.

In the *next decade* (by 1985) we can look forward to meeting the fifth billion of our fellow humans.

By the end of this century we can expect 6.5 to 7.5 billion people on our globe at the present rate of growth. And if current rates were to prevail, our lineal descendants would, during the following century, populate the earth with 37 billion folks. . . . a number staggering to even our most fanciful imagination.

Take some key countries: *India*—now with a population of 650 million and growing by twelve million plus per year—can look to the year 2000 to having over a billion people within her borders.

Bangladesh—a nation the size of the State of Wisconsin—is expected to have almost as many people within its borders by the year 2000 as now populate the entire United States of America. *Mexico*—our good neighbor to the south, with 48 percent of her population under the age of 15—will have approximately 1.3 billion inhabitants in another century if present population trends continue.

And so it goes in nearly every developing country of the world— the unrelenting geometry of human growth! Even though population growth continues to be rapid and is causing severe problems in parts of the world today, rising affluence now has emerged as another claimant on the world's food-producing resources. The impact of population growth on the demand for food is easy to understand. A 3 percent increase in population generates a 3 percent increase in the demand for food, but the impact of rising affluence complicates the picture and is not as easily understood. One method of measuring the affluence factor is in terms of per capita grain requirements. For example, in the less developed countries, approximately 400 pounds of grain per year is available to the average person, nearly all of which must be consumed directly merely to meet minimal food energy needs. Very little of this grain can be converted into livestock products. Contrast this example to the average North American who uses nearly a ton of grain per year. Of this ton, less than 200 pounds is consumed directly as bread, pastry, and breakfast cereal. The remaining 1800 pounds plus is consumed indirectly in the form of meat, milk and eggs.

Thus, the average North American currently uses up five times as many agricultural resources as the average Indian, Nigerian or Colombian.

The combined effect of population growth and rising affluence is accelerating world food demand at rates without precedent in history. At the turn of the century, the annual increase in the global demand for cereals was approximately four million tons per year. By 1950 it was about 12 million tons per year. Twenty years.later, as of 1970, the world demand for cereals was expanding by 30 million tons per year—the equivalent of the annual wheat crops of Canada, Australia, and 'Argentina combined. Most importantly, this increase in demand is incessant, occuring in years of good weather and bad weather alike.

The eminent statesman and philosopher from the British Isles, C. G. Snow, speaking in Fulton, Missouri, in the late 1960's stated that he had little reason to believe that the Developing World (the so-called "Third World") would be able to head off a collision between "soaring population" and a "limited food supply." He went on to forewarn "most informed opinions believe that the collision is going to take place. At best, this will mean local famine to begin with; at worst the local famines will spread into a sea of hunger." Lord Snow went on to further predict an initial collision date sometime between 1975 and 1980. It now appears that his prediction was tragically accurate. The "local famines" began in 1973. During 1974, conservative estimates are that somewhere between 200 and 400 million of our fellow human beings will stare starvation directly in the face. Over 10 million persons—most of them children five years of age and under—will perish as a direct result of too little food to eat.

Whether these "local famines will spread into a sea of hunger" depends, amongst other things, on the response of our own and other governments.

The Department Operations Subcommittee offers the following observations on the subject of population as it relates to food and nutrition:

The Subcommittee has found that a great deal of progress has been made in understanding the interrelationships of health, nutrition, and population. However, it appears that our overseas experiences may dictate major changes in traditional approaches and assumptions. There is little doubt that available food supplies from exporting nations such as ours will likely go to countries who can pay. This, of course, increases the likelihood for nutritional disasters to occur and short term food distribution programs will continue to be necessary. This also suggests we must become more judicious than we have been in past patterns of mass shipments of food to chronically deficient areas. The ability of the poor to feed themselves must be developed, which requires effort and attention to mechanisms for proper distribution.

The Subcommittee found that in all probability, the world can expect more, rather than less, disasters associated with malnutrition. The world food crisis will not disappear spontaneously or soon, and maybe never.

The Subcommittee observed from field studies that have recently been conducted that there is a basis for hope, but solutions will probably have to come from the hard, slow process of developing services at village levels and not from simple mass distribution of food. Researchers have found that the greatest probable cause of death, disability, and retarded development around the world today is a synergism between malnutrition and common infections. Potential retardation of growth and development because of malnutrition has even more serious implications for national development than high mortality or morbidity. Obviously, poorly nourished individuals have low productivity because they are not strong enough to work. More significant still are recent findings on reduced physical and mental development—i.e., prenatally and during infancy, children seem susceptible to retardation due to malnutrition even though it is not yet clear how much of the brain damage is biological and how much is due to lack of stimulation that one fails to receive during important stages of growth.

Nonetheless, there is clearly a direct interaction between health, nutrition, and population. Family planning appears to be one of the most effective measures for improving health and nutrition. In fact, around the world, a large number of births per family and short birth intervals are associated with high mortality and morbidity, and population growth interferes with health and nutrition programs. Conversely, better health and nutrition is an important factor in reducing the rate of population growth. Birth rates and death rates both have to decline, and the objective is to have a minimal lag between them. Field research indicates that people will not stop having children until they are certain that those they already have are going to survive so that they will be assured of having someone to support them when they become aged and unable to care for themselves. Consequently, the Subcommittee concludes that while we should maintain strong international support for population programs, we should also begin to emphasize more strongly our support for health and nutrition programs.

The Subcommittee suggests further that our Government and our people carefully consider these policy goals:

(a) A goal of global population stabilization by the year 2000 be established based on providing every woman in the developing world of childbearing age with the information and contraceptive assistance necessary for her to voluntarily space or limit the size of her family.

(b) A goal of at least one population census in every developing nation by 1985, giving particular attention to data relevant to planning and formulation of population policies.

(c) A goal of research of the broadest nature relating to the social, cultural, and economic determinants of population growth as well as the scientific development of more effective contraceptive devices.

(d) A goal of a major global program of education, information, and training on population subjects and population areas.

(e) A goal for the adoption of an individual population policy by every member nation of the United Nations by 1976 based on the individual needs and problems of each sovereign country.

Factors Related to Production

On the supply side of the equation, three sets of factors are beginning to affect efforts to augment world food output as rapidly as is necessary:

1. Technical and financial constraints are limiting the rapid expansion of food production, particularly beef and soybeans.

2. All four of the major resources necessary to produce food—land, water, energy, and fertilizer—are now in short supply.

3. In a growing number of situations the pressures of growing

demand for food are beginning to undermine the ecology of major food producing systems.

The inability to achieve technological breakthroughs in critical areas is a significant constraint in the expansion of food supplies. In the case of beef, agricultural scientists have not been able to devise any commercially viable means of producing more than one calf per cow per year. For every animal entering the beef production process one additional animal must be fed and otherwise maintained. A breakthrough in this area does not appear to be imminent according to beef production experts.

Another example of technological limitation is the inability of scientists to dramatically increase per acre yield of soybeans. Soybeans are a major source of high quality protein for livestock and poultry throughout the world and in East Asia they are consumed directly as food by perhaps a billion people. Soybeans are therefore extremely important in economic terms. They have become the leading export of the United States, surpassing not only more traditional farm exports such as wheat and corn, but also highly technological items such as electric computers and jet aircraft. Yet since 1950, soybean yields per acre have increased by only about 1 percent per year, while corn yields have increased by nearly 4 percent per year. Thus the world gets more soybeans only by planting more acres to soybeans. As of 1973 one of every six acres of United States farmland was planted to soybeans, as idled cropland disappears in the United States. The inability to achieve a soybean yield breakthrough may create serious global supply problems.

The world is now also in a uniquely serious situation regarding the supply of land, water, energy, and fertilizer. For the first time in modern history there are shortages of each of these critical agricultural resources. From the beginning of agriculture until about 1950, most of the year-to-year increase in world food output came from expansion of the area under cultivation. Since 1950, however, the major increases, probably four-fifths of the current gains in output, are attributable to intensification of cultivation on existing cropland. Most of the good cropland in the world is already under cultivation. There are currently about 3.5 billion acres of cropland in the world including all tree crops, regular fallow and rotational pasture. The U.S. Department of Agriculture and the Food and Agriculture Organization estimate that about 6.6 billion acres of potentially arable land exist in the world. The estimated cost of reclaiming substantial new lands would be phenomenal—in the neighborhood of $450 billion. About 70 percent of the earth's surface is water. Of the remaining 30 percent which is land (33 billion acres), one-twentieth is under polar ice or tundra, one-fifth is mountain chains, one-tenth is in subpolar regions, one-fourth is desert, and only slightly more than one-tenth is currently cropland. The inescapable conclusion is that food production from the 3.5 billion acres currently under cultivation must be dramatically increased if mass starvation of many of the world's citizens is to be avoided.

The 1974 world food supply-demand equation is precariously balanced. A poor harvest in any major producing country—the United

States, the Soviet Union, India or China is sure to send economic
shock waves, not only throughout the food sector of the world economy,
but as it fuels the fires of inflation throughout its other sectors as well.
The vulnerability of the supply-demand balance to the weather suggests that the climate itself might well replace pollution as the dominant global environmental concern.

The principal constraint on efforts to expand world food supplies
during the final years of this century may well be water and climate,
rather than land. In many regions of the world fertile agricultural land
is still available, provided that water can be found to make it productive, but most of the rivers that lend themselves to damming and to
irrigation have already been developed. Thus, while the world's
irrigated areas expanded by nearly 3 percent annually between 1950
and 1970, it will probably grow at barely 1 percent a year in the final
remaining years of this century. Since water is becoming an increasingly scarce commodity, man will have to pay more attention to the
efficiency with which crops, particularly cereals, use water.

Climatic trends can cause radically different consequences in various
countries. A temperature change of a degree or two downward in the
latitudes above 40° north in North America may not sound very im-
pressive, but such a change could completely eliminate wheat and
corn production in growing districts of Canada during the deterioration. At the same time in some areas of the United States the wheat
and corn crop yields could increase.

Ecological implications of highly intensive food production efforts
must be considered. New signs of agricultural stress appear almost daily
as the growing demand for food presses against our ecosystem's finite
capacities. Interventions by early agricultural men were local in effect,
but the technological intrusions of modern agriculture often have
global consequences. Efforts to expand the food supply, either by
expanding the area under cultivation or intensifying cultivation
through the use of agricultural chemicals and irrigation, bring with
them troublesome and disturbing ecological consequences. Accelerating soil loss, problems caused by irrigation and eutrophication of
streams and lakes due to increased use of chemical fertilizers are pressing ecological dangers associated with efforts to increase food production. Enlarging livestock herds for food and draft power has caused
overgrazing and the inevitable erosion that follows. Nature requires
centuries to create topsoil and man can destroy it in only a few years.
Deforestation has been followed by erosion in many parts of the world.

Damming the Nile at Aswan expanded the irrigated area for producing cereals but largely eliminated the annual deposits of rich alluvial
silt on fields in the Nile valley, forcing farmers to rely more on chemical
fertilizers. Additionally, interrupting the flow of nutrients into the Nile
caused a precipitous decline in the fish catch there.

Efforts to intensify agricultural yields also have adverse environmental consequences. The water runoff from agricultural land carries
chemical fertilizer with it, raising the nutrient content of streams and
lakes throughout the world, causing them to eutrophy. Thousands of
freshwater lakes are threatened throughout North America and
Europe and increasingly in poor countries where fertilizer use in rice
paddies is resulting in eutrophication of local lakes and ponds, depriv-

ing them of fish, a traditional source of animal protein. The cost to mankind of losing these lakes is staggering.

The market price of food reflects only a portion of the true cost of food production. An unwillingness to tolerate some of the environmental costs of indefinitely expanding the food supply is beginning to translate into constraints on food production. Many countries have banned, or severely limited the use of DDT, dieldrin, and other chlorinated hydrocarbons, a group of cheap highly effective pesticides. In the United States, a growing number of State and local governments are banning the use of phosphates in detergents because of eutrophication. No one knows how many species of birds, fish, and mammals must be sacrificed to achieve a moderate increase in the world's food supply. We do know that as the number of people in the world increases, the number of extant species goes down. In the long run, willingness to pay the total true costs of expanding the world's food supply will surely diminish.

Increasing world food production also requires a substantial increase in the amount of *energy* available for doing so. The recent tripling of the world price of energy is certain to affect future food production prospects, but no one can yet foresee exactly how. In the more modern agricultural systems, such as that of the United States, the amount of energy now used to produce food exceeds by several times the amount of food energy the crops themselves yield. But as energy-intensive as farm production is, it consumes less than one-fourth of the energy used in the United States food system. The rest is used to transport, process, preserve, and distribute the food. In the developing countries, the future availability of energy will have a profound effect on efforts to provide adequate nutrients, for large increases in energy imports will be necessary if food production in these nations is to increase rapidly.

Fertilizer is in very short supply. The outlook in this case also is for generally higher prices in the future. One reason for the fertilizer shortage is a lag in the construction of new production facilities; but even when supply catches up with demand, the rising cost of energy will undoubtedly keep fertilizer prices well above the historical level. The production of nearly all of the world's nitrogen fertilizer utilizes natural gas or naphtha as a raw material. In addition, the manufacturing process is an energy intensive one requiring large amounts of electrical power. The combination of soaring energy prices, the enormous capital requirements needed to create new production facilities, and the time required to bring new facilities into production means that nitrogen fertilizer will be in critically short supply for many years at least.

World Food Stocks

Since World War II the world has been fortunate to have, in effect, two major food "reserves"—one in the form of grain stocks in the principal exporting countries, and the other in the form of reserve cropland, virtually all in the United States. These two "reserves" have provided a valuable degree of price stability, since their size could be adjusted to compensate for production fluctuation. Most importantly, they have provided a critical safety valve when crop failures or droughts have created major unexpected import needs, as in India or the Soviet Union.

Grain stocks, including substantial quantities of both foodgrains and feedgrains, are most commonly measured in terms of carry-over stocks—the amount in storage at the time the new crop begins to come in. World carry-over stocks are concentrated in a few of the principal exporting countries, namely, the United States, Canada, Australia, and Argentina. Since 1960, world grain stocks have fluctuated from a high of 155 million metric tons to a low of about 100 million metric tons. When these stocks drop to 100 million tons, severe shortages and strong upward price pressures develop. Although 100 million tons appears to be an enormous quantity of grain, it represents a mere 8 percent of annual world grain consumption, or less than one month's global needs—clearly an uncomfortably small working reserve and a perilously thin buffer against the vagaries of weather and plant diseases. As world consumption expands by some 2.5 percent annually, so should the size of working stocks; but over the past two decades, stocks have dwindled while consumption has continued to climb.

The second major source of stability in the world food economy throughout much of the postwar period was the reserve of idle U.S. cropland. For the past dozen years or so, the Government has paid to keep roughly 50 million acres idled under farm programs. Although this source of supply cannot be tapped as quickly as the grain stocks, most of this acreage can be brought back into production within 12 to 18 months once the decision to do so has been made.

In recent years, the need to draw down grain reserves and to utilize the reserve cropland has occurred with increasing frequency. This first happened during the food crisis years of 1966 and 1967, when world grain reserves were reduced to a dangerously low level and the United States brought back into production a small portion of its 50 million idle acres. It happened again in 1971 as a result of the corn blight in the United States. In 1973, in response to growing food scarcities, world grain reserves once more declined, and the United States again resorted to cultivating its idle cropland—but to a much greater extent than on either of the two previous occasions. Government decisions in early 1973 permitted much of the idled cropland to come back into production, and in 1974 no Government payments will be made for keeping cropland fallow.

Global stocks fell close to 100 million tons in 1973, and still further in 1974. Thus world grain reserves have dropped to their lowest level in more than two decades, although the world's population has increased by half in the interim. The sum of global reserve stocks and the potential grain production of idle cropland gives a good indication of the actual total reserve capability in the world food economy in any given year. Taking this total as a percentage of total world grain consumption provides a rough estimate of global food security for the year. The world is now in a situation of extreme vulnerability. In 1973 and 1974, world reserve capabilities in relation to consumption needs have fallen far below any previous level in the postwar era, plummeting from the equivalent of 95 days of world consumption in 1961 to only 26 days in 1974.

From the end of World War II until quite recently, world prices for the principal temperate zone farm commodities such as wheat, feedgrains, and soybeans have been remarkably stable. Since in the years ahead world food reserves may be chronically low and the idled crop acreage in the United States may be further reduced or even disappear entirely, very volatile world prices for the important food commodities can probably be expected.

World Food Reserves—The Policy Question

The subject of world food reserves is one which has been debated for many years from many different points of view. To say the least, this is a controversial topic with many ramifications, and the Subcommittee does not intend to pass on the merits of the various proposals now pending in the Congress. However, to give the readers of this report some idea of the issues involved and the degree of controversy surrounding this subject, we at this point insert portions of testimony presented to the Subcommittee by the American Farm Bureau Federation and the National Farmers Union which outline widely differing opinions on grain reserves.

EXCERPT FROM AMERICAN FARM BUREAU FEDERATION TESTIMONY

Government-managed reserve stocks of farm commodities are both unnecessary and undesirable.

The costs of a reserve managed by U.S. Government—either independently or as a part of an international program—almost certainly would exceed the benefits. The costs include adverse effects on farmers and higher taxes for all taxpayers. Government-managed reserve stocks also can have adverse effects on consumers by delaying the increases in production which are needed from time to time. The historical record indicates that periods of short supplies are relatively rare in American agriculture. The costs of holding reserves for infrequent shortfalls in production are substantial. In the present period of relatively short supplies it is easy to forget the public resentment which developed against the Government farm program a few years ago when carrying charges on Commodity Credit Corporation stocks amounted to over $1 million per day.

A reserve inevitably becomes a part of the supply-demand equation and buyers know that rules established to protect market prices are always subject to change. Thus reserves tend to depress average farm prices. Combining a reserve program with higher government support prices in an effort to offset the price-depressing effects of reserve stocks would be a step backward toward a Government-managed agriculture in which the Government would have to decide what is to be produced and who is to produce it.

A Government-managed reserve program is not needed for the protection of our customers either here or abroad. Domestic consumers have a great deal of protection in the productivity, diversity, and flexibility of American agriculture. While we are opposed to Government-managed reserve stocks we believe needed reserves can, and should, be maintained by farmers, handlers, and processors. The existing Government loan programs make an important contribution to the maintenance of farmer-owned reserve stocks whenever production exceeds current domestic consumption and exports. Farmers and the trade have demonstrated that they will maintain larger reserves if the U.S. Government does not take over this function. Domestic processors and foreign buyers also can protect their needs through advance contracts. Importing countries are free to maintain their own reserves and should be encouraged to do so.

It is sometimes argued that U.S. reserves are needed to facilitate food aid to the less developed countries. Farm Bureau believes that foreign aid programs are worthwhile as a contribution to peace and the welfare of the entire world. We also believe that emergency food relief needs should have the highest priority in foreign aid programs. We do not, however, agree that such programs require the maintenance of Government-managed reserve stocks. Food aid can be made available to less developed countries through purchases in the open market, either here or abroad, without adopting an approach that inevitably would lead to a Government-managed agriculture.

EXCERPT FROM NATIONAL FARMERS UNION TESTIMONY

Food is produced seasonally and the seasons are uncertain. They are marked by drought and flood and the invasion of pestilence. Yet there is a remedy for the uncertainty of the seasons, and the shortages that may result. It is a remedy universally agreed upon, not only for shortages but for surpluses which work such havoc in the farm economy. The remedy is *reserves*.

Reserves are the second innovation of the age of agriculture the logical follow-up to production itself. Nor are reserves limited to agriculture. They are used in every essential pursuit—ranging from metals to money—to fill needs in times of shortages, to change surpluses from curse to salvation. In other words, reserves are the essential device that must be used to stabilize a market in which supplies may at one time be in short supply, or in long supply at other times.

We are told that reserves are too costly. But let me emphasize to you: we can accumulate reserves only when we have surpluses. What is the cost? The cost of reserves is only this—*the cost of not having a farm depression.*

A second aspect of the physical reality of food is that it cannot be produced evenly over the surface of the earth. The basic resources for production—top soil and water—are unevenly available. And so is the ability to produce—knowledge and technology—unevenly available.

Thus, a requirement to assure food for all is trade—not for the purpose of enriching a few, not merely for the purpose of balancing payments—but to get the food from where it is to where it is needed, on acceptable and reasonable terms. This, we believe in Farmers Union, is achievable under international commodity agreements between the producing and consuming nations of the world.

As illustrated by these statements, there is no clear-cut answer to this issue upon which even two major farm groups can agree.

We would tend to support a "world food security plan" expanding upon present multilateral food assistance efforts to permit countries to contribute assistance in the form of food, money, fertilizer, or other real resources for which the donating country is best able to participate in such an effort. For example, the oil-producing countries of the Middle East would be encouraged to contribute from their large monetary reserves which they are earning from their oil exports. Similarly the Soviet Union and Japan might make their contributions in whole or in part in the form of fertilizer for which they have particular plentiful production capabilities.

Summary

Building quietly and ominously these days is a voice that will rock the world in our lifetime, and that voice articulates the world food and people equation. . . . and it is to our blessed land of abundance from across the threshold of scarcity that this voice cries.

Will Americans discover too late that Thomas Malthus is a 200-year-old alarmist whose time has finally arrived?

The Subcommittee concludes that unless present trends in population growth and food production are significantly altered, a food crisis that will have the potential to affect everyone from every walk of life will hit with more impact than the energy crisis of 1973–74. Unfortunately most of the citizens of this and every country of the world are yet unaware of the phenomenal problem that looms on the horizon, and if the hearings held by the Subcommittee and this followup report can serve to make people at least aware of what the statistics show we are headed for, our goal will have been achieved. Americans, who heretofore have been rather complacent about this subject, inasmuch as abundant food supplies have been available at low prices in years past and since the growth rate of our population has slowed considerably, cannot afford to sit idly by thinking that this problem does not affect us. Did you ever stop to think, for example, what the effects on our national security would be if, say, the governments of three or four major countries collapsed due to a shortage of food, resulting in riots in the streets and an overthrow of the government? Can we live in peace in a whole world neighborhood of sick and hungry people?

The United States of America, comprising approximately 5 to 6 percent of the world's population, consumes more than 40 percent of the world's resources. The demand for food, like the demand for oil, metals, minerals, and other resources, is obviously going to skyrocket, and that rocket is going to be fueled by fires of inflation and joblessness.

Can we boil the complex issues down to a very elementary proposition, namely tradeoffs and sacrifices? How do we manage the demands? What formula do we use to determine who gets how much of what we have? We have to decide to what extent the interest of certain groups, among others, taxpayers, consumers, farmers, domestic industry, foreign customers, and the humanitarian interest, are served and/or sacrificed. Let us further examine this statement. Our country has, throughout its history, operated our political and social systems within the perimeters of abundance and has seldom had to cope with the politics of scarcity. But last summer, Americans were forced to cope with scarcities and found it none too pleasant. Price controls were applied to beef. Export controls were set on soybeans. Import restrictions on nearly all commodities were lifted. Humanitarian food shipments under Title II of Public Law 480, our Food for Peace program, were suspended.

These central contemporary questions arise: Should we limit the amount of commodities we export from this country at the expense of our balance of trade and humanitarian interests so we can have "cheap food" here at home; or should we sell all of the commodities we can on the world market to bolster our balance of trade and strengthen the dollar and our economy at the expense of American consumers who will have to pay higher prices for food and hungry people around the world who don't have money to pay for food and will starve as a result; or should we give away large quantities of food to feed hungry people and save lives around the world at the expense of the American taxpayer who would be called upon to finance such a venture and the American consumer who would have to pay higher food prices as a result; or should we establish large governmentally or internationally held and controlled grain reserves which quite possibly could be used against the best interests of the American farmer who in turn would probably reduce production due to a lack of incentive to produce, at the expense of the American consumer who again would have to pay higher food prices and the American taxpayer who would be called upon to finance the largest portion of any such undertaking?

The aforementioned alternatives briefly outline the question of whose interests are to be served or sacrificed before any conclusive policy can be forthcoming. However, the Subcommittee is certain that the U.S. Government can no longer afford to take a piecemeal approach to food policy as we have done in past years. The problem with the piecemeal approach is that it never allows for all of the pieces to really be put together and thus have never solved the puzzle. What is needed is an integrated social policy approach in the formulation, debate, and implementation of the policy position to be taken by the United States. An integrated social policy approach sees the issue of food in terms of its relationship to the other elements of socio-economic-political development in a highly interdependent world. Income distribution, health care systems, literacy programs, land reform in the agricultural sector, employment policies in the industrial sector, encouragement of savings among the poor, and the possibility of political participation by all sectors—these are some of the elements which give people a stake in society and thus motivates them to do something for the sake of society and for themselves, namely to have smaller families. Additionally, issues such as world prices (inflation), trade, preferential tariffs, international money structures, et cetera, should be taken into consideration. In other words, the issue is much broader than just a question of food supply and demand or population, and all factors which might conceivably enter into the picture as previously stated should be discussed.

World Food Conference

(Texts of the Declaration and of the 22 resolutions
adopted by the World Food Conference held in Rome
in November 1974.)

DECLARATION ON THE ERADICATION OF HUNGER AND MALNUTRITION [1]

The World Food Conference, convened by the General Assembly of the United Nations [2] and entrusted with developing ways and means whereby the international community, as a whole, could take specific action to resolve the world food problem within the broader context of development and international economic cooperation, *adopts the following*

Universal Declaration on the Eradication of Hunger and Malnutrition

Recognizing that:
(i) The grave food crisis that is afflicting the peoples of the developing countries where most of the world's hungry and ill-nourished live and where more than two thirds of the world's population produce about one third of the world's food—an imbalance which threatens to increase in the next ten years—is not only fraught with grave economic and social implications, but also acutely jeopardizes the most fundamental principles and values associated with the right to life and human dignity as enshrined in the Universal Declaration of Human Rights; [3]
(ii) The elimination of hunger and malnutrition, included as one of the objectives in the United Nations Declaration on Social Progress and Development, [4] as well as the elimination of the causes that determine this situation are the common objectives of all nations;
(iii) The situation of the peoples afflicted by hunger and malnutrition arises from their historical circumstances, including social inequalities, including in many cases alien and colonial domination, foreign occupation, racial discrimination, *apartheid* and neo-colonialism in all its forms, which continue to be among the greatest obstacles to the full emancipation and progress of the developing countries and all the peoples involved;
(iv) This situation has been aggravated in recent years by a series of crises to which the world economy has been subjected, such as the deterioration in the international monetary system, inflationary increase in import costs, the heavy burdens imposed by external debt on the balance of payments of many developing countries, rising food demand partly due to demographic pressure, speculation, and a shortage of and increased costs of essential agricultural inputs;
(v) These phenomena are considered within the framework of the on-going negotiations on the Charter of Economic Rights and Duties of States, and urging the General Assembly of the United Nations unanimously to agree upon and to adopt a Charter that will be an effective instrument for the establishment of new international economic relations based on principles of equity and justice;
(vi) All countries, big or small, rich or poor, are equal. All countries have the full right to participate in the decisions on the food problem;
(vii) The well-being of the peoples of the world largely depends on the adequate production and distribution of food as well as the establishment of a world food security system which would ensure adequate availability and reasonable prices of food at all times, irrespective of periodic fluctuations and vagaries of weather and free of political and economic pressures, and should thus facilitate, amongst other things, the development process of developing countries;

---

[1] Adopted by the Conference at its 16th meeting on 16 November 1974.
[2] Resolution 3180 (XXVIII) of 17 December 1973.
[3] General Assembly resolution 217 A (III) of 10 December 1948.
[4] General Assembly resolution 2542 (XXIV) of 11 December 1969.

(viii) Peace and justice encompass an economic dimension helping the solution of the world economic problems, the liquidation of under-development, offering a lasting and definitive solution of the food problem for all peoples and guaranteeing to all countries the right to implement freely and effectively their development programmes. To this effect, it is necessary to eliminate threats and resort to force and to promote peaceful co-operation between States to the fullest extent possible, to apply the principles of non-interference in each others internal affairs, full equality of rights, respect of national independence and sovereignty as well as to encourage the peaceful co-operation between all States, irrespective of their political, social and economic systems. The further improvement of international relations will create better conditions for international co-operation in all fields which should make possible large financial and material resources to be used, *inter alia*, for developing agricultural production and substantially improving world food security;

(ix) For a lasting solution of the food problem all efforts should be made to eliminate the widening gaps which today separate developed and developing countries and to bring about a new international economic order. It should be possible for all countries to participate actively and effectively in the new international economic relations by the establishment of suitable international systems, where appropriate, capable of producing adequate action in order to establish just and equitable relations in international economic co-operation;

(x) Developing countries reaffirm their belief that the primary responsibility for ensuring their own rapid development rests with themselves. They declare, therefore, their readiness to continue to intensify their individual and collective efforts with the view to expanding their mutual co-operation in the field of agricultural development and food production including the eradication of hunger and malnutrition;

(xi) Since, for various reasons, many developing countries are not yet always able to meet their own food needs, urgent and effective international action should be taken to assist them, free of political pressures, consistent with the aims and objectives of the Declaration on the Establishment of a New International Economic Order [5] and the Programme of Action [5] of the sixth special session of the General Assembly of the United Nations.

The Conference consequently solemnly proclaims:

1. Every man, woman and child has the inalienable right to be free from hunger and malnutrition in order to develop fully and maintain their physical and mental faculties. Society today already possesses sufficient resources, organizational ability, and technology and hence the competence to achieve this objective. Accordingly, the eradication of hunger is a common objective of all the countries of the international community, especially of the developed countries and others in a position to help.

2. It is a fundamental responsibility of Governments to work together for higher food production and a more equitable and efficient distribution of food between countries and within countries. Governments should initiate immediately a greater concerted attack on chronic malnutrition and deficiency diseases among the vulnerable and lower income groups. In order to ensure adequate nutrition for all, Governments should formulate appropriate food and nutrition policies integrated in over-all socio-economic and agricultural development plans based on adequate knowledge of available as well as potential food resources. The importance of human milk in this connexion should be stressed on nutritional grounds.

3. Food problems must be tackled during the preparation and implementation of national plans and programmes for economic and social development, with emphasis on their humanitarian aspects.

4. It is a responsibility of each State concerned, in accordance with its sovereign judgment and internal legislation, to remove the obstacles to food production and provide proper incentives to agricultural producers. Of prime importance for the attainment of these objectives are effective measures of socio-economic transformation by agrarian, tax, credit and investment policy reform and the reorganization of rural structures, such as the reform of the conditions of ownership, the encouragement of producer and consumer co-operatives, the mobilization of the full potential of human resources, both male and female, in the developing countries for an integrated rural development and the involvement of the small farmers, fishermen and the landless workers in attaining the required food

---

[5] General Assembly resolutions 3201 and 3202 (S–VI) of May 1, 1974

production and employment targets. Moreover, it is necessary to recognize the key role of women in agricultural production and rural economy in many countries, and to ensure that appropriate education, extension programmes and financial facilities are made available to women on equal terms with men.

5. Marine and inland water resources are today becoming more important than ever as a source of food and economic prosperity. Accordingly, action should be taken to promote a rational exploitation of these resources, preferably for direct human consumption, in order to contribute to meeting the food requirements of all peoples.

6. The efforts to increase food production should be complemented by every endeavour to prevent wastage of food in all its forms.

7. To give impetus to food production in developing countries and in particular in the least developed and most seriously affected among them, urgent and effective international action should be taken, by the developed countries and other countries in a position to do so, to provide them with sustained additional technical and financial assistance on favourable terms and in a volume sufficient to their needs on the basis of bilateral and multilateral arrangements. This assistance must be free of conditions inconsistent with sovereignty of the receiving States.

8. All countries, and primarily the highly industrialized countries, should promote the advancement of food production technology and should make all efforts to promote the transfer, adaptation and dissemination of appropriate food production technology for the benefit of the developing countries and to that end they should *inter alia* make all efforts to disseminate the results of their research work to Governments and scientific institutions of developing countries in order to enable them to promote a sustained agricultural development.

9. To assure the proper conservation of natural resources being utilized or utilizable for food production, all countries must collaborate in order to facilitate the preservation of the environment, including the marine environment.

10. All developed countries and others able to do so should collaborate technically and financially with the developing countries in their efforts to expand land and water resources for agricultural production and to assure a rapid increase in the availability, at fair costs, of agricultural inputs such as fertilizers and other chemicals, high-quality seeds, credit and technology. Co-operation among developing countries, in this connexion, is also important.

11. All States should strive to the utmost to readjust, where appropriate, their argicultural policies to give priority to food production recognizing, in this connexion, the interrelationship between the world food problem and international trade. In the determination of attitudes toward farm support programmes for domestic food production, developed countries should take into account, as far as possible, the interest of the food exporting developing countries, in order to avoid detrimental effect on their exports. Moreover, all countries should co-operate to devise effective steps to deal with the problem of stabilizing world markets and promoting equitable and remunerative prices, where appropriate through international agreements, to improve access to markets through reduction or elimination of tariff and non-tariff barriers on the products of interest to the developing countries, to substantially increase the export earnings of these countries, to contribute to the diversification of their exports, and apply to them, in the multilateral trade negotiations, the principles as agreed upon in the Tokyo Declaration including the concept of non-reciprocity and more favourable treatment.

12. As it is the common responsibility of the entire international community to ensure the availability at all times of adequate world supplies of basic foodstuffs by way of appropriate reserves including emergency reserves, all countries should co-operate in the establishment of an effective system of world food security by :

participating in and supporting the operation of the Global Information and Early Warning System on Food and Agriculture ;

adhering to the objectives, policies and guidelines of the proposed International Undertaking on World Food Security as endorsed by the World Food Conference ;

ear-marking, where possible, stocks or funds for meeting international emergency food requirements as envisaged in the proposed International Undertaking on World Food Security and developing international guidelines to provide for the co-ordination and the utilization of such stocks ;

co-operating in the provision of food aid for meeting emergency and nutritional needs as well as for stimulating rural employment through development projects.

All donor countries should accept and implement the concept of forward planning of food aid and make all efforts to provide commodities and/or financial assistance that will ensure adequate quantities of grains and other food commodities. Time is short. Urgent and sustained action is vital. The Conference, therefore, calls upon all peoples expressing their will as individuals, and through their Governments and non-governmental organizations, to work together to bring about the end of the age-old scourge of hunger.

The Conference affirms:

The determination of the participating States to make full use of the United Nations system in the implementation of this Declaration and the other decisions adopted by the Conference.

RESOLUTIONS ADOPTED BY THE CONFERENCE

RESOLUTION I. OBJECTIVES AND STRATEGIES OF FOOD PRODUCTION

The World Food Conference,

Recalling General Assembly resolution 3201 (S–VI) and 3202 (S–VI) of 1 May 1974, concerning the Declaration and the Programme of Action on the Establishment of a New International Economic Order and the subsequent ECOSOC resolution 1911 (LVII) on its implementation, as adopted.

Recalling General Assembly Resolution 3180 (XXVIII) of 17 December 1973 on the World Food Conference,

Recognizing that past trends in food production and productivity in the majority of developing countries have been unsatisfactory, for reasons, among others, of inadequate socio-economic structures, insufficient investment funds, paucity of trained manpower, and unfavourable trade relations,

Noting that if these trends were to continue the expected increase in the demand for food in these countries will raise their import requirements to unmanageable proportions, aggravate malnutrition and intensify human suffering.

Expressing concern at the inadequate performance of agriculture, including livestock and fisheries, in many developing countries in relation to the targets of the Second United Nations Development Decade and their own national objectives, at the new constraints created by the scarcity of inputs and at the inadequacy of the present level of resources including development assistance flowing to agriculture in these countries,

Considering that agricultural production in the developing countries requires the availability of inputs at reasonable prices.

Stressing that an increase in agricultural productivity and sustained expansion of food production in these countries at a rate much faster than in the past is essential in order to meet the rapidly growing demand for food, due to rising population and incomes, the requirements for security stocks and the need to raise the consumption by undernourished people to universally accepted standards,

Recognizing the importance of fish products for the improvement of quality of human diet and the potential for increased fish production especially in developing countries.

Recognizing that in many developing countries there is considerable scope for increased production through bringing new land under cultivation or through more intensive use of land already under cultivation,

Recognizing that in many developing countries large quantities of food are lost between the farm field and the consumer and that the deterioration in the nutritional value of food before it reaches the consumer is a serious problem ;

Considering that conditions in certain developed countries are favourable for the rapid increase of food production and recognizing that some countries can produce more food than they need and thus are able to export ; that reliance on this production to supply the growing needs of the developing countries and some developed countries is increasing ; that for years these exporting countries have been concerned that production at full capacity could create undesirable surpluses and thus depressed markets, which would deprive farmers of incentives to invest and to produce, and that in view of the present and prospective demand for food in the world, such a concern may no longer be relevant,

Stressing the urgent need for greater efforts by the developing countries themselves and for increased regional, sub-regional and international co-operation for agricultural[1] development in these countries, as part of the International Development Strategy for the Second United Nations Development Decade,

Stressing the importance, in selecting the measures to be taken to achieve the urgently needed increases in food output, of taking into account the need for the most efficient use of land and water resources, the short and long-term effects of alternative technologies on the quality of the environment,

Affirming that in order to solve the food problem, highest priority should be given to policies and programmes for increasing food production and improving food utilization in developing countries, so as to achieve a minimum agricultural growth rate of 4 per cent per annum, placing appropriate emphasis on (i) providing adequate supplies of essential inputs, such as fertilizers, pesticides, quality seeds, farm and fishery equipment and machinery, fuel, breeding stock and water; (ii) ensuring sufficient incentives to farmers; (iii) developing rural infrastructures, including storage, processing, transportation, marketing, input supply systems, credit and educational and social amenities; (iv) conservation and improvement of existing cultivated and cultivable land; (v) reclamation and development of new land; (vi) promoting research training and extension; (vii) progressive social and structural transformation of agriculture; (viii) active participation of the rural population, particularly small farmers and landless workers in the development process, and (ix) providing the necessary financial resources.

1. *Resolves* that all governments should accept the removal of the scourge of of hunger and malnutrition, which at present afflicts many millions of human beings, as the objective of the international community as a whole, and accept the goal that within a decade no child will go to bed hungry, that no family will fear for its next day's bread, and that no human being's future and capacities will be stunted by malnutrition.

2. *Calls on* the government of each developing country to:
    (i) accord a *high* priority to agricultural and fisheries development;
    (ii) formulate food production and food utilization objectives, targets and policies, for the short, medium and long-term, with full participation of producers, their families, and farmers' and fishermen's organizations, taking into account its demographic and general development goals and consistent with good environment practices;
    (iii) take measures for agrarian reform and a progressive change in the socio-economic structures and relationships in rural areas; and
    (iv) develop adequate supporting services for agricultural and fisheries development, including those for education, research, extension and training, marketing, storage and processing, transport, as well as credit facilities and incentives to enable producers to buy the required inputs;

3. *Calls on all governments* able to furnish external assistance to substantially increase their official development assistance to agriculture in developing countries, especially the least developed and the most seriously affected countries, including capital assistance on soft terms, technical assistance, transfer of appropriate technology and programme loans for imports of essential inputs;

4. *Requests* governments to make arrangements whereby developing countries will have access to inputs such as fertilizer, pesticides, agricultural machinery and equipment in sufficient quantity and at reasonable prices;

5. *Urges* governments to respond to the appeal of the Secretary-General of the United Nations for contributions to the Special Programme, the urgent implementation of which is essential for ensuring progress in resolving the food problem of the developing countries seriously affected by the economic crisis, and to contribute generously to the International Fund for Agricultural Development proposed by the Conference;

6. *Urges* the developed countries concerned to adopt and to implement agricultural policies which encourage the early expansion of food production while taking into account a satisfactory level of income for producers and world food requirements and the need of maintaining reasonable prices for consumers, such policies should not impede or delay the increase in food production by developing countries, both for domestic consumption and for export;

7. *Requests* all countries to reduce to a minimum the waste of food and of

---

[1] Including livestock and fisheries.

agricultural resources, in particular land, water and all forms of energy ; and to ensure the rational utilization of fisheries resources ;

8. *Calls on* the regional economic commissions to continue their important contribution to the task of stimulating co-ordinated economic development in their respective regions, by co-operating in the efforts in this direction that the countries in those regions are making ;

9. *Urges* FAO in consultation with UNDP and other relevant international institutions, with due regard for national sovereignty :

(*a*) to formulate economic, social, physical and biological criteria for selecting suitable additional areas for food production,

(*b*) to make an inventory, on the basis of these criteria, of the areas most suitable for additional production,

(*c*) to make an inventory of resources for financing additional production, and

(*d*) to indicate ways and means for carrying out programs and projects for additional food production ;

10. *Requests* the World Bank, Regional Banks, UNDP, FAO, UNIDO and other international agencies, through modification of their existing policies and criteria as appropriate, to substantially increase their assistance for agriculture and fisheries in developing countries giving priority to programmes and projects aimed at benefiting the poorest groups of the population and placing equal emphasis on both economic and social benefits ; simplify and streamline the procedures for the granting of such assistance ; and mobilize the support of the entire international community including non-governmental organizations, for the urgent task of overcoming hunger and malnutrition.

RESOLUTION II. PRIORITIES FOR AGRICULTURAL AND RURAL DEVELOPMENT

The World Conference,

Recognizing that self-reliance, relying on the masses of people, tapping fully the potentialities of the country and striving in accordance with each country's respective conditions for the maximum possible degree of self-sufficiency in basic foods is the fundamental approach to the solution of the food problem of developing countries,

Recognizing the urgent need for expanding and improving the productivity base of agriculture through fuller and more efficient utilization of land and water resources, through application and adaptation of improved technology consistent with the local ecological conditions, and through agrarian reforms and other appropriate socio-economic changes in the organization of rural communities,

Recognizing the vital importance of mobilizing the people through their organizations for rural development, and particularly of involving small farmers and landless labourers in the planning and operation of programmes aimed at improving their living standards and those of their families and at a more equitable distribution of income,

Stressing the severe problem of rural unemployment and under-employment,

Emphasizing the critical need for the strengthening of the administrative capacity of government organizations and of rural infrastructures, down to the village level including housing and health services, agricultural extension and communication and other family well-being services, and for greatly expanded rural education and technical and vocational training programmes, particularly the need for universal literacy,

Recognizing the important role of women in rural life, in the production, processing, marketing and consumption of food, in family nutrition, in decisions on family size and child spacing and in child care and education, the need to involve them fully in the process of rural development, and the implications thereof for education and extension,

Affirming that a determining element in rural development and in reducing rural unemployment, is the capacity of the rural community to expand, intensify, and diversify its activities in crop production, animal husbandry, forestry, fisheries, agro-allied and other rural-based industries and public works programmes, and that in support of these, the necessary production structure and infrastructure needs to be established,

Noting that no single pattern of social, economic or institutional set-up can be applicable to all countries, that the concept of integrated rural development

is sufficiently flexible for countries to design operational strategies appropriate
to their own circumstances, and recalling the efforts made in promoting the
concept of integrated rural development,

1. *Calls on* governments to bring about appropriate progressive agrarian reforms
in accordance with the political objectives and administrative capabilities of
each country, adequate means of information and motivation and other institutional improvements in rural areas aimed at employment and income generation,
at organizing, activating and assisting the rural population, including nomads,
for participation in integrated rural development and at eliminating exploita-
tive patterns of land tenure, credit and marketing systems where they still
prevail, calls on them to improve credit marketing and inputs distribution
systems and recommends that existing and experienced institutions and organizations in the developed countries should be mobilized as much as possible to take
part in agricultural development work, and also to make all efforts to carry
out Economic and Social Council Resolution 1707 (LIII) on Agrarian Reform;

2. *Invites* governments to promote the development of cooperative organizations
and other associations for the mass of farmers and rural workers for agricultural
and rural development and for generating greater self-reliance, self-sufficiency
and motivation;

3. *Requests* all governments to intensify their efforts in both formal and non-
formal education of rural people with emphasis on what is relevant to their
needs, taking into account the special role of women in agriculture and rural
life in many societies, and to aim at the elimination of illiteracy within a
decade;

4. *Calls on* each country to identify and implement with greater financial and
policy support such food production and rural development programmes as are
best suited to its specific national and regional characteristics and circumstances
and which are required to achieve its national and international food production
objectives, bearing in mind the development of appropriate technology, and the
establishment of price relationships which will lead to increased incomes;

5. *Calls on* UNDP, IBRD, FAO and other international and bilateral agencies
to review their criteria for financial, technical and other assistance for integrated rural development; to give greater importance to social criteria so as to
implement broader and longer-range programmes of rural development; and if
necessary improve their technical and administrative capacity for implementing
these programmes;

6. *Urges* governments, UNDP and the other international and bilateral agencies
to co-operate in accelerating the planning and implementation of integrated rural
development programmes and to devote greatly expanded resources to these
activities;

7. *Calls on* FAO and other United Nations organizations concerned to collect,
evaluate and disseminate the results and experience from past and ongoing rural
development programmes, to determine the suitability of these programmes in
bringing about both expending agricultural production and social integration.

RESOLUTION III. FERTILIZERS

The World Food Conference,
Recognizing the vital role of fertilizers in increasing food production, the
urgency of eliminating the current global shortage of fertilizers, and the necessity
of ensuring on a continuing basis the adequate and regular supply of fertilizers to
all countries,

Recognizing further that the present international prices of fertilizers reflect
to a considerable extent their scarcity value and are threatening food production
efforts in developing countries,

Noting the recent increased activity of the international community in respect
of fertilizers, including the establishment of the FAO Commission on Fertilizers,
the International Fertilizer Supply Scheme, the International Fertilizer Development Centre in the USA, the important activities of the IBRD and UNIDO and
the funding operations of the United Nations Emergency Operation,

Taking note of the Economic and Social Council resolution 1836, of the proposal
by Sri Lanka and the Economic and Social Commission for Asia and the Pacific,
and of the proposal by Mexico which were designed to ensure the availability of
scarce and essential agricultural inputs like fertilizers.

Taking note of the growing awareness of the importance of fertilizers as an
appropriate instrument for external assistance in increasing food supplies in
developing countries, both on a bilateral and multilateral basis,

Stressing the need for increased and coordinated international efforts to improve fertilizer availability, particularly to developing countries, and define the elements of an effective international fertilizer policy,

Recognizing also that increasing availability and applications of fertilizer in developing countries need to be promoted in conjunction with the use of other inputs and rural services, and taking into account the Conference Resolutions on related inputs such as pesticides and seeds,

1. *Recommends* that during the current period of supply shortages and high prices, the international organizations and bilateral aid agencies significantly intensify their effort to meet the needs of developing countries, particularly the least developed and those most seriously affected by economic crisis, through increased material and financial support to the International Fertilizer Supply Scheme and by stepping up bilateral efforts, so as to bridge the gap in supply as estimated by the Scheme from time to time;

2. *Calls upon* developed countries, international agencies and others in a position to do so to extend assistance in the form of grants and concessional loans to enable developing countries to import urgently needed fertilizers and raw materials;

3. *Recommends* that FAO, UNIDO and IBRD jointly organize a programme to assist developing countries to improve the efficiency of their fertilizer plant operations coordinating with agencies providing assistance for this purpose;

4. *Urges* international institutions, developed countries and others in a position to do so to provide financial assistance, technical assistance, technology and equipment on favorable terms, to build required additional fertilizer production capacities in appropriate developing countries that possess oil and natural gas, phosphate rock and/or other natural resources such as coal, in other developing countries where specific local factors justify such investments, and also to assist all developing countries with storage facilities, distribution services and other related infrastructures;

5. *Requests* that interested countries and parties actively explore the possibilities for setting up cooperative ventures in the fertilizer field among countries producing fertilizer raw materials, countries with established fertilizer production industries and fertilizer consuming countries with a view to the promotion of more economic and stable fertilizer production and supply systems, and to consider any other measures that may be needed to channel adequate investments into the fertilizer field;

6. *Requests* the FAO Commission on Fertilizers, in collaboration with the member states of the United Nations and the other international organizations concerned such as UNIDO and IBRD, to undertake as a matter of urgency an authoritative analysis of the long term fertilizer supply and demand position in order to provide the elements of a world fertilizer policy which would include the overall aim of avoiding cyclical imbalances between supply and demand, help ensure that fertilizer prices are stabilized at reasonable levels and would enable developing countries to obtain fertilizers they need for their food and agricultural production;

7. *Requests* that all countries should introduce standards for ensuring fertilizer quality and policies and measures for the promotion of the most efficient and effective use of available fertilizers including the application of mineral fertilizers as well as alternative and additional sources of plant nutrients such as organic fertilizers, legume crops and other means of biologically fixing nitrogen and recycling of wastes and combining fertilizer use with other improved agricultural practices; it also recommends that each fertilizer consuming nation call upon its citizens voluntarily to reduce non-critical uses of fertilizer toward making available more fertilizers for food·production in developing countries.

8. *Recommends* the intensification of international efforts in the transfer of technical knowledge, particularly on the intermediate level, in order to increase production and to make more effective use of fertilizers, including the improvement of extension services and training of farmers in all countries, as well as research on methods to augment soil fertility and plant growth through the development of improved mineral fertilizers, greater utilization of locally available plant nutrients, of different types of organic fertilizers, biological fixation of nitrogen, on micro-elements, and on food crop varieties that are efficient in the uptake of plant nutrients from the soil.

RESOLUTION IV. FOOD AND AGRICULTURAL RESEARCH, EXTENSION AND TRAINING [1]

The World Food Conference,
Recalling the General Assembly Resolution 3202 (SVI) of 1 May 1974, relating to the Programme of Action concerning the Establishment of a New International Economic Order, as adopted,
Recalling further the General Assembly Resolution 3168 (XXVIII) of 17 December 1973, by which the Assembly requested the strengthening of economic, scientific and technical cooperation between Member States;
Considering that coordinated basic and applied research conducted in, or for the benefit of, the developing countries, in all fields of food and agricultural development, both technical and socio-economic, is vital to increasing food, agricultural and fisheries production and the optimum utilization of resources, and must therefore enjoy high priority at the national, regional and international levels;
Expressing its concern at the inadequate amount of basic and particularly of applied research directed to developing new agricultural technology suited to the needs of developing countries, especially tropical and sub-tropical areas; as well as at weaknesses in adaptive research, training, and extension to achieve more effective transfer and utilization of both existing and new technology, especially in fields related to food production and utilization under the local environmental, agricultural, and socio-economic conditions in each country;
Noting that much of current research both lacks coordination and makes inadequate use of important information already available from research in ecologically comparable regions;
Recognizing that the paucity of trained technical personnel at various levels required both for the conduct of research and for the transmission of the results of research to agricultural producers is a major constraint in increasing agricultural production; and recalling the recommendations on this subject made by the First World Conference Agricultural Education and Training (Copenhagen 1970).
Affirming its conviction that strengthening research, technical training, and the extension and dissemination of research results to all agricultural and marine producers, and especially to small farmers and fishermen in line with the national goals of developing countries, must be accorded a priority merited by its crucial role in providing new means of increasing food and agricultural production;
1. *Urges* all governments to evaluate the scope and organization of their national agricultural research, training, and extension programmes, and their linkages with relevant universities, international and regional institutions, and agro-industry research efforts, with a view to taking all necessary measures (including additional financial provision) to strengthen national programmes to cover priority areas of food and agricultural production more adequately, including *inter alia* environmental and socio-economic considerations;
2. *Invites* countries which enjoy a high level of development of scientific agriculture to ensure that no onerous conditions or limitations are placed on the transfer of agricultural technology, which might impede its ready acquisition and assimilation by the developing countries;
3. *Requests* the concerned national, regional, and international research institutions to intensify their efforts to examine the possibilities of new as well as traditional food crop, livestock and fisheries production systems, and the potential for the development of water resources and the efficient use of land, water, fertilizer and other inputs for significantly increasing food production in the developing countries; to improve the nutritional quality of both conventional and non-conventional foods; to investigate the problems connected with opening up of new lands in the light of diverse land use requirements, ecological and tenure systems and the need to conserve soil fertility; and, in close cooperation with extension services, to develop studies aimed at a better understanding of the motivation of the rural populace and thus to assist them in improved participation in the benefits to be gained from the application of research results;
4. *Recommends* the strengthening and expansion of programmes relating to the survey, conservation and effective utilization of agricultural resources, particularly of soil, water and plant and animal genetic resources; and *urges* the rapid establishment of a global network of plant genetic resource centres and the extension of this to animal genetic resources.

---

[1] Agriculture is here taken as including production of plants, livestock, and fish.

5. *Recommends* the stepping-up of cooperative goal-oriented basic research programmes, involving research centres of developed countries, international and regional research institutes, and suitable institutions in developing countries on problems relating to the development of appropriate technology for increasing productivity, improving marketing and reducing costs of production; examples of such research are: biological nitrogen fixation, utilization of solar and geophysical energy, production physiology for raising yield ceilings, plant introduction and genetic breeding using wide germ plasm resources, and development of new human and animal food sources.

6. *Recommends* that the concerned national and international institutions intensify basic and applied research regarding

(i) the impact of different ecological conditions, particularly climate, weather and their variability, on agricultural production in various climatic zones and particularly in tropical and climatically marginal (e.g. semi-arid and arid) land areas,

(ii) the application of meteorological information and knowledge in planning agricultural research and land-use and management systems, including the development of alternative cropping strategies to suit different weather conditions so as to minimize the adverse effects of aberrant weather and encourage production patterns in tune with the climatic potential.

7. *Recommends* the rapid expansion of applied research in national, regional and international research centres, so as to bring about a continuing rise in the economic yield and nutritional value of plants and farm animals, taking into account the need to improve biological efficiency so as to economize in inputs, without detriment to the long-term production potential of specific farming systems;

8. *Recommends* that research, possibly on a regional basis, be undertaken in order to develop coastal fisheries and marine and inland aquaculture to the fullest; and urges developed fishing nations to provide developing countries with the necessary technical assistance for the exploitation, management, processing and marketing of these resources;

9. *Recommends* the following early action with a view to reinforcing and improving the co-ordination of research efforts directed to these goals and the rapid dissemination of results to agricultural producers:

(i) that FAO undertake the systematic collection, and dissemination of data on current research, and the results of research already carried out in the developing countries, and that additional resources be provided for this purpose and for permitting the exchange of experience and data between existing centres;

(ii) that the resources of the Consultative Group on International Agricultural Research, co-sponsored by FAO, UNDP, and the World Bank, be substantially enlarged to enable it to augment the number and scope of international and regional research programmes in and for the developing countries, with the objective of complementing and helping to strengthen research in the developing countries through promoting co-operative research networks, assisting in adaptive research at the national level and in training programmes, and the dissemination of research information at all levels; and *further recommends* that the Technical Advisory Committee and the Consultative Group study the feasibility of an international programme on the use of remote sensing techniques in agriculture, including the use of data from Earth Resources Satellites;

(iii) that consideration shall be given by FAO, UNDP and the World Bank to establishing a co-ordinated programme for the improvement of extension systems:

(iv) that extensive adaptive research programmes be developed involving testing in farmers' fields the economic and viability of new technology and thereby tailoring recommendations to suit specific locations, farming situations and socio-economic conditions; and subsequently the organization of widespread on-farm demonstrations ranging from small plot demonstrations to whole villages of water-shed demonstrations; and that whole village or other appropriate pilot projects be developed and implemented jointly by agricultural and social scientists so as to bring about an understanding of the institutional and socio-economic requirements of new technology;

(v) that priority be given to, and increased resources made available for, the development of agricultural education and training at all levels, in order that the required training programmes can be provided—including training of research and extension workers in management techniques, special basic and in-service technical training for graduate and middle-level extension personnel, and farmers' training, including programmes for rural women and children, aiming at the achievement of an integrated educational system for the rural population within an appropriate political and social framework;

(vi) that all countries co-operate in special measures aimed at reducing the loss of specialized technical personnel from the developing countries;

(vii) that means be found to facilitate the acquisition by developing countries, under favourable terms, of the equipment required for agricultural research and experimental development activities, including better access to the world's germ plasm resources, and

(viii) that to support these recommendations national, regional and international resources devoted to agricultural research, extension, and training in and for developing countries should be increased severalfold in real terms by 1985.

RESOLUTION V. POLICIES AND PROGRAMMES TO IMPROVE NUTRITION

The World Food Conference,

Considering that large numbers of people, particularly the less advantaged in many countries, lack adequate and appropriate food resulting in adverse effects on their health, their development and their ability to learn and work for basic livelihood; whereas overconsumption among the affluent not only impairs their health but also contributes to reducing the food availability for less advantaged groups and furthermore, large food resources are used to feed animals,

Recognizing that malnutrition is closely linked to widespread poverty and inadequate social and institutional structures, and that its effects are aggravated by infectious diseases and the lack of environmental sanitation; and that increased agricultural production and increased incomes may not by themselves lead to improved nutrition; and that to this end a more just and equitable distribution of food and incomes is essential, among nations as well as within countries among their various social categories,

Recognizing that information on food consumption patterns and on their consequences for the nutrition and health status of the majority of the population in developing countries is insufficient and inadequate, and that improved knowledge about how to prevent malnutrition through better use of available food resources. including human milk, is essential.

Considering the relationship which often exists between child and mother, malnutrition and too-close pregnancies,

Recognizing that food and nutritional aspects are generally not sufficiently taken into account in the formulation of national development plans,

Considering the need for improving nutrition in all countries and that the present consumption patterns of the affluent need not be taken as a model,

Recommends

1. That all governments and the international community as a whole, in pursuance of their determination to eliminate within a decade hunger and malnutrition formulate and integrate concerted food and nutritional plans and policies aiming at the improvement of consumption patterns in their socio-economic and agricultural planning, and for that purpose assess the character, extent and degree of malnutrition in all socio-economic groups as well as the preconditions for improving their nutritional status;

2. That FAO, in cooperation with WHO, UNICEF, WFP, IBRD, UNDP, and UNESCO, assisted by PAG, prepare a project proposal for assisting governments to develop intersectoral food and nutrition plans; this proposal to be communicated to the FAO Council at its mid-1975 session through its Food and Nutrition Policy Committee, and to the governing bodies of the other interested agencies;

3. That governments, with their own resources, supplemented with food, financial and technical assistance from multilateral or bilateral external sources, and in close cooperation with agricultural production programmes initiate new or strengthen existing food and nutrition intervention programmes, on a scale large enough to cover on a continuing basis a substantial part of the vulnerable groups;

4. That governments include nutrition education in the curricula for educational programmes at all levels and that all concerned in the fields of agriculture health and general education be appropriately trained to enable them to further the nutrition education of the public within their domains;

5. That governments strengthen basic health, family well-being and planning services and improve environmental conditions, including rural water supplies and the elimination of water-borne diseases; and provide treatment and rehabilitation of those suffering from protein-energy malnutrition;

6. That governments consider the key role of women and take steps to improve their nutrition, their educational levels and their working conditions; and to encourage them and enable them to breast-feed their children;

7. That governments review special feeding programmes within the context of their food and nutrition strategies to determine desirability and the feasibility of undertaking such new programmes, or improving existing ones, particularly amongst the vulnerable groups (children, pregnant and nursing mothers), but also for school children, workers and others; such programmes should promote increased local food production and processing thereby stimulating local initiative and employment and should also include an element of nutrition-education;

8. That the international agencies, non-governmental agencies and countries which are in a position to provide funds and foods for this purpose, should provide assistance to governments who will request such aid in order to introduce in the period 1975-76, emergency programmes for supplementary feeding of a substantial number of the malnourished children with due attention to basic health and other essential services for the welfare of all children at risk;

9. That governments should explore the desirability and feasibility of meeting nutrient deficiencies, through fortification of staples or other widely-consumed foods, with amino-acids, protein concentrates, vitamins and minerals, and that, with the assistance of WHO in cooperation with other organizations concerned, should establish a world-wide control programme aimed at substantially reducing deficiencies of vitamin A, iodine, iron/folate, vitamin D, riboflavine, and thiamine as quickly as possible;

10. That FAO, in association with other international and non-governmental organizations concerned, undertakes an inventory of vegetable food resources other than cereals, such as roots, tubers, legumes, vegetables and fruits, including also those from unconventional sources, and that it studies the possibility of increasing their production and consumption, particularly in countries where malnutrition prevails;

11. That governments take action to strengthen and modernize consumer education services, food legislation and food control programmes and the relevant aspects of marketing practices, aiming at the protection of the consumer (avoiding false and misleading information from mass-media and commercial fraud), and that they increase their support of the Codex Alimentarius Commission;

12. That the joint FAO/WHO food contamination monitoring programme, in cooperation with UNEP, be further developed in order to provide early information to the national authorities for appropriate action;

13. That a global nutrition surveillance system be established by FAO, WHO and UNICEF to monitor the food and nutrition conditions of the disadvantaged groups of the population at risk, and to provide a method of rapid and permanent assessment of all factors which influence food consumption patterns and nutritional status;

14. That governments consider establishing facilities and funds for applied nutrition research related to economic, cultural, social and medical aspects of production, processing, preservation, storage, distribution and utilization of food and that FAO, WHO and UNICEF arrange for an internationally coordinated programme in applied nutritional research including establishing priorities, identifying appropriate research centres and generating the necessary fundings;

15. That governments should associate, wherever practicable, non-governmental organizations whose programmes include nutrition-related activities, with their nutritional efforts, particularly in the areas of food and nutrition programmes, nutrition education and feeding programmes for the most vulnerable groups.

RESOLUTION VI. WORLD SOIL CHARTER AND LAND CAPABILITY ASSESSMENT

The World Food Conference,

Noting that land resources are limited and that of the total land area of the world only a small percentage is currently used to feed the world population which is likely to double by the end of the century,

Considering that meeting the food requirements of mankind including the eradication of malnutrition, entails:

the intensification of crop production including multiple cropping, where-
ever this can be safely accomplished,

the bringing into cultivation of new lands, wherever conditions for sustained cropping prevail, with a view to considerably increasing the land
areas used for food production,

the establishment and better utilization of grasslands,

Conscious of the dangers of soil degradation resulting from inadequate measures
for intensifying crop production and grazing, particularly in areas which are
exposed to water and wind erosion, or salinity and alkalinity,

1. *Recommends* that Governments apply appropriate soil protection and conservation techniques in conjunction with the measures they take to intensify
crop production and grazing and bring new lands into cultivation;

2. *Recommends* that FAO, UNESCO and UNEP, in cooperation with WMO,
and other competent international organizations, and in consultation with Governments concerned, prepare without delay an assessment of the lands that can
still be brought into cultivation, taking proper account of forestry for the protection of catchment areas of land required for alternative uses. Such an assessment should take into account primarily the hazards of irreversible soil degradation as well as the order of magnitude of costs and agricultural and other inputs
required;

3. *Urges* that the Food and Agriculture Organization of the United Nations
select the most appropriate ways and means to establish a World Soil Charter
which would be the basis for an international cooperation towards the most
rational use of the world's land resources.

RESOLUTION VII. SCIENTIFIC WATER MANAGEMENT: IRRIGATION, DRAINAGE AND
FLOOD CONTROL

The World Food Conference,

Recognising the vital role of water in agricultural development and consequently of completing projects under construction, improving existing irrigation
systems and developing new irrigation facilities in developing countries,

Recognising that extending the area under assured irrigation has become particularly urgent, since variability in weather and climate is becoming an increasingly important factor in influencing the world food situation,

Noting that considerable ground and surface water resources are yet to be
exploited and that available evidence on benefit/cost is favourable to their development and utilisation,

Noting that a large number of irrigation schemes are operating at low levels
of efficiency,

Noting also that extensive irrigated areas have gone out of cultivation or their
production capabilities have been reduced due to waterlogging, salinity and
alkalinity,

Noting that colossal damage to crops due to floods has become an increasingly
recurring phenomenon in some regions, calling for urgent action with respect to
control measures,

Noting that efficient water conservation and use will be essential for increasing
agricultural production in semi-arid and arid areas, as well as for desert creep
control,

Considering that the principal obstacles to fully exploiting the potential water
resources and adopting effective drainage and flood control measures are shortage of financial resources, equipment and trained manpower, to ensure regional
cooperation and to evolve ecologically sound policies,

1. *Recommends* urgent action to be taken by governments and international
agencies such as FAO and WMO to implement the following:

(*a*) Undertake, wherever needed, exhaustive climatic, hydrological and
irrigation potential, hydro-power potentials and desert creep surveys;

(*b*) Rapid expansion of irrigation capacities in areas where surface water
and/or groundwater reserves are available for rational exploitation, so as
to facilitate both the improvement of productivity and intensity of cropping;

(*c*) Development of techniques for the safe utilization of brackish water
for food production in areas where sweet surface/groundwater is not available;

(*d*) Reclamation of areas affected by waterlogging, salinity and alkalinity and prevention of salinisation of irrigated areas;

(*e*) Identification of groundwater resources, exploration of the economic
feasibility of using non-conventional sources of water and research and

development efforts in the most economical use of water with such techniques as drip and sprinkler irrigation in arid areas where shortage of water, rather than land, is the limiting factor in crop production;

(f) Sound exploitation of groundwater resources, water harvesting and conservation in the soil profile and in run-off farm ponds together with techniques for the efficient use of the water thus made available in semiarid and in drought-prone areas;

(g) Flood protection and flood control measures, including watershed management and soil conservation to mitigate the damage to crops in high rainfall and flood-prone areas; to render where feasible, the flood-free period into a major cropping season through development of lift irrigation and groundwater exploitation;

(h) Establishment of suitable drainage systems and appropriate steps to control salinity in swampy areas as well as in areas exposed to tidal inundation;

(i) Taking all necessary measures and developing techniques to combat desert creep;

2. *Calls on* international institutions and bilateral and multilateral aid agencies to provide substantially increased external assistance to enable the developing countries to undertake rapidly action set out under paragraph 1;

3. *Urges* governments and international agencies to assess and make appropriate arrangements for meeting the energy requirements for irrigation and to encourage intensive research on using solar hydro-electric power, geo-thermal and wind energy in agricultural operation;

4. *Urges* governments and international agencies to strengthen and where necessary to initiate national, regional research and training in all aspects of water technology related to specific farming systems and to improve the administration and management of water delivery systems;

RESOLUTION VIII. WOMEN AND FOOD

The World Food Conference,

Considering that the major part of the required increase in food production must occur in the developing countries if the present tragedy of starvation and malnutrition for uncounted millions is not to continue,

Recognizing that rural women in the developing world account for at least fifty per cent of food production,

Knowing that women everywhere generally play the major role in procurement and preparation of food consumed by their families,

Recognizing the important role of the mother in the health development of the future generation through proper lactation and furthermore that mothers in most cultures are the best source of food for their very young children,

Reaffirming the importance of the World Health Assembly resolution on lactation in May this year,

1. *Calls on* all governments to involve women fully in the decision-making machinery for food production and nutrition policies as part of total development strategy;

2. *Calls on* all governments to provide to women in law and fact the right to full access to all medical and social services particularly special nutritious food for mothers and means to space their children to allow maximum lactation, as well as education and information essential to the nurture and growth of mentally and physically healthy children;

3. *Calls on* all governments to include in their plan provision for education and training for women on equal basis with men in food production and agricultural technology, marketing and distribution techniques, as well as consumer, credit and nutrition information;

4. *Calls on* all governments to promote equal rights and responsibilities for men and women in order that the energy, talent and ability of women can be fully utilized in partnership with men in the battle against world hunger.

RESOLUTION IX. ACHIEVEMENT OF A DESIRABLE BALANCE BETWEEN POPULATION AND FOOD SUPPLY

The World Food Conference,

Recognizing that the increasing demand for food is related in particular to the unprecedented population growth, which has doubled the world's population in a single generation,

Realizing that despite improved agricultural technology, an appreciable share of the human race continues to be seriously undernourished, and that many millions face actual starvation,

Bearing in mind that land and water resources are limited and further that due to underdevelopment of such resources in developing countries, it is becoming increasingly difficult to meet the food needs of a rapidly growing world population,

Recalling that in recent months in Bucharest a consensus was reached on a World Population Plan of Action,

Stressing that the increases in supply of food can be achieved only by economic development.

Now calls on all governments and on people everywhere not only to make every possible effort to grow and equitably distribute sufficient food and income so that all human beings may have an adequate diet—a short-range goal which priority and the best techniques might make possible—but also to support, for a longer-term solution, rational population policies ensuring to couples the right to determine the number and spacing of births, freely and responsibly, in accordance with national needs within the context of an overall development strategy.

RESOLUTION X. PESTICIDES [1]

The World Food Conference,

Recognizing that pesticides are in short supply, particularly in developing countries, and are important inputs for improving agricultural and livestock production, storage and distribution, and in health,

Recognizing the need for adequate measures to ensure the production and supply of appropriate pesticides and application equipment at reasonable prices and to increase the efficiency of pesticides use,

Noting the urgent need to examine alternative methods of pest control, including cultural practices and biological control,

1. *Recommends* that international coordination be established to facilitate the supply for developing countries or their common control organizations with a maximum assurance under favourable economic conditions of necessary pesticides and equipment and advice on their efficient and safe use, including wherever possible the encouragement of local manufacture, and the establishment of adequate revolving reserve stocks to cater for any emergencies;

2. *Recommends* a coordinated programme including the necessary elements of supply, information, training, research and quality control, to increase the efficiency of protection measures;

3. *Recommends* a strong continuing programme of research into the mechanism of resistance in both plants and pests, especially in tropical and sub-tropical areas on the development of integrated pest management for major cropping systems, on the residual effects of pesticides in soils, water, crops, livestock, environment and human habitat;

4. *Calls on* FAO in cooperation with UNEP, WHO and UNIDO to convene on an urgent basis an *ad hoc* consultation, including member governments and industry, to recommend ways and means to give effect to the intentions of this resolution, including the supply-demand information that FAO has been collecting, the investment required in pesticides and equipment supply, the standardization of regulatory procedures and environmental rules, examination of alternative methods of pest control and to take follow-up action.

RESOLUTION XI. PROGRAMME FOR THE CONTROL OF AFRICAN ANIMAL TRYPANOSOMIASIS

The World Food Conference,

Recognizing the importance of African animal trypanosomiasis as a major limiting factor to rural development in general and animal production in particular in a large number of African countries,

Taking note that progress in trypanosomiasis and tsetse control techniques now makes possible the implementation of large-scale operations,

Recognizing that the effective implementation of an internationally coordinated programme for the control of African animal trypanosomiasis could open up vast areas of land for animal and crop production thus providing the potential for

---

[1] Includes insecticides, herbicides, fungicides, acaricides, rodenticides, avicides, growth regulators and other pest control measures.

greatly increased animal protein and other food supplies both to overcome deficits in the African continent and to provide surpluses for export,

Recognizing the socio-economic benefits which would accrue to rural populations from such a programme, including a significant contribution to the control of human trypanosomiasis,

Taking note that trypanosomiasis and tsetse control should be considered as the first phase of an integrated plan of economic development to be followed by projects covering appropriate land and water conservation and utilization, including forestry, pasture improvement, livestock management, animal health, livestock marketing and processing, as well as training in their various fields,

1. *Recommends* that FAO in cooperation with the governments of the countries concerned, interested international organizations and specialized research institutes, and with the support of bilateral and multilateral assistance agencies, launch as a matter of urgency a long-term programme for the control of African animal trypanosomiasis as a project of high priority;

2. *Calls for* immediate establishment of a small coordinating unit at FAO Headquarters to start the first phase of the programme devoted to training, pilot field control projects and applied research, in preparation for future large-scale operations;

3. *Recommends* that FAO take immediately the necessary steps to mobilize the funds and services required for the programme.

RESOLUTION XII. SEED [1] INDUSTRY DEVELOPMENT

Recognizing the urgent need to increase agricultural production in many countries to meet worldwide food demand,

Recognizing the importance which a secured supply of viable seeds of high genetical physical purity of high-yielding and adapted varieties has to increasing crop production and productivity,

Affirming therefore that the development of seed industries should be given high priority in national agricultural development strategies,

Stressing the need that some countries experiencing frequent emergencies such as drought, flooding, typhoons, etc., which cause severe crop damage, will have to establish adequate regional and/or national seed reserve stocks to satisfy the need of adequate seed supplies for the subsequent season,

Stressing the increasing international linkages in crop research and in the trade of seeds and the need to guard against introduction of seed-borne pests and diseases,

1. *Urges* the governments of developing countries to make short and long-term commitments of manpower, institutional and financial resources for seed industry development in their national agricultural development plans;

2. *Requests* interested countries and parties to introduce policies and measures for the production, processing, quality control, distribution, marketing, legislation, promotion and education of farmers in the utilization of quality seed;

3. *Recommends* that the international assistance of the FAO Seed Industry Development Programme be strengthened, so that natural seed production and utilization efforts, both for domestic use and exports, including the training of competent technical and managerial manpower, can be furthered to meet demands.

RESOLUTION XIII. INTERNATIONAL FUND FOR AGRICULTURAL DEVELOPMENT

The World Food Conference,

Recognizing the need for substantial increase in investment in agriculture for increasing food and agricultural production in the developing countries;

Recognizing that provision of an adequate supply and proper utilization of food are the common responsibility of all members of the International Community; and

Recognizing further that the prospects of the world food situation call for urgent and co-ordinated measures by all member countries;

Resolves that:

1. An International Fund for Agricultural Development should be established immediately to finance agricultural development projects primarily for food production in the developing countries;

---

[1] "Seed" in this resolution refers to both sexually and vegetatively propagated planting materials.

2. All developed countries and all those developing countries that are in a position to contribute to this Fund should do so on a voluntary basis;

3. The Fund should be administered by a Governing Board consisting of representatives of contributing developed countries, contributing developing countries, and potential recipient countries, taking into consideration the need for equitable distribution of representation amongst these three categories and ensuring regional balance amongst the potential recipient representations;

4. The disbursements from the Fund should be carried out through existing international and/or regional institutions in accordance with the regulations and criteria to be established by the Governing Board;

5. The Secretary-General of the United Nations should be requested to convene urgently a meeting of all interested countries mentioned in paragraph 3 and institutions to work out the details, including the size of, and commitments to, the Fund;

6. The Fund should become operative as soon as the Secretary-General of the United Nations determines, in consultation with representatives of the countries having pledged contributions to the Fund, that it holds promise of generating substantial additional resources for assistance to developing countries and that its operations have a reasonable prospect of continuity.

RESOLUTION XIV. REDUCTION OF MILITARY EXPENDITURES FOR INCREASING FOOD PRODUCTION

The World Food Conference,
Recalling General Assembly Resolution 3180 (XXVIII), which stipulates that the principal purpose of the World Food Conference is to devise ways and means by which the international community as a whole may deal concretely with the world food problem,

Recalling further General Assembly Resolution 3121 (XXVIII), establishing that the contributions to the World Food Programme must be augmented by substantial additional contributions from other sources,

Stressing heading 2 "Food" of General Assembly Resolution 3202 (VI), on a Programme of Action on the Establishment of a New International Economic Order,

Considering also General Assembly Resolution 2667 (XXV), 2831 (XXVI) and 3075 (XXVIII) "Economic and social consequences of the armaments race and its extremely harmful effects on world peace and security",

Recalling also General Assembly Resolution 3093 (XXVIII), on "Reduction of the military budgets of States permanent members of the Security Council by 10 percent and utilization of part of the funds thus saved to provide assistance to developing countries",

Noting FAO Resolution 3/73 which recognizes that the guaranteeing of world food security is the joint responsibility of the entire international community,

Considering with concern that there is a severe world food crisis which must be confronted energetically by all states,

Recalling with equal concern that the Report of the Group of Experts on Disarmament and Development (A/9770) estimates that more than 200 thousand million dollars are spent annually for military purposes, which shows the enormous disproportion between the military expenditures and the present goals of agriculture development aid,

Calls on the states participating in the Conference to take the necessary measures for the most rapid implementation of the Resolutions of the General Assembly and other organs of United Nations pertaining to the reduction of military expenditures on behalf of development, and to allocate a growing portion of the sums so released to the financing of food production in developing countries and the establishment of reserves to deal with emergency cases.

RESOLUTION XV. FOOD AID TO VICTIMS OF COLONIAL WARS IN AFRICA

The World Food Conference.
Recalling resolution 3118 (XXVIII) of the General Assembly of the United Nations regarding assistance to populations in colonial territories and other relevant United Nations resolutions,

Recalling resolution 1892 (LVII) of the Economic and Social Council on the implementation of the Declaration on the Granting of Independence to Colonial Territories and Peoples,

Noting with satisfaction the decisions adopted by the twenty-fifth and twenty-sixth sessions of the Intergovernmental Committee of the World Food Programme for providing assistance in all its forms to these territories,

Bearing in mind the progress achieved so far in the process of total independence of territories under Portuguese administration,

Taking into account the repressive measures employed by the former fascist-colonialist Portuguese regime during the wars of national liberation in Guinea-Bissau, Mozambique and Angola,

Gravely concerned about the destruction and devastation of the agricultural potential of these countries and the serious food shortage prevailing in these countries,

Aware that the populations in these countries have been deprived in the past of any assistance from the United Nations or from the United Nations family of organizations due to the former Portuguese policy,

1. *Requests* the Director-General of FAO and the Executive Director of WFP to take immediate action to intensify food aid to the populations of Guinea-Bissau, Cape Verde, Mozambique, Angola, Sao Tome and Principe;

2. *Requests* the Secretary-General of the United Nations and all the executive heads of organizations within the United Nations system to take all necessary measures to assist the national liberation movements or the governments of these countries to formulate a comprehensive plan of national reconstruction;

3. *Invites* all Governments and non-governmental organizations to give their assistance to compensate for the manifold damage arising out of the struggles for national liberation.

RESOLUTION XVI. GLOBAL INFORMATION AND EARLY-WARNING SYSTEM ON FOOD AND AGRICULTURE

The World Food Conference,

Recognizing that the capacity of Governments to take prompt and appropriate measures to deal with food shortages would be enhanced by the furnishing by all countries of timely and adequate information concerning the current and prospective crop and food situation, and further recognizing the growing interdependence of countries in this respect,

Stressing the urgent need for establishing on a world-wide basis a Food Information and Early Warning System which would aim at (a) identifying countries and regions where acute food shortages and malnutrition problems are thought to be imminent; (b) monitoring world food supply-demand conditions so as to enable Governments to take timely and appropriate measures; and (c) contributing to the effective functioning of the proposed International Undertaking on World Food Security,

Recognizing the important role of a comprehensive and timely flow of information and forecasts on the situation and prospects for agricultural production, import requirements, export availabilities, livestock health, inputs and trade in meeting the requirements of world food security and market stability, at equitable and remunerative prices in a constantly changing food and agriculture situation,

Noting that a world information system requires a regular supply of reliable reports and observations,

Recognizing that the areas most severely affected by food shortages, for which it is particularly important to have timely and adequate information, are often those which do not possess the necessary resources and techniques to supply the information needed for the proper functioning of the System and recognizing also that the problem of inadequate food information and data collection in developing countries is largely a result of inadequate institutions,

Noting that the Governments of all major food producing and consuming countries have expressed their willingness in principle to participate in expanding the existing information arrangements into a more comprehensive and global system, and also noting the importance of strengthening the information functions of FAO, International Wheat Council and other international organizations concerned with food and agriculture,

Welcoming the action being taken by FAO to strengthen its food information and early warning systems following a decision by the FAO Conference in 1973,

1. *Resolves that* a Global Information and Early Warning System on Food and Agriculture (hereinafter referred to as the "System") should be established and agrees that FAO is the most appropriate organization to operate and supervise the System;

2. *Requests* FAO, in co-operation with other concerned international organizations, particularly the International Wheat Council, to formulate arrangements necessary for the establishment of the System, and to submit them for final approval by Governments participating in the System;

3. *Requests* all Governments to participate in the System and extend full co-operation, on a voluntary and regular basis, by furnishing as much current information and forecasts as possible, including current information and forecasts obtained from the statistics and regular studies which are published, initially on basic food product, including in particular wheat, rice, coarse grains, soybeans, and livestock products and, to the extent practicable, other important food products and other relevant aspects of their food supply and demand situation affecting world food security, such as prices and production of inputs and equipment required for agricultural production, the food industry and livestock health, taking account of and respecting in full the sovereign rights of Governments in this regard;

4. *Requests* Governments to take steps, where necessary, to amplify and otherwise improve their data collection and dissemination services in these fields; and further requests FAO, WMO, WHO, the Intergovernmental Bureau for Informatics and other multilateral and bilateral sources to urgently assist interested Governments with technical and financial assistance on particular aspects in strengthening existing arrangements for data collection and dissemination in the fields of food production, nutritional levels at various income levels, input supplies, meteorology and crop/weather relationships, on a national or regional level as appropriate, and to co-ordinate this section with that of the World Food Council provided for in Conference resolution XXI on arrangements for follow-up action;

5. *Requests* that the information thus collected be fully analysed and disseminated periodically to all participating Governments, and for their exclusive use; it being understood that, where requested, certain information provided by Governments would be disseminated in aggregate form particularly in order to avoid unfavourable market repercussions;

6. *Requests* the World Meteorological Organization, in co-operation with FAO (a) to provide, as a part of the System, regular assessments of current and recent weather on the basis of the information presently assembled through the World Weather Watch, so as to identify agriculturally significant changes in weather patterns; (b) to expand and establish joint research projects particularly in arid and semi-arid areas, to investigate weather/crop relationships taking account of the effect of soil moisture conditions; (c) to strengthen the present global weather monitoring systems in regard to the adequacy of meteorological observations, and data processing systems, at the national and regional levels, in order to make them directly relevant to agricultural needs; and (d) to encourage investigations on the assessment of the probability of adverse weather conditions occurring in various agricultural areas, and on a better understanding of the causes of climatic variations.

RESOLUTION XVII. INTERNATIONAL UNDERTAKING ON WORLD FOOD SECURITY

The World Food Conference,
Stressing the urgent need for ensuring the availability at all times of adequate world supplies of basic food-stuffs particularly so as to avoid acute food shortages in the event of widespread crop failure, natural or other disasters, to sustain a steady expansion of food consumption in countries with low levels of per capita intake, and offset fluctuations in production and prices.

Recognizing that very low levels of world food stocks, primarily cereals, pose a serious threat to consumption levels and make the world too dependent on the vagaries of weather,

Welcoming the progress already made through FAO towards developing a common approach for attaining the objectives of world food security, and noting that all major food producing and consuming countries support these objectives,

Reaffirming the common responsibility of the entire international community in evolving policies and arrangements designed to ensure world food security, and in particular in maintaining adequate national or regional stocks as envisaged in the proposed International Undertaking on World Food Security,

Recognizing that universal participation of all producing and consuming countries is essential for the achievement of the global objectives of world food security, and stressing the importance of adherence to the objectives, policies and guidelines of the proposed International Undertaking by all Governments, taking account of its voluntary nature and the sovereign rights of nations,

Recognizing the difficulties currently faced especially by the developing countries in building up stocks through lack of adequate domestic supplies in excess of current consumption needs, the present high prices of foodgrains in world markets and the constraints imposed by serious balance of payments difficulties, which require an immediate increase in the food production of the developed countries while the developing countries are simultaneously assisted to increase their food production and build up their own stocks,

1. *Endorses* the objectives, policies and guidelines as set out in the text of the proposed International Undertaking on World Food Security,[1] *invites* all Governments to express their readiness to adopt them and *urges* all Governments to co-operate in bringing into operation the proposed International Undertaking as soon as possible ;

2. *Calls for* the early completion by the FAO bodies of the operational and other practical arrangements required for the implementation of the proposed International Undertaking, including the examination of practical economic and administrative problems involved ;

3. *Invites* Governments of all major food, primarily cereals, producing, consuming and trading countries to enter as soon as possible into discussion in appropriate international fora, with a view to accelerating the implementation of the principles contained in the proposed International Undertaking on World Food Security, and also with a view to studying the feasibility of establishing grain reserves to be located at strategic points ;

4. *Urges* Governments and the concerned international and regional organizations to provide the necessary technical, financial and food assistance in the form of grants or on specially favourable terms to develop and implement appropriate national food stocks policies in developing countries, including the extension of storage and transport facilities, within the priorities of their national development programme, so that they are in a position to participate effectively in a world food security policy.

RESOLUTION XVIII. AN IMPROVED POLICY FOR FOOD AID

The World Food Conference,

Recognizing that, while the ultimate solution to the problem of food shortages in developing countries lies in increased production in these countries, during the interim period food aid on grant basis and any additional food transfers on concessional or agreed-upon terms to developing countries will continue to be needed, primarily for meeting emergency and nutritional needs, as well as for stimulating rural employment through development projects,

Stressing the importance of evolving a longer-term food aid policy to ensure a reasonable degree of continuity in physical supplies,

Noting that contrary to earlier expectations, the year 1974 has failed to bring the good harvest needed for the replenishment of stocks and re-establishment of a reasonable degree of security in world food supplies, and expressing concern that most developing countries will not be able to finance their increased food import bills in the immediate period ahead.

Stressing that food aid should be provided in forms consonant with the sovereign rights of nations, neither interfering with the development objectives of recipient countries nor imposing the political objectives of donor countries upon them.

Emphasizing further the paramount importance of ensuring that food aid is provided in forms which are voluntary in nature and are consistent with the agricultural development plans of recipient countries with the ultimate aim of promoting their long-term development efforts and ensuring that it does not act as a disincentive to local production and cause adverse repercussions on the domestic market or international trade, in particular of developing countries,

Taking note with interest of the work of the General Assembly at its twenty-ninth session on the subject of strengthening the Office of the United Nations Disaster Relief Co-ordinator, in particular in relation to disaster preparedness and pre-disaster planning,

Recognizing the need to increase the resources of the World Food Programme, so as to enable it to play a greater and more effective role in rendering develop-

---

[1] E/CONF.65/4, chapter 14, annex A.

ment assistance to developing countries in promoting food security and in emergency operations, and also recognizing the need to increase the resources of UNICEF, to enable it to play a greater role in meeting the food needs of children in emergency operations,

1. *Affirms* the need for continuity of a minimum level of food aid in physical terms, in order to insulate food aid programmes from the effects of excessive fluctuations in production and prices;

2. *Recommends* that all donor countries accept and implement the concept of forward planning of food aid, make all efforts to provide commodities and/or financial assistance that will ensure in physical terms at least 10 million tons of grains as food aid a year, starting from 1975, and also to provide adequate quantities of other food commodities;

3. *Requests* that interested cereals exporting and importing countries as well as current and potential financial contributors meet as soon as possible to take cognizance of the needs and to consider ways and means to increase food availability and financing facilities during 1975 and 1976 for the affected developing countries and, in particular, for those most seriously affected by the current food problem;

4. *Urges* all donor countries to (a) channel a more significant proportion of food aid through the World Food Programme, (b) consider increasing progressively the grant component in their bilateral food aid programmes, (c) consider contributing part of any food aid repayments for supplementary nutrition programmes and emergency relief, (d) provide, as appropriate, additional cash resources to food aid programmes for commodity purchases from developing countries to the maximum extent possible;

5. *Recommends* that the Intergovernmental Committee of the World Food Programme, reconstitute as recommended in Conference resolution XXI on arrangements for follow-up action, be entrusted with the task of formulating proposals for more effective co-ordination of multilateral, bilateral and non-governmental food aid programmes and of co-ordinating emergency food aid;

6. *Recommends* that Governments, where possible, earmark stocks or funds for meeting international emergency requirements, as envisaged in the proposed International Undertaking on World Food Security, and *further recommends* that international guidelines for such emergency stocks be developed as a part of the proposed Undertaking to provide for an effective co-ordination of emergency stocks and to ensure that food relief reaches the neediest and most vulnerable groups in developing countries;

7. *Recommends* that a part of the proposed emergency stocks be placed at the disposal of the World Food Programme, on a voluntary basis, in order to increase its capacity to render speedy assistance in emergency situations.

RESOLUTION XIX. INTERNATIONAL TRADE, STABILIZATION AND AGRICULTURAL ADJUSTMENT

The World Food Conference,

Recognizing the interrelationship between the world food problem and international trade, and the role which international trade based on mutual and equitable benefits can play in solving the world food problem, including its development aspects,

Bearing in mind that the instability in the world agricultural markets as reflected in excessive fluctuations of prices and the uncertainty about availability of agricultural products in world markets benefits neither the producer nor the consumer countries and has negative impacts on their economies, particularly of developing countries,

Bearing in mind also that this instability seriously affects the planning of export opportunities and of import requirements,

Considering the need for stability in world markets for food, taking full account in this respect of the interests of developing importing countries which cannot afford high prices for their imports and the interests of developing exporting countries to have increased access to markets for their exports and recalling in this connexion the International Strategy for the Second United Nations Development Decade and the United Nations General Assembly Programme of Action on the Establishment of a New International Economic Order,

Recognizing the role of on-going activities of UNCTAD, GATT, FAO, the International Wheat Council and other international organizations which have a direct or indirect concern with the questions of expansion and access to markets and pricing policy,

Emphasizing the urgent need for food deficit developing countries to have available food inports at stable and reasonable prices,

Endorsing the view that increasing interdependence of the economies of individual countries necessitates a global concept of agricultural adjustment,

Bearing in mind that the international trade of agricultural and especially food products has been restricted by various tariff and non-tariff barriers as well as by other restrictions which impose a heavy burden on the balance of payments, particularly of developing countries and that these problems have been aggravated by inflation and monetary crises,

Bearing in mind that the foreign exchange earnings of the majority of developing countries are predominantly dependent on exports of agricultural and food products and recognizing that the share of these developing countries in the world agricultural exports, already modest, is continuously declining,

Bearing also in mind that the provision of agricultural inputs at reasonable and stable prices has a fundamental effect upon enhancing stability in the markets of agricultural products exported by developing countries,

Underlining the importance of national measures such as agrarian reforms, market organization, development of infrastructure, etc., for allowing the benefit of possibilities created by trade expansion to accrue to the poorer sections of the rural population,

1. *Calls upon* all Governments to co-operate in promoting a steady and increasing expansion and liberalization of world trade with special reference to food products and an improvement in the welfare and living standards of all peoples, in particular those of developing countries: accordingly, requests all Governments to co-operate, *inter alia*, towards the progressive reduction or abolition of obstacles to trade and all discriminatory practices taking into account the principle of most-favoured nation treatment as applicable in GATT and towards the improvement of the international framework for the conduct of world trade; to these ends, co-ordinated efforts shall be made to solve in an equitable way the trade problems of all countries taking into account ,the specific trade problems of the developing countries;

2. *Urges* Governments to take measures aimed at securing additional benefits for the international trade of developing countries so as to achieve a substantial increase in their foreign exchange earnings, the diversification of their exports, the acceleration of the rate of growth of their trade, taking into account their development needs, an improvement in the possibilities for these countries to participate in the expansion of world trade and a balance more favourable to developing countries in the sharing of the advantages resulting from this expansion, through, in the largest possible measure, a substantial improvement in the conditions of access for the products of interest to the developing countries and, wherever appropriate, measures designed to attain stable, equitable and remunerative prices particularly for food and agricultural products;

3. *Calls upon* all Governments to co-operate in taking measures to prevent speculative practices aimed at destabilization of markets and attaining of extra profits;

4. *Calls upon* Governments to devise in the appropriate organizations, effective steps for dealing with the problem of stabilizing world markets particularly for food-stuffs and especially through international arrangements aimed, *inter alia*, at increasing food production, particularly in developing countries, alleviating food shortages, ensuring food security, and promoting prices which are remunerative to producers and fair to consumers and which gave particular attention to the interests of developing countries as importers and exporters;

5. *Urges* UNCTAD to intensify its efforts in considering new approaches to international commodity problems and policies and in elaborating further the proposals for an overall integrated programme for commodities, with particular reference to foodstuffs to give priority consideration to recommendations including a time-table of work for appropriate action at an early date;

6. *Requests* the responsible international bodies to give the highest possible priority to speed up the consultations and negotiations within agreed time limits for reaching agreements on reduction or elimination of barriers and restrictions in international trade and enabling substantially improved access of agricultural and food products of developing countries to the markets of developed countries in accordance with basic objectives guiding the comprehensive multilateral trade negotiations within the framework of the GATT as agreed upon in Tokyo, including the concept of non-reciprocity and of special and more favourable treat-

ment through **differential measures in favour of** developing countries through negotiations, where this is feasible and appropriate;

7. *Requests* all developed countries to implement, improve and enlarge their schemes under the Generalized System of Preferences and to consider its extension to food and agricultural commodities, including those which are processed or semi-processed;

8. *Urges* the Governments participating in the intensive *ad hoc* consultations on commodities, as well as other Governments, to make determined efforts to achieve substantial and concrete results in the fields of access to markets and pricing policy and recommends to all Governments to take concrete action on proposals made in the intensive consultations which are accepted by them;

9. *Calls upon* Governments of developed countries, in the determination of attitudes towards farm support programmes for domestic food production, to take into account as far as possible the interests of the food exporting developing countries, in order to avoid detrimental effects to their exports;

10. *Requests* the developed countries to enable and facilitate to the extent possible the expansion of food and agricultural imports from developing countries, in competition with domestic production, thus providing a fair and reasonable opportunity to increase their export earnings and to allow developing countries which export to these developed markets to plan their production and exports on a forward basis;

11. *Reaffirms* the importance given by the member countries of the FAO to international agricultural adjustment and the need for Governments to work together toward greater consistency in their national and regional policies bearing on future changes in food and agriculture;

12. *Requests* that FAO take full account of the discussions and decisions of the World Food Conference in formulating and implementing the proposed strategy of the international agricultural adjustment;

13. *Requests* the Governments of developed countries and international organizations concerned to increase the field assistance to the developing countries in export promotion activities and mechanisms, and in training of agricultural marketing and trade personnel taking due account of the diversification process and development needs;

14. *Calls upon* countries and organizations concerned to devote special attention to the solution of the problems facing developing countries in the matter of transportation of food-stuffs;

15. *Invites* the developing countries to expand their mutual economic co-operation and invites the developed countries and the international organizations concerned to maintain and expand their support for economic co-operation among developing countries;

16. *Stresses* the need for measures assuring the poorer sections of the rural population of their share in the opportunities and benefits offered by trade expansion;

17. *Requests* the World Food Programme and other international organizations concerned to give priority to the use of cash resources available for multilateral or bilateral food aid for purchases in developing countries at competitive world market prices and terms;

18. *Urges* the developed countries and other countries concerned and international financial institutions concerned to give favourable consideration to the provision of adequate assistance to developing countries in cases of balance-of-payments difficulties arising from fluctuations in export receipts or import costs, particularly with regard to food;

19. *Requests* the Governments of all countries and international organizations concerned, when considering all the subjects contained in this resolution, to give the highest possible priority and the most favourable terms to the least developed, land-locked and island developing countries and to developing countries most seriously affected by economic crises.

RESOLUTION XX. PAYMENT OF TRAVEL COSTS AND OTHER RELATED EXPENSES TO
REPRESENTATIVES OF NATIONAL LIBERATION MOVEMENTS

The World Food Conference,

Recalling resolution 1892 (LVII) of 8 August 1974 of the Economic and Social Council. and in particular paragraph 2(d).

Recalling further resolution XX of the World Population Conference,

Decides to request the General Assembly to defray all travel costs and other related expenses of representatives of the national liberation movements who have participated in the World Food Conference.

RESOLUTION XXI. EXPRESSION OF THANKS

The World Food Conference,
Recognizing the gravity of the world food problem and national and international efforts to find adequate solutions thereof,
Convinced that the world Food Conference which took place at Rome from 5 to 16 November 1974 represents a major contribution to the efforts of the United Nations as well as the international community to find urgent solutions to the immediate and long-term problems of food shortages, hunger and malnutrition,
Expresses its deep appreciation to the President of the Republic of Italy, Mr. Giovanni Leone and to all the people of the Republic of Italy for hosting the World Food Conference at Rome, and for their generous hospitality and great contribution to the successful completion of the work of the Conference.

FOLLOW-UP ACTION

RESOLUTION XXII. ARRANGEMENTS FOR FOLLOW-UP ACTION, INCLUDING APPROPRIATE OPERATIONAL MACHINERY ON RECOMMENDATIONS OR RESOLUTIONS OF THE CONFERENCE [1]

The World Food Conference,
Recognizing that an assurance of adequate world food supplies is a matter of life and death for millions of human beings,
Appreciating the complex nature of the world food problem, which can only be solved through an integrated multi-disciplinary approach within the framework of economic and social development as a whole.
Considering that collective world food security within the framework of a world food policy should be promoted and its concept further defined and elaborated, so that it should foster the acceleration of the process of rural development in developing countries as well as ensure the improvement of international co-operation,
Appreciating the need to co-ordinate and strengthen the work of the international agencies concerned, and to ensure that their operational activities are co-ordinated in an effective and integrated world food policy,
Recognizing in particular the need for improved institutional arrangements to increase world food production, to safeguard world food security, to improve world food trade, and ensure that timely action is taken to meet the threat of acute food shortages or famines in the different developing regions,
1. *Calls upon* the General Assembly to establish a World Food Council, at the ministerial or plenipotentiary level, to function as an organ of the United Nations reporting to the General Assembly through the Economic and Social Council, to serve as a co-ordinating mechanism to provide over-all, integrated and continuing attention for the successful co-ordination and follow-up of policies concerning food production, nutrition, food security, food trade and food aid, as well as other related matters, by all the agencies of the United Nations system;
2. *Takes note* of the fact that interagency meetings between the Secretary-General of the United Nations and the heads of the specialized agencies provide an opportunity for considering necessary constitutional amendments to improve the functioning of the United Nations system;
3. *Requests* that the present resolution be taken into account in such consultations with a view to facilitating its early implementation;
4. *Recommends* that:
(*a*) The World Food Council should consist of . . . members, nominated by the Economic and Social Council and elected by the General Assembly, taking into consideration balanced geographical representation. The Council should invite the heads of United Nations agencies concerned to attend its sessions;
(*b*) The Council should elect its President on the basis of geographical rotation and approve its rules of procedure. It should be serviced within the framework of FAO, with headquarters at Rome;

---

[1] Adopted by the Conference at its 16th meeting on 16 November 1974.

(c) The Council should review periodically major problems and policy issues affecting the world food situation, and the steps being proposed or taken to resolve them by Governments, by the United Nations system and its regional organizations, and should further recommend remedial action as appropriate. The scope of the Council's review should extend to all aspects of world food problems in order to adopt an integrated approach towards their solution;

(d) The Council should establish its own programme of action for co-ordination of relevant United Nations bodies and agencies. While doing so, it should give special attention to the problems of the least developed countries and the countries most seriously affected;

(e) The Council should maintain contacts with, receive reports from, give advice to, and make recommendations to United Nations bodies and agencies with regard to the formulation and follow-up of world food policies;

(f) The Council should work in full co-operation with regional bodies to formulate and follow-up policies approved by the Council. Committees to be established by these regional bodies should be serviced by existing United Nations or FAO bodies in the regional concerned;

5. *Recommends* further that the FAO establish a Committee on World Food Security as a standing committee of the FAO Council. The Committee should submit periodic and special reports to the World Food Council. The functions of the Committee on World Food Security should include the following:

(a) to keep the current and prospective demand, supply and stock position for basic food-stuffs under continuous review, in the context of world food security, and to disseminate timely information on developments;

(b) to make periodic evaluations of the adequacy of current and prospective stock levels, in aggregate, in exporting and importing countries, in order to assure a regular flow of supplies of basic food-stuffs to meet requirements in domestic and world markets, including food aid requirements, in domestic and world markets, including food aid requirements, in time of short crops and serious crop failure;

(c) to review the steps taken by Governments to implement the proposed International Undertaking on World Food Security;

(d) to recommend such short-term and long-term policy action as may be considered necessary to remedy any difficulty foreseen in assuring adequate cereal supplies for minimum world food security;

6. *Recommends further* that the Intergovernmental Committee of the World Food Programme be reconstituted so as to enable it to help evolve and co-ordinate short-term and longer-term food aid policies recommended by the Conference, in addition to discharging its existing functions. The reconstituted Committee should be called, and function as, the Committee on Food Aid Policies and Programmes. The Committee should submit periodical and special reports to the World Food Council. The functions of the Committee on Food Aid Policies and Programmes should include the following:

(a) to provide a forum for intergovernmental consultations on national and international food aid programmes and policies, with particular reference to possibilities of securing improved co-ordination between bilateral and multilateral food aid;

(b) to review periodically general trends in food aid requirements and food aid availabilities;

(c) to recommend to Governments, through the World Food Council, improvements in food aid policies and programmes on such matters as programme priorities, composition of food aid commodities and other related subjects;

7. *Recommends further* that the Governing Board of the proposed International Fund for Agricultural Development should submit information periodically to the World Food Council on the programmes approved by the Board. The Board should take into consideration the advice and recommendations of the Council;

8. *Recommends* that the World Food Council should receive periodic reports from UNCTAD, through the Economic and Social Council, on the world food trade situation, as well as on the effective progress to increase trade liberalization and access to international markets for food products exported by developing countries. UNCTAD should take into consideration the advice and recommendations of the Council on these matters. The Council should also seek to arrange for the receipt of relevant information from the GATT. In its recommendation on

World Food Council

*The U.N. General Assembly Dec. 17, 1974 took the following action to
form a World Food Council and endorse the recommendations of the World
Food Conference.*

Date: 17 December 1974   Meeting: 2323
Adopted without vote   Report: A/9886/Add. 1

The General Assembly,
Recalling its resolution 3180 (XXVIII) of 17 December 1973, in which it
recognized that the principal task of a world food conference consisted in developing ways and means whereby the international community as a whole could
take specific action to resolve the world food problem within the broader context
of development and international economic co-operation.
Further recalling its resolutions 3201 (S–VI) and 3202 (S–VI) of 1 May 1974
on the Declaration and the Programme of Action on the Establishment of a New
International Economic Order,
Having considered the report of the World Food Conference,[63] held in Rome
from 5 to 16 November 1974 and Economic and Social Council decision 59 (LVII)
thereon,
Considering that urgent action should be taken by the international community
on the resolutions adopted at the World Food Conference,
1. *Takes note with satisfaction* of the report of the World Food Conference;
2. *Commends* the Secretary-General of the United Nations, the Secretary-
General of the World Food Conference, and the Director-General of the Food
and Agriculture Organization of the United Nations for their contributions to
the success of the Conference, and expresses its appreciation to the Government
of Italy as host of the Conference;
3. *Endorses* the Declaration on the Eradication of Hunger and Malnutrition
and the resolutions adopted at the World Food Conference;
4. *Calls upon* Governments to take urgent action to implement the resolutions
adopted at the World Food Conference and to achieve the goals established
therein;
5. *Requests* the Secretary-General and the executive heads of the subsidiary
organs of the General Assembly and of the specialized agencies to take expedi-
tious action in line with the resolutions adopted at the World Food Conference;
6. *Invites* the organizations of the United Nations system to consider the
resolutions adopted at the World Food Conference on an urgent basis and to take
the necessary steps for their effective implementation;
7. *Establishes* a World Food Council at the ministerial or plenipotentiary level
to function as an organ of the United Nations, reporting to the General Assembly
through the Economic and Social Council and having the purposes, functions
and mode of operation set forth in resolution XXII of the Conference;
8. *Decides* that the World Food Council shall consist of 36 members nominated
by the Economic and Social Council and elected by the General Assembly for
a term of three years, taking into consideration balanced geographical representation,[64] with one-third of the members retiring every year, retiring members to be
eligible for re-election;
9. *Requests* the Economic and Social Council to nominate the members of the

---

[63] F/5587 and Add. 1–4.
[64] The members of the World Food Council shall be elected according to the following
pattern:
    (a) Nine members from African States;
    (b) Eight members from Asian States;
    (c) Seven members from Latin American States;
    (d) Four members from Socialist States of Eastern Europe;
    (e) Eight members from Western European and other States.

food trade matters, the Council should pay particular attention to the resolutions and recommendations of the Conference;

9. *Requests* the FAO to initiate urgent steps, through its Commission on Fertilizers, for following up on Conference resolution . . . on Fertilizers, and to take appropriate initiatives with respect to fertilizers, pesticides, fungicides and herbicides, working in close co-operation with UNIDO and IBRD, and other agencies. The FAO Commission on Fertilizers should submit periodic reports to the World Food Council, and should be guided by the advice and recommendations of the Council;

10. *Requests* FAO to examine its ability to follow up on Conference resolution XVI on the Global Information System and Early-Warning System in Food and Agriculture, with a view to recommending to the FAO Council, at its sixty-fifth session in 1975, any new arrangements which may be necessary with respect to its activities in this field, and to initiate whatever other arrangements may be necessary to facilitate global coverage as called for by the above-mentioned resolution, drawing upon the help in this regard of ECOSOC, if necessary, as well as that of the International Wheat Council and other organizations. Periodic reports on progress should be submitted to the World Food Council;

11. *Requests* the Economic and Social Council to consider on an urgent basis, and make recommendations, whether or not rearrangements in the United Nations system or new institutional bodies may be justified in order to ensure effective follow-up on Conference resolution V on nutrition, examining nutritional activities within bodies such as the United Nations, the specialized agencies, in particular FAO and WHO, UNICEF, and the World Food Programme, and also giving appropriate attention to nutritional programmes being conducted on a bilateral basis;

12. *Requests* the Consultative Group on International Agricultural Research (CGIAR) and the Technical Advisory Committee to assume leadership in following up on the research aspect of Conference resolution IV on research;

13. *Requests* FAO, IBRD, UNDP and other relevant international organizations and interested Governments to investigate the desirability of introducing an organizational approach, along the lines of the Consultative Group—Technical Advisory Committee for Agricultural Research, for other sectors such as extension, agricultural credit and rural development;

14. *Requests* the IBRD, FAO and UNDP to organize a Consultative Group on Food Production and Investment in Developing Countries (CGFPI), to be composed of bilateral and multilateral donors and representatives of developing countries, chosen as in the case of the CGIAR, to be staffed jointly by the IBRD, FAO and UNDP, and *invites* this Consultative Group to keep the World Food Council informed of its activities to increase, co-ordinate, and improve the efficiency of financial and technical assistance to agricultural production in developing countries;

15. *Recommends that* the main functions of the CGFPI should be (a) to encourage a larger flow of external resources for food production, (b) to improve the co-ordination of activities of different multilateral and bilateral donors providing financial and technical assistance for food production and (c) to ensure a more effective use of available resources;

16. Anticipating the possibility that such measures as may be agreed to provide financial assistance to developing countries for procurement of food and necessary food production inputs, particularly fertilizers and pesticides, and for investment in food production and distribution systems, may not fulfill all needs, *requests* the Development Committee established by the IBRD and IMF to keep under constant review the adequacy of the external resources available for these purposes, especially to the less advantaged countries, and to consider in association with the CGFPI new measures which may be necessary to achieve the required volume of resources transfers.

World Food Council at its resumed fifty-seventh session for election by the General Assembly at its current session;

10. *Decides* that the first meeting of the World Food Council shall be convened not later than 1 July 1975, and for this purpose the members of the Council shall undertake necessary consultations as soon as possible;

11. *Requests* the Secretary-General, in consultation with the Director-General of the Food and Agriculture Organization of the United Nations, to take immediate action for establishing a secretariat for the World Food Council, as set forth in resolution XXII of the World Food Conference;

12. *Decides* to review, at its thirtieth session, actions taken to resolve the world food problem as a result of the World Food Conference and, to this end, requests the Secretary-General to submit a report to the General Assembly at that session on the implementation of the resolutions of the Conference;

13. *Further requests* the Secretary-General to convene urgently a meeting of all interested countries, including the representatives of the contributing developed countries, the contributing developing countries and the potential recipient countries, and all interested institutions, to work out the details of an International Fund for Agricultural Development as envisaged in resolution XIII of the World Food Conference, bearing in mind operative paragraph 6 of that resolution.

ELECTION OF 36 MEMBERS OF THE WORLD FOOD COUNCIL

At its 2323rd plenary meeting, on 17 December 1974, the General Assembly, without balloting, elected the following 36 States which had been nominated by the Economic and Social Council to serve on the World Food Council: Argentina, Australia, Bangladesh, Canada, Chad, Colombia, Cuba, Egypt, France, Gabon, Germany (Federal Republic of), Guatemala, Guinea, Hungary, India, Indonesia, Iran, Iraq, Italy, Japan, Kenya, Libya, Mali, Mexico, Pakistan, Romania, Sri Lanka, Sweden, Togo, Trinidad and Tobago, United Kingdom, United States, USSR, Venezuela, Yugoslavia and Zambia.

Lots were then drawn to select 12 members to serve on the Council for three years, 12 members to serve for two years and 12 members to serve for one year.

The 12 member States selected to serve for three years are: Chad, Egypt, Hungary, Iran, Italy, Japan, Kenya, Sri Lanka, Sweden, Trinidad and Tobago, United Kingdom and Venezuela.

The 12 States selected to serve for two years are: Australia, Colombia, Cuba, France, Guatemala, Guinea, India, Libya, Mali, Pakistan, Romania and the Soviet Union.

The 12 States selected to serve for one year are: Argentina, Bangladesh, Canada, Gabon, Germany (Federal Republic of), Indonesia, Iraq, Mexico, Togo, Yugoslavia, United States and Zambia.

Index